Germany Today

Politics and Policies
in a Changing World

Christiane Lemke
Leibniz University Hannover

Helga A. Welsh
Wake Forest University

ROWMAN & LITTLEFIELD
Lanham • Boulder • New York • London

Executive Editor: Susan McEachern
Assistant Editor: Rebeccah Shumaker
Senior Marketing Manager: Kim Lyons

Credits and acknowledgments for material borrowed from other sources, and reproduced
with permission, appear on the appropriate page within the text.

Published by Rowman & Littlefield
A wholly owned subsidiary of The Rowman & Littlefield Publishing Group, Inc.
4501 Forbes Boulevard, Suite 200, Lanham, Maryland 20706
www.rowman.com

Unit A, Whitacre Mews, 26-34 Stannary Street, London SE11 4AB, United Kingdom

British Library Cataloguing in Publication Information Available

Library of Congress Cataloging-in-Publication Data Available
ISBN 978-1-4422-2996-9 (cloth : alk. paper)
ISBN 978-1-4422-2997-6 (pbk. : alk. paper)
ISBN 978-1-4422-2998-3 (electronic)

∞™ The paper used in this publication meets the minimum requirements of
American National Standard for Information Sciences—Permanence of Paper
for Printed Library Materials, ANSI/NISO Z39.48-1992.

Printed in the United States of America

Brief Contents

Contents

Tables and Figures

TABLES

Tables and Figures

FIGURES

Abbreviations

AfD	Alternative for Germany
AKP	Justice and Development Party
ALFA	Alliance for Progress and Renewal
BDA	Confederation of German Employers' Association
BDI	Federation of German Industry
CAP	Common Agricultural Policy
CDU	Christian Democratic Union of Germany
CEAS	Common European Asylum System
CETA	Comprehensive Economic and Trade Agreement
CFSP	Common Foreign and Security Policy
CJEU	Court of Justice of the European Union
CME	Coordinated Market Economy/ies
CPSU	Communist Party of the Soviet Union
CSCE	Conference on Security and Cooperation in Europe
CSU	Christian Social Union
DGB	German Trade Union Federation
DM	German Mark (Deutsche Mark)
EC	European Community
ECB	European Central Bank
ECJ	European Court of Justice
ECSC	European Coal and Steel Community
ECU	European Currency Unit
EEAS	European External Action Service
EEC	European Economic Community
EFSF	European Financial Stability Facility
EMS	European Monetary System
ENP	European Neighborhood Policy
EP	European Parliament

EU	European Union
Euratom	European Atomic Energy Community
FDGB	Free German Trade Union Federation
FDP	Free Democratic Party
G-8; G-7	Group of Eight (Canada, France, Germany, Italy, Japan, Russia, United Kingdom, United States); Group of Seven (without Russia)
GDP	Gross Domestic Product
GDR	German Democratic Republic
GIZ	German Society for International Cooperation
HR	The High Representative of the Union for Foreign Affairs and Security Policy
ICC	International Criminal Court
ILO	International Labor Organization
IMF	International Monetary Fund
ISAF	International Security Assistance Force
KPD	Communist Party of Germany
LGBT	Lesbian, Gay, Bisexual, and Transgender
LME	Liberal Market Economy/ies
MEP	Member of European Parliament
MMP	Mixed-Member Proportional System
MP	Member of Parliament
NATO	North Atlantic Treaty Organization
NGO	Nongovernmental Organization
NPD	National Democratic Party of Germany
NSA	US National Security Agency
NSDAP	National Socialist German Workers Party
OECD	Organisation for Economic Co-operation and Development
OPEC	Organization of the Petroleum Exporting Countries
OSCE	Organization for Security and Co-operation in Europe
Pegida	Patriotic Europeans against the Islamization of the Occident
PHARE	Poland and Hungary: Assistance for Restructuring of the Economy
PPP	Purchasing Power Parity
SED	Socialist Unity Party of Germany
SPD	Social Democratic Party of Germany
TTIP	Transatlantic Trade and Investment Partnership
UK	United Kingdom of Great Britain and Northern Ireland
UKIP	United Kingdom Independence Party
UN	United Nations
UNHCR	United Nations High Commissioner for Refugees
US	United States
WASG	Labor and Social Justice–The Electoral Alternative
WTO	World Trade Organization

Authors' Notes

Throughout the book we clarify our terminology, but the following short lexicon defines basic constructs.

European (Economic) Community vs. European Union. The history of European integration has been accompanied by name changes. What we call the European Union (EU) today started as three distinct communities: the European Coal and Steel Community (ECSC), the European Economic Community (EEC), and the European Atomic Energy Community (Euratom). They merged into the European Community (EC) in 1967. With implementation of the Maastricht Treaty (1993), the three communities became one pillar of the newly founded European Union (EU). The Treaty of Lisbon (2009) made the EU the legal successor to the EC. Most authors use *EU* when referring to the history of European integration, and we follow this convention, applying EEC or EC only to describe distinct historical developments prior to 1993.

European Union treaties. Major EU policy decisions are often implemented through treaties, normally named after the city in which they were signed (e.g., Maastricht, Amsterdam). The literature dates them differently, some noting the year they were signed; others, the year they were ratified, and still others when they came into force. We use the year the treaty came into effect.

Federal. Germany is a federal state, and the term *federal* (in German: *Bund*) is part of many compound nouns that relate to politics. Some of them are federal army (*Bundeswehr*), federal government (*Bundesregierung*), federal chancellor (*Bundeskanzler*), federal president (*Bundespräsident*), federal state (*Bundesland*), Federal Constitutional Court *(Bundesverfassungsgericht)*, Federal Parliament (*Bundestag*), and Federal Council (*Bundesrat*). For readability, we usually omit the prefix, but in the case of the German national parliament, the *Bundestag*, and the representative body of the *Länder*, the *Bundesrat*, we follow convention and use their full German names.

Federal Republic of Germany. When the western zones of occupation merged in May 1949, they were designated the Federal Republic of Germany. East and West Germany unified in October 1990 as the Federal Republic of Germany. Depending on context, *Federal Republic of Germany* can apply to pre-unification West Germany or the unified Germany after 1990.

German Democratic Republic. In October 1949, the German Democratic Republic (GDR) was established; it ceased to exist when it unified with the Federal Republic of Germany in October 1990. It is usually referred to as East Germany or GDR.

Government vs. administration. In the United States, the executive branch of government and its officials are called the administration (e.g., the Obama administration). Throughout Europe, including Germany, the term *government* is used (e.g., the Merkel government).

State vs. Land. The word *state* is variously used as a synonym for country (e.g., the German state) and a territorial unit within a country (state of Bavaria), but it can also refer to the system of public institutions that rules a territory and people. In German, the latter meaning is most common; the other two predominate in the English-speaking world. To avoid confusion, we generally use the German term *Land* (singular) or *Länder* (plural) to designate the subnational units, but at times, we also refer to them as states.

Unification vs. reunification. Both unification and reunification are commonly used to refer to the merger of East and West Germany in October 1990. Both are correct. We use *unification* because it makes clear that the current Federal Republic of Germany never existed, since Germany lost some of its territory at the end of World War II.

Preface

This book was coauthored by two political scientists raised and educated in the former West Germany. We have published on different aspects of German history and politics and conducted academic careers on both sides of the Atlantic. Some aspects of our socialization inform our insider–outsider perspective and may be worth pointing out.

We grew up in a divided Germany. We remember the building of the Berlin Wall and the precarious place of East and West Germany at the center of the Cold War. Our academic careers first focused on the communist German Democratic Republic (GDR), and like everyone else, we were surprised and excited when the Berlin Wall fell and German unity became reality. We have followed the difficult struggles and distinct successes of the merger with personal and professional interest since 1990.

Our generation was also shaped by the cultural, political, and economic influence of the United States and the presence of its armed forces in West Germany and West Berlin. Christiane Lemke was a high school exchange student in California in 1967–68; Helga Welsh was a graduate exchange student at the University of Iowa in 1979–80. Today, Lemke regularly shuttles between the United States and Germany and teaches in both locations; Welsh is a dual citizen of the United States and Germany and resides and teaches in North Carolina.

Both personal and national experiences shape attitudes toward European integration. We belong to a generation of Germans that has benefited from European unification; it opened new opportunities for the nation and its citizens. For us, Europeanization has entailed travel across borders, moving between cultures and languages in a Europe first separated by ideologies and, after 1989, reunited. These developments shaped our scholarship and intellectual interests. We have worked with scholars and students in Western

Europe and the formerly communist-ruled East, and perhaps not surprisingly, we believe in a closely integrated Europe.

We would like to thank our student assistants at Wake Forest University, who helped with the research and preparation of the manuscript: John Archie, Mimi Bair, and Ana Hincu. Friends and colleagues provided insightful feedback on individual chapters: Phillip Ayoub, Tobias Hof, Konrad H. Jarausch, Sylvia Maier, Holger Moroff, David Patton, and Angelika von Wahl. The Transatlantic Masters Program at the University of North Carolina at Chapel Hill and its administrative director, Katie Lindner, most graciously invited us to present our project at an earlier stage. We are grateful for the editorial help of Julie Edelson; her queries always challenged us to clarify what we thought was clear. Susan McEachern at Rowman & Littlefield and her editorial team combined insights, patience, and encouragement. We thank the external reviewers for their valuable input. Remaining shortcomings are our own.

Our transatlantic research and collaboration would have been impossible without the support of several institutions: the Leibniz University of Hannover, the University of North Carolina at Chapel Hill, Wake Forest University, and the German Academic Exchange Service (DAAD). Christiane Lemke thanks her family for their encouragement throughout the project. Helga Welsh extends her special gratitude to Ron Pardue. His unwavering support makes a difference every day.

We dedicate this book to our students on both sides of the Atlantic. They inspire and challenge us. We hope that they and scholars grappling with German and European politics find our analysis both instructive and thought-provoking.

Chapter 1

The German Polity in Context

KEY TERMS

Berlin Wall
critical junctures
division of Germany
East-West dichotomies
Europeanization
German Question
globalization

historical institutionalism
Holocaust
interdependence
normality
Sonderweg
unification crisis
unification process

Introducing readers to the politics of a specific country is never an easy undertaking, especially if the subject is very familiar to the authors. What should be highlighted, and what left out? Should we focus on distinctive or representative features? In what order should we present them to make their logic clear, particularly when they are interrelated? How do continuity and change mesh in political culture, institutions, and policy making? An introduction to a country's politics and policies typically covers the relevant historical background, institutional structures, and policy areas, yet for each country, the rationale and resulting focus will differ.

This book is prompted by six crucial features that make understanding the subject valuable; they are introduced in this chapter and will be examined throughout:

- Germany's relevance to contemporary European history and contemporary politics;
- the place of German institutions in the canon of comparative politics;

- German approaches to contemporary challenges that affect most Western democracies;
- lessons of the Holocaust in contemporary German discourse, institutions, and policies;
- Germany's division into two states that represented political polar opposites during the Cold War and their unification after more than four decades; and
- the overlapping and interlocking dynamics of unification, Europeanization, and globalization that have shaped German politics and policies since the 1990s.

Understanding Germany's place in the world, its institutions, and discourses today requires understanding its centrality in twentieth-century history. We begin our brief overview by outlining some major junctures and the debates surrounding them and conclude by defining our approach to the book's content.

A FRACTURED HISTORICAL NARRATIVE

Germany's tortuous path to a modern democratic polity was shaped at crossroads where political institutions, policies, and political culture were recast (see table 1.1). Its historical narrative reads like a modernist experiment in contrasting viewpoints.

In 1918, Germany abandoned monarchical authoritarianism, but efforts to secure democracy in the so-called Weimar Republic (1919–33) failed in the coming decades, with dramatic consequences for the country and the world. In 1933, Adolf Hitler came to power. The period from 1933 to 1945 sets Germany apart from other European countries due to its prosecution of genocide: more than six million Jews and another five million non-Jewish victims, including, but not limited to, Sinti and Roma, gay people, resistance fighters, people with handicaps, Christian pastors, communists, and trade unionists were murdered methodically. Hitler's dictatorship was one of the most brutal in the twentieth century and, together with Stalin's Soviet Union, inspired Hannah Arendt's (1958) typology of totalitarian regimes. They relied heavily on propaganda, cult of personality, centralization of power, and use of ideology to mobilize and control the populace. They exerted violence and repressed civil and political liberties. World War II redrew the political, economic, social, and ethnic map of Europe and brought immeasurable suffering and destruction.

In the aftermath, the Cold War between the Western allies and the USSR soon led to the establishment of two separate states on German soil. In both,

Table 1.1. Critical Junctures in Modern German History

Period	Official Name	Political System	Structure	Party System (national representation)
1871–1918	German Reich	authoritarian monarchy	monarch and chancellor, federal	Five major parties with many subgroups
1919–33	German Reich/ Weimar Republic	democracy	parliamentary with a strong president, federal	extreme and polarized multiparty system
1933–45	Third Reich	totalitarian (fascism)	personalistic/ supremacy of the Führer, unitary	one-party system
1949–90	Federal Republic of Germany (West Germany)	democracy	parliamentary, federal	moderate multiparty system
1949–90	German Democratic Republic (East Germany)	totalitarian-authoritarian (communist)	supremacy of the general secretary of the SED/ Politburo; personnel overlap between party and state structures, unitary (since 1952)	one party system with communist party (SED) and three other officially sanctioned parties (bloc parties)
1990–	Federal Republic of Germany	democracy	parliamentary federal system, bicameral	moderate multiparty system

new political systems were designed with input and oversight from the occupying powers to achieve particular goals. In the Federal Republic of Germany, a Western-style democracy succeeded; in the German Democratic Republic, contrary to what its name suggests, a communist system took hold. This division would last forty years. Unexpectedly the peaceful revolution in East Germany opened the door to unification in 1990.

This cursory overview notes the moments that inform enduring debates about Germany's place in European history. How could it be one of the instigators in World War I and be responsible for World War II? How could it stoop to perpetrate a genocide singular in its international reach, extermination methods, and primary target, Jewish citizens who seemed integrated into its society? How could it emerge from utter destruction and successfully remake its political culture and political institutions? Its success in achieving a consolidated democracy, first as West Germany and now as unified Germany, illustrates the possibility of "practical redemption from moral disaster" while raising questions about the impetus for change. "Did the Germans really learn from their catastrophe and reject the negative patterns that led them and their neighbors to disaster? Was the subsequent transformation primarily a product of total defeat, a result of transnational processes of modernization, or the outcome of their own decision, based on contrition?" (Jarausch 2006a, 17).

If the answers to these questions are not simple, Germany's path after 1945—its division into two states at the center of the East-West conflict and ultimate unification—was never straightforward. Considering challenging domestic and international developments, crucial decisions could have yielded different outcomes. Based on the appeal of the West to many German citizens in both former states, the temptation to portray it as a success story and communist East Germany as a failure fails to acknowledge achievements and misguided policies in both. Only in hindsight can we ascertain the democratic stability and cultural transformation in West Germany and now the unified Germany, summarized in the titles of two books on the history of the Federal Republic, *Die geglückte Demokratie* (*The Successful Democracy*) by Edgar Wolfram (2006) and Konrad H. Jarausch's *After Hitler: Recivilizing Germans 1945–1995* (2006a).

In most, if not all, histories of post–World War II Germany, East Germany is explored relatively briefly and mostly functions as a foil to highlight democratic development in the West; its dictatorial features serve as a negative template. After 1990, a rich literature initially focused on dissent and the role of the Soviet Union in imposing and maintaining communist rule, repression, and top-down communist elite structures, but soon studies shed light on the everyday lives of East German citizens, shaped by compromises, sacrifices, and achievements (Port 2013). These differentiated accounts are a necessary supplement and highlight changes over time, patterns of accommodations, and agency. They also contribute to our understanding of identity problems after unification, when many East Germans felt that their lives under communism were not only misconstrued but also diminished by Western perceptions. Cognizant of these discussions, we only touch on them insofar as they shaped contemporary Germany.

UNIQUE, EXCEPTIONAL, OR JUST DIFFERENT?

Special Path and the German Question

In the first half of the twentieth century, Germany moved from monarchy to democracy to dictatorship. In the second half, it was divided into a Western-oriented democratic state and a Soviet-oriented communist state and unified some forty years later after a "peaceful revolution." Do these convoluted historical developments make Germany exceptional? Can it ever atone for its past and become normal? How useful are the concepts *exceptional* and *normal*, which are fraught with definitional and operational difficulties? As Shafer (1999) points out, the more we dissect a feature, the more unique it becomes. We should also inquire, as he does, into the purpose of declaring something unique or different. Such categorizations always require careful selection of the units of comparison. Are the terms *exceptional* or *special* applied to, or even promoted in, a country to suggest that its features should be emulated (positive exceptionalism) or never repeated (negative exceptionalism)?

Any reference to exceptionalism is associated with scholarship about the United States, a country whose creation, according to the narrative woven around it, has been seen as trailblazing. However, it is also applied to settings as diverse as Russia and Japan. Germany's historical path in the nineteenth and the first half of the twentieth century exhibits distinct features that historians have frequently subsumed under the term *special path* (*Sonderweg*). In an opposing interpretation, David Blackbourn and Geoff Eley (1984) assert that there is no one path to democracy; while in some ways, German political development in the nineteenth century may have been different, its social and economic development was similar to that in other European countries. The record should not be misinterpreted in seeking the historical origins of Nazism.

Most scholars now reserve the term special path "for the (comparative) discussion of one basic and startling fact"—that is, Germany's evolution into a "fascist and totalitarian state"—and it should be applied only in comparison to those states in the West "with which Germany likes to compare itself," mostly France and the United Kingdom (Kocka 1988, 10). Late nation-state building from above in 1871 and a bureaucratic tradition based on authority, according to Kocka, contribute more to our understanding of the Weimar Republic's failure than the rise of National Socialism. US historian Helmut Walser Smith (2008, 236) emphasizes the unit of comparison. Germany's lack of singularity does not make authoritarianism, nationalism, and anti-Semitism less important in its historical trajectory. On the other hand, Heinrich August Winkler (2007, 586), a German historian, argues that the "anti-western *Sonderweg* of the German Reich came to an end in 1945" whereas the "post-national

Sonderweg of the old Federal Republic and the internationalist *Sonderweg* of the GDR" ended in 1990.

The special path debate has focused on Germany's historical development in comparison to France and the United Kingdom. In contrast, the so-called *German Question* refers to the country's size and place in the heart of Europe and its shifting political borders. Branded in the nineteenth century, the term described efforts to overcome the fractured landscape of territories and movements to create a (German) nation-state. In 1945, the German Question was refocused on how a divided Germany would continue this pursuit. What role would the victorious allies—France, the United States, the United Kingdom, and the Soviet Union—allow it to play in international affairs? How much power could Germany have without destabilizing Europe? How would it atone for the crimes committed under Hitler's rule?

When East and West Germany unified in October 1990, the German Question seemed settled; both unity and freedom were achieved. However, British and US commentators revived the term to ask how Germany would deal with its new unified status. Would it be steadfast in its pursuit of Europeanization, or should we fear a Germanized Europe? When the latter did not materialize, the term faded out of use until Germany emerged as the unsolicited but undisputed leader of the European Union (EU). Now, the question has been turned on its head: Is Germany willing and able to accept a leadership role in European affairs (Ash 2013)? Alternatively, reacting to Germany's controversial role in the euro crisis Roger Cohen (2015) wrote, "Yes, the German Question is back. Is German domination compatible with further European integration or will it prove a fracturing force?" Hans Kundnani (2015) similarly asserts a return of the German question with potentially destabilizing features. Today's German question, according to Kundnani, is based on economic, not political, power. The country "is unique in its combination of economic assertiveness and military abstinence. In a sense, therefore, it may be the purest example of a 'geo-economic power' in the world today" (105).

The Quest for Normality

On both sides of the aisle, Germany's role in the heart of Europe invites scrutiny, expectations, and, at times, trepidation. The shadow of the Third Reich and the Holocaust remains and raises another question: Will Germany ever be considered a normal country? *Normality* is an elusive concept that depends on individual perceptions. It is a reputation that "must be sought out and earned; it is not something granted" automatically (Bittner 2014). Germany has shared the quest for normality with Japan, another aggressor in

World War II, but not Italy, and at times, the terminology has been connected to post-Soviet Russia and Cuba.

Christian Wicke (2015, 3) asserts that "the question of normality . . . became *the* German question" after World War II and "a magic word among the provincial orchestrators of the West German identity project." Being fully sovereign, stable, trustworthy, secure in its borders, and willing to pursue its national interests like other countries in Europe were cornerstones of Chancellor Helmut Kohl's political agenda from 1982 to 1998. German unification marks the watershed in the search for normality. For some, the Holocaust and its legacies will forever deny Germany normal status, while for others, the new normality is unsettling, or at least, getting used to it will take time. Such reasoning applies especially to Germany's role in the EU. Its long-standing, unequivocal support for European integration was widely perceived as extraordinary. Now that its national interests are expressed with newfound confidence, some foreign observers are leery (Maull 2011, 113). Joachim Gauck ("Interview with Joachim Gauck" 1995, 1229) wanted the unified Germany to be a mature nation. Ultimately, whether we grant Germany's new normality, evade clear answers, or use qualifiers, our responses are rooted in our perception of Germany's history and how the country has processed the lessons of the past.

Transitional justice refers to legal and nonlegal measures to address past human rights abuses and can include monetary reparations, public apologies, trials, truth-finding commissions, and dismissals from public office. The term is hardly used in German discourse, which tends to focus on the lengthy and complex process of "dealing with" or "working through" the past. A brief look at Germany's approach to its difficult past reminds us that transformative processes are neither straightforward nor confined to a particular moment, even if the result moved the country from subject to object of transitional justice (Betts 2005). Initially, observers wondered how Germany would address the atrocities committed during Hitler's rule. Peter Graf Kielmannsegg (2000, 643) suggests that the relatively quick return to "normal" life after World War II helped to rebuild Germany and to anchor democracy but also acted as a stumbling block to openly addressing the burden of the past. Shame and guilt were repressed.

Generational change, the emergence of the 1968 student movement, the role of television in bringing Nazi trials and the US-made miniseries "Holocaust" into West German living rooms, and the internationalization of Holocaust memory and human rights abuses more generally elicited public and private conversations about the crimes of the Nazi regime and the cooperation of its citizens. As younger cohorts moved into positions of political power, they often brought a new moral approach to politics and political leadership.

Now many scholars point to the nation's exemplary approach in dealing with its troubled past. Policies and practices include a growing preoccupation with memory culture in the form of museums, memorials, and commemorative dates; explicit consideration of the Nazi past in public discourse, political education, and the media; the establishment of far-ranging restitution and compensation schemes; the pursuit of criminal trials; the development of institutional safeguards against a recurrence of dictatorship; reconciliation efforts toward neighbors who suffered under Nazi occupation; and, last but not least, a shift in values and beliefs manifest in many areas of policy making.

Unification brought the task of dealing with the legacy of yet another cruel dictatorship, this time communist, and the move of the capital to Berlin unlocked opportunities to present a new Germany, fully cognizant of the past. Residents and visitors encounter an impressive array of commemorative sites, unparalleled in any other German city. They call to mind many historical ruptures, from monarchy to republic, from Nazi dictatorship and Holocaust to postwar division to unification and democratic consolidation. The Holocaust memorial next to the Brandenburg Gate, the memorial to the murdered Sinti and Roma next to the Reichstag, and a small memorial to homosexuals who perished in Nazi concentration camps count among the most prominent postunification *lieux de mémoire*. Others, such as the Berlin Wall Memorial Site, which includes a walking trail along the "death strip" once separating the eastern from the western part of the city, remind visitors of the communist past.

FROM PARTITION TO UNITY

Beginning and End of the Cold War

The partition into two separate states is no more than a historical fact for many readers of this book, but for many German citizens, it is lived memory. Founded in May and October 1949, respectively, their establishment was the result of utter defeat in World War II, division into four zones of occupation in 1945, and the outbreak of the Cold War in 1947. The Soviet Zone of Occupation turned into the communist-governed, USSR-dominated GDR; the US, British, and French occupation zones merged into a democratic, Western-oriented Federal Republic of Germany. What began as a transitory arrangement was soon set in stone, literally and symbolically, after the Berlin Wall was erected in August 1961. The symbolic Iron Curtain was made concrete. It marked the end of the immediate postwar period during which the division was hotly contested. System competition between East and West played out in discourse and policies. Starting in the 1960s, both East and West Germany finally set out to consolidate their respective regimes.

Change began some twenty years later. Once the Soviet Union under CPSU General Secretary Mikhail Gorbachev (1985–1991) cut the short leash on which it kept its satellites in Central and Eastern Europe, Poland and Hungary led the way in dismantling the communist regimes that had ruled them since the late 1940s. Other communist leaders clamped down, not least the hardline East German Erich Honecker, but discontent could not be contained. A wisecrack that would be repeated in graffiti and posters captured the diffusion of rebellion across borders and the acceleration of events. British historian Timothy Garton Ash (1990) told dissident writer and later Czech president Václav Havel, "In Poland it took ten years, in Hungary ten months, in East Germany ten weeks: perhaps in Czechoslovakia it will take ten days!" The dominoes did not stop with Czechoslovakia; all European communist regimes toppled. None survived. The collapse took most people by surprise and attracted the rapt attention and admiration of much of the world.

Actions by the communist Hungarian leadership proved crucial to turn the events in East Germany. When they gave the green light to open the borders to Austria in summer 1989, thousands of East German tourists used this route to escape to West Germany. When the East German regime ended travel to Hungary, hundreds of its determined citizens stormed the West German embassy in Prague and demanded safe passage to West Germany. Simultaneously, mass protests in East German cities called for democratic reforms. Once-crucial sectors associated with the communist regime recognized the futility of opposing reform, yet long-anticipated personnel changes among top leadership did not stop the protests. Political circumstances were close to a significant change when the once-unthinkable happened: by accident, the Berlin Wall opened on November 9, 1989 (Sarotte 2014). Despite initial disbelief, this joyous event unleashed an avalanche of emotions, events, and developments. Within weeks, protesters who had demanded change by chanting "we are the people" added the refrain "we are one people," insisting on not only democratic rights but also a merger of the two German states. Almost overnight, unification was on the agenda.

The opening of the Berlin Wall constituted the unofficial end of the Cold War, which exposed opportunities and risks. In particular, it demanded swift answers to the question: What would and should be Germany's place in this new European order? Events unfolded in rapid succession and accelerated pressure on decision makers at home and abroad; all were caught by surprise. The United States, under President George H. W. Bush, quickly took the lead in endorsing a unified Germany. France, under President François Mitterrand, supported the project but wished to gain time before far-reaching decisions were made. The United Kingdom, under the leadership of Prime Minister Margaret Thatcher, was more skeptical, if not hostile, toward the idea of a unified Germany. Mikhail Gorbachev, the Soviet leader, needed prodding but, confronted with the possible collapse of the GDR, gave his assent to unification (Zelikov and Rice 1995; Bozo 2005).

Pressure mounted when the Alliance for Germany, a coalition of political parties, won the first democratic election with the promise of rapid unification with the West. Continuous mass migration from east to west, the instability of the Soviet Union, and East Germans' expectations for a swift increase in their standard of living heightened consciousness of a window of opportunity that could not be ignored.

The modalities of the merger were negotiated under real and perceived time pressure in two separate but overlapping arenas. At the domestic level, in "marathon negotiations" representatives of the German states hammered out the details of the so-called *Unification Treaty*, a process at times bypassing the customary lengthy decision-making channels. On the international level, German unity required the consent of the Allied Powers—France, the Soviet Union, the United Kingdom, and the United States—since the outbreak of the Cold War prevented the signing of a peace treaty after World War II. Between May and September 1990 they negotiated the Two-Plus-Four Treaty with the two German states. A few days after its signing on September 12, 1990, a positive vote by the East German parliament removed the last hurdle for the Unification Treaty to take effect on October 3, 1990. East Germans discarded their old regime and statehood simultaneously.

The day of German Unity, an annual holiday, marked the end of a period of extraordinary politics, highlighted by unusual arrangements, such as the roundtable negotiations, when communist leaders finally sat down with members of the opposition; a hastily arranged first democratic election; and a flurry of decision making at the national and international levels. Rapid, unanticipated change coupled with the need for action supported a return to the proven; few East Germans and even fewer West Germans wanted to engage in a drawn-out debate on the future shape of Germany. High uncertainty justified a no-experiment policy (Welsh 2010, 534–35). Germany remained in NATO and the process of transferring West German political and economic systems to the East could begin in earnest.

Unification Process

Formal unification was just one, albeit crucial, step in the long process of uniting "what belongs together," as former Chancellor Willy Brandt put it.

The gigantic political and economic social engineering project in the eastern part of the country took unanticipated turns and had no master plan; very few variables could be controlled.

"In the beginning," writes Iwona Irwin-Zarecka, associating the period after the fall of communism in Central and Eastern Europe with Genesis, "it all looked quite simple. Enthusiastic crowds took on a grand memory demolition job; the Berlin Wall came down and so did many monuments, portraits of Lenin disappeared with the red flags, streets and towns changed names, history books went into garbage bins, museums of revolution shut their doors forever. . . . The initial euphoria was not to last" (1993, 33). Although referring to the complex "groundwork of recovering Eastern Europe's history" (36), her statement has broader implications. Citizens everywhere in the region had to absorb the fact that economic modernization would take time and involve hardship. Democratic freedom, political competition, and marketization of the once-planned economy created winners and losers. Expectations about what the United States and Western Europe would do to assist in these difficult transition years were disappointed.

In Germany, media headlines emphasized the differences between East and West to reacquaint citizens who had been separated by the Iron Curtain and to indicate the magnitude of the task ahead. German-American historian Fritz Stern (1993; 2005) said the unified Germany had been given a "second chance" at democracy after the failed Weimar Republic (1919–33) but, a few years later, lamented that "pain and disappointment" marred its first few years. Jubilation yielded to the reality that new opportunities and freedoms for eastern Germans would require difficult economic and social adjustments and that western Germans could not expect politics as usual. Most citizens of the old Federal Republic were at ease with the post–World War II borders, identified with Western European integration, eagerly internalized the limits on international military responsibility, and basked in their economic accomplishment. Elites and citizens accepted the adage calling West Germany an economic giant but a political dwarf, and their frustration built when confronted with the financial cost of unification and the difficult task of reforming the East.

East Germans, on the other hand, wanted to acquire the economic and political status of West Germans, but many soon felt slighted by their western compatriots. Some critics thought the accession process resembled colonization. While this metaphor diminishes East German input in and ownership of the processes that shaped the merger, it highlights the perception of western dominance and arrogance. In the end, citizens on both sides of the previous border felt alienated from one another. This outcome should not have come as a surprise. Unification was a step into the unknown and always contained a built-in tension in calling attention to the differences between the two Germanies while attempting to eliminate them. Talk of a *unification crisis* ensued, peaking around the mid-1990s, but by the end of the decade other problems affecting both parts of the country emerged. Reforms in such policy areas as the labor market, the pension system, education, and healthcare were overdue, delayed and accentuated by the merging of East and West. Nevertheless, despite selective nostalgia, East and West Germans overwhelmingly, though at times grudgingly, agree that unification has been good.

HISTORICAL LEGACIES AND POLITICAL INSTITUTIONS

A country's history shapes political institutions, political culture, and policies. It creates national symbols and traditions and leaves a trail of often unresolved legacies and conflicts. To this day, Germany's place in the historical trajectory of Western European powers, the rise of National Socialism, World War II, and the Holocaust are focal points in debates about its identity, policy styles, the features of its polity, and its role in Europe. Many debates over topics ranging from foreign and security policy to abortion and asylum hark back to lessons learned and responsibilities inherited from these dark experiences. Its polity is likewise shaped by memories of the failed democracy of the Weimar Republic and the experience of two dictatorships, Nazi and communist. To understand political institutions and politics in Germany today requires reflection on the history that shaped them. Which factors contributed to the successful remaking of the Federal Republic of Germany?

The theory of institutionalism helps to conceptualize the trajectories. The scholarly literature distinguishes a rational choice, sociological, and *historical institutionalism*, but in reality, these categories are "border crossing" (Thelen 1999). Rational choice institutionalism focuses on the strategic interactions of political actors who make decisions according to what they perceive as in their best interests. Sociological institutionalism is less concerned with explaining the self-interest of political actors but emphasizes changing societal norms and culture and their impact on political behavior. Historical institutionalism, our approach, falls in between: "If you think that history and ideas matter, institutions structure actor's choices but are subject to change by actors themselves, and real people make decisions that are not always efficient or purely self-interested, then you probably are a historical institutionalist" (Steinmo 2008, 136). Inclusive, transparent, and accountable institutions are widely praised as the basis of stable and prosperous democracies, but no one set of institutions guarantees such positive outcomes. Scholars ask which formal institutional arrangements best fit a particular setting and how they structure political behavior. Choices are shaped by different historical trajectories and the preferences of political leaders; no "one size fits all."

Historical institutionalism also assumes that institutions, once created, tend to be durable and path dependent; that is, continuity is preferred over other options, and change follows the logic of the known and proven, although, once again, the boundaries of continuity and change are flexible. After 1945, learning from the past meant melding traditional institutional features with significant innovations. After 1990, stability won out over major change. Most features of the united Germany follow the West German path. In any case, choosing between change and continuity requires an awareness of long time frames. Continuity and incremental change are characteristics of policy making; rapid, dramatic change is the exception, while stagnation is often a sign of crisis and/or enforced stability. Even stable democracies routinely encounter political challenges, often triggered by economic and/or social developments, some urgent, some lingering before actions ensue. Domestic stimuli, fueled by dissatisfaction with prevailing political and/or economic developments, feed change, and sparks from abroad can ignite action. Historical and political narratives must balance national with international priorities, but domestic agents and structures often win out; at best, external stimuli and pressures frame national decisions. Such challenges are not unusual. Crisis management and continuous adaptation to a changing political environment are the bread and butter of politics and policy making. How politicians respond to them is determined by place and time. Gradualism and incrementalism have been hallmarks of institutional and policy change in the history of the Federal Republic. Adaptations take time and may be interrupted by periods of stagnation or bursts of activity.

DEFINING KEY TERMS

This book examines the intersection of domestic and international influences to account for challenges and transformations in Germany. It emphasizes the period since 1990, framing the analysis within post–World War II developments. The manuscript was completed in the summer of 2017, but some newer developments were added, including the outcome of the 2017 national election. The book's cover draws attention to Germany's place in the geographical, political, and cultural map of Europe. German politics and policies are interpreted as the outcome of enduring institutional configurations and political preferences, influenced and challenged by three interrelated processes: unification, Europeanization, and globalization. A few words about their meaning are in order.

Unification

History is often measured in sizable swaths; separation into a communist-governed East Germany and a democratic West Germany turned out to be a forty-year interlude. Indeed, a few years after the demise of the GDR, its history was relegated to the back burner. A similar fate befell its dramatic regime change. Most Germans remember—more and more vaguely—their initial sense of disbelief and joy when the Berlin Wall was breached on November 9, 1989.

The unification process can be broken down into three stages: the sprint toward unity in 1990; the early 1990s, when most decisions about merging the two states were made and implemented; and the return to normal politics and a more gradual assimilation of political, economic, social, and cultural developments. Navigating uncharted waters, they challenged assumptions on both sides of the former Iron Curtain. Whether and to what extent they affected Germany's international role, its institutions, and policies will be analyzed in the following chapters. We will also show that change occurred both in competition and in tandem with Europeanization and globalization.

Europeanization

As far back as the High Middle Ages, the diffusion of naming and marriage patterns, coins, written contracts, religious symbols and rituals, and cultural canons, often imparted by newly formed universities, marked the birth of Europe (Bartlett 1993). Since then, Europeanization has been intimately connected to the spread of cultural icons, traditions, ideas, and norms in Europe and abroad. In all cases, the degree of penetration of these transnational processes differs considerably with location and policy area. Transnational diffusion continues to define who is perceived as inside or outside of Europe.

In contrast to historical examples associated with violent conquest, post–World War II efforts to integrate Europe rely on the voluntary transfer of sovereignty attributes to the EU. No longer defined by the ideological East-West divide, European polities and societies have become more diverse and multilayered. In the EU alone, twenty-four languages and many more regional dialects are spoken. Increased cross-border trade and organized political responses to globalization have challenged traditional ways of coping with economic crises.

Today, the term *Europeanization* is most often associated with the impact of European institutions on EU members' domestic institutions, policies, and policy processes. The transformation of the nation-states (twenty-eight in 2017, pending the exit of the United Kingdom) includes transnational features, such as closer policy coordination on the European level, joint representation with other EU countries in international organizations, and cooperation in foreign and security policy. However, the resulting policies and practices are not confined to member states; nonmembers, such as Switzerland and Norway, are affiliated through many formal and informal channels.

In reaction to increasingly complex globalization forces, the EU aimed to position itself as an international actor. It represents a bloc of countries that individually and collectively participate in major international organizations, such as the World Trade Organization (WTO), the International Labor Organization (ILO), and the United Nations (UN). It is claiming its place among the major world powers while allowing its member states to guard their own foreign policy priorities and traditions, a process characterized by cooperation as much as competition and dissent.

The EU's impact includes regulations and benchmarks that will be adapted and implemented in the member states, which are not simply recipients but political actors. Depending on policy area, countries can act as trendsetters, fence-sitters, or foot-draggers in designing or promoting EU policies. Thus, Europeanization is a two-way process, top-down and bottom-up, and highly differentiated based on country and policy area. Furthermore, political leaders spend considerable time consulting, debating, and deciding with their counterparts in other EU member states; the transnational networks of domestic political parties and interest groups increasingly operate at both the domestic and European levels. As a result, Europeanization has taken on deeper and new meaning, and separating the national from the supranational has become increasingly difficult in many policy areas. Throughout the book, we use the term *Europeanization* to refer to processes that foster shared values, institutional adaptions, and policy changes in many European countries. Direct and indirect actions by the EU serve as their major motor, but transnational networks and communication also encourage diffusion and emulation across borders.

Globalization

The concept of globalization became prominent in the 1990s, but the guiding ideas and transnational connections are much older (James and Steger 2014). Historians dispute whether it emerged in the sixth or the thirteenth century, but most agree that the two most important waves took place in the eighteenth century and, after an interruption between world wars, the second half of the twentieth century. A consensus holds that global interactions intensified and accelerated toward the end of the twentieth century with innovations in transportation and communication.

Globalization refers to the interconnection and universalization of cultural, economic, and social exchanges but is most often associated with economic and financial transactions. Germany's stake in them is based on its role as Europe's leading exporter and one of the four leading exporters in the world. Critics of globalization point to the loss of sovereignty, job outsourcing, environmental damage, economic exploitation, and rise in economic inequality. Supporters argue that globalization is conducive to the spread of knowledge and technology, the promotion of free trade, and the internationalization of human rights and democracy.

Globalization complicates governing: the extent and pace of change require political steering, but politicians are less able to control decision making; global integration and the dispersal of decision-making structures go hand in hand (Maull 2015). In many policy arenas, such as global warming, international trade, and migration, today's answers must be national, European, and global.

PLAN OF THE BOOK

Chapter 1 makes a case for the study of German politics and offers a backdrop for understanding the momentous changes that Germany has experienced since 1990. It traces German unification, contrasting the expectations and reality that followed, and links this process to European integration and globalization. Chapter 2 introduces the major political institutions and situates them in a comparative framework. Political parties are essential actors, and chapter 3 analyzes their role, electoral trends, and elite composition. Political institutions do not act in a vacuum; they acquire legitimacy through the citizenry. Different patterns of political participation constitute the core of chapter 4, but we also pay special attention to citizens' activities, political culture, and changing attitudes toward gender and religious affiliation.

Immigration and the integration of foreigners are topics of high priority for all Western European countries. German society is more pluralistic than ever, and chapter 5 outlines its stumbling path toward encompassing immigrants and its ongoing struggles to address mass migration and the integration of foreigners. German power is most often defined as an economic power, and we analyze the characteristics that distinguish its economic system in chapter 6.

European integration has been the fulcrum of German foreign policy. Its significance for Germany's identity and its role in international relations is explained in chapter 7. Chapter 8 turns to Germany's role in global politics, emphasizing its evolution from bystander to active participant while maintaining key aspects of its civilian-power approach. The final chapter summarizes some of our findings and charts future prospects. Throughout, we compare distinctive German features with trends experienced by other advanced democracies, mostly in Western Europe.

Chapter 2

Power Distribution in
a Complex Democracy

KEY TERMS

Bundesrat

Bundestag

chancellor

coalition government

consensual vs. majoritarian democracy

constitution writing

defensive democracy

federal constitutional court

federalism

federal president

judicialization

multilevel governance

semisovereign state

veto players

Institutions, defined as laws, formal and informal rules, and formal organizations, such as governmental entities and political parties, are the core of democratic political systems. Historically, once created, they tend to be rather durable and path dependent. Initial choices become entrenched, and since the costs of reversal are unknown, any attempt at alteration encounters resistance.

While some German political institutions, such as federalism, are long-lived, the system tolerates innovation and adaptation. After 1945, learning from the past meant significantly revising traditional governmental features. After unification, stability won out; demands for a radical departure from the proven West German model were muted, and the system survived relatively unscathed. However, institutions had to be upgraded, not only to absorb the impact of EU decision-making procedures and the need to implement EU policies in national and subnational contexts, but also to respond to changing domestic circumstances.

In this chapter, we examine the pillars of the political system: the constitution, the executive, the legislature, and the judiciary. We explain Germany's parliamentary and federal systems by highlighting its major features and debates. Our comparative framework examines both broad trends and distinctive German characteristics. We describe formal institutions and politics in action to illustrate a system that has been called complex, interlocking, semisovereign, and consensual, to cite just a few of the adjectives. We borrow the term "complex democracy" from the essay collection edited by Volker Schneider and Burkard Eberlein (2015) to capture the unique blending of party dominance (described in chapter 3), coalition government, multifaceted center and periphery relations, prominent Constitutional Court, and strong intermediary institutions that distinguishes Germany's political system.

BACKGROUND

Choices made in the aftermath of utter defeat in 1945 reflected institutional and policy patterns and lessons from the past, both good and bad. West Germany shouldered the burdens left by the Nazi state, which included large-scale reparations to its victims and shaping reconciliation policies (Feldman 2012). Democracy, individual rights, and rule of law were the new priorities. In the east, the communist state's founding principles were antifascism and collectivism in the private and public spheres. The two states pursued similar goals—recovery from World War II, economic and political stability—quite differently, and in the Cold War decades, global competition between democracy and communism reinforced their divergent paths.

The peaceful overthrow of the communist regime in 1989 soon gave way to calls for German unity. The two constitutional options for merging the two German states were adhering to and extending the West German Basic Law to the eastern part of the country (Art. 23) or writing a new constitution (Art. 146). Article 23 of the West German Basic Law of 1949 had kept the possibility of a unified Germany alive by stating, "for the time being, this Basic Law shall apply in the territory of the Länder Baden, Bavaria, Bremen, Greater Berlin, Hamburg, Hesse, Lower Saxony, North Rhine-Westphalia, Rhineland-Palatinate, Schleswig-Holstein, Württemberg-Baden, Württemberg-Hohenzollern. It shall be put into force for other parts of Germany on their accession." Some East German dissidents advocated substantial amendments or even a new constitution, but West German elites and the public clearly favored maintaining the proven model. The West German constitution was retained and only amended to reflect minor concessions that resulted from unification. No assembly convened to draft a new constitution, and no referendum was held; rather, each of the newly founded East German Länder parliaments voted to accede to the West German federation. This legal provision paved the way for swift unification.

The Unification Treaty, signed on August 31, 1990, laid out the merger framework, which largely duplicated the government structure of the old Federal Republic. "In times of crisis or deep uncertainty," Kathleen Thelen writes (2004, 292), "political actors often specifically eschew experimentation and instead fall back on familiar formulas—resulting in institutional reproduction, not change." Institutional structures resist change even during times of normal politics. Coupled with the asymmetry in resources and population (the population ratio between West and East Germany in 1990 was 4:1), the ready-made model of West German institutions was transferred to the east with minor modifications. Wade Jacoby (2001, 189) playfully summed it up: "To put it metaphorically, although the East Germans were allowed to order their own meal, the menu was limited, substitutions were not welcome, and the chefs were easily insulted if the specials were ignored."

In an important symbolic move, the Unification Treaty designated Berlin the new capital but left open whether it would resume its prior role as the seat of government or whether Bonn would keep this distinction. A heated debate across party lines ensued. Those favoring relocation saw it not only as returning Berlin to its historical place but also as an important symbolic gesture toward including eastern Germans. Those in favor of Bonn harnessed a different kind of symbolism: its association with a successful democracy. They evoked Berlin's associations with past upheavals and Nazi rule and pointed to the considerable costs the move would involve, money that would be better spent on rebuilding the east.

In June 1991, at the end of a marathon debate of over ten hours, a slim majority of Members of Parliament (MPs) (338:320) opted for Berlin as the capital and the seat of government. In the final negotiations, as a gesture of goodwill and compromise, some ministries and federal agencies were kept in Bonn. The recommendation that the Bundesrat, the federal chamber, should remain in Bonn was initially respected but revised in September 1996 to ensure close communication and smooth functioning of the two houses of parliament. Construction delayed the move of governmental institutions to Berlin, which finally took place in 1999–2000.

The prospect of building a new government quarter almost from scratch is a rare opportunity, and it took place under unique circumstances. The Berlin Wall, erected in August 1961, divided the city, creating a desolate no-man's land in its center. Once demolished, it left prime real estate for new construction. How would the unified Germany present itself? To use Stefan Sperling's apt description, "architecture expresses a form of governing" (2013, 7). In capitals around the world, the location, size, and style of government buildings project power and prestige and aim to join the past with the present, those who govern with those who are governed. Berlin is no exception, but designers and politicians were more ambitious; the structures would express a democratic and open Germany. Architects in forty-four countries submitted more than 800 proposals to the design competition. The winning concepts emphasized transparency and links between the executive and legislature and the eastern and western parts of Berlin. Transparency was expressed by the expansive use of glass, most strikingly in the dome above the Reichstag, which now houses the Bundestag, the seat of parliament. Directly across is the chancellor's office, so parliament and the head of government face each other, symbolizing mutual control as much as cooperation. The layout links eastern and western territory and executive and legislative buildings in the so-called *Band des Bundes* (ribbon or band of the Federation). From a bird's-eye view, they represent a unit; a stroll on ground reinforces accessibility and short distances. Spacious office buildings for MPs, meeting facilities for parliamentary committees, a nearby press center, and a building specially designed as a preschool for government employees' children reinforce the idea of a "working parliament." The extensive display of installations, sculptures, and paintings by world-renowned artists sheds new light on history and politics; "green" construction emphasizes sustainability. These architectural designs illustrate how ideas can create and construct institutions; functionality and symbolism go hand in hand.

Within a short time, Berlin has retaken its place among the major European cities, known not only as the thriving capital and seat of government but also as a place of commemoration and architectural innovation. It is a hub for business start-ups, research, higher education, cultural vibrancy, and diversity. The one-time principal conductor of its Philharmonic Orchestra, Englishman Sir Simon Rattle, summarized its special flair as "60 percent Germany, 38 percent New York, and the rest Wild West" (*Deutschland Magazine* 2007). The traditional advertising slogan "Berlin is worth a visit" rings true; it is among the top tourist destinations in Europe.

THE CONSTITUTION AND CONSTITUTIONAL DESIGN

It is common to try to engineer power distribution and political outcomes through institutional choices, such as electoral systems and various checks and balances. Crafting new constitutions now often includes external expertise. In 1948, when the West German constitution was under discussion, the vocabulary of institutional design and constitutional engineering had not been coined, but they were practiced, and the occupying powers, primarily US officials, played a crucial, if mostly informal, role in initiating and monitoring the talks. The sixty-five elected delegates (sixty-one men and four women) from the Länder who convened in the Parliamentary Council to write the new constitution were diverse and had experienced the tumultuous years of the Weimar democracy firsthand. The lessons of the past would dictate principles. They avoided the term *constitution* in favor of Basic Law (*Grundgesetz*) since it would be a transitory, purely western arrangement, but from its adoption on May 23, 1949, only its geographic reach was provisional. The commitment to democracy and the rule of law was conceived as permanent (Heun 2011, 10), and the writers made clear their intention to act "on behalf of those Germans to whom participation was denied." The goal of eventual unification "by free self-determination" stood alongside the desire "to serve the peace of the World as an equal partner in a united Europe" (preamble). After unification, the Basic Law was retained and the preamble revised to highlight Germany's "determination to promote world peace as an equal partner in a united Europe."

Thus, Western allies and West German politicians took the lead in formalizing the division of the two separate states, thereby accelerating ongoing preparations for a new constitution in the Soviet Zone of Occupation. A constitutional committee drawn from the German People's Council (*Deutscher Volksrat*), an all-German institution, prepared a draft that was adopted in June 1949. Its structure and goals were similar to those of the West German constitution, including use of the Weimar constitution as a reference point. It established the principles of a federal and parliamentary system, but in reality, any pretense of democracy quickly vanished as it was interpreted according to the ideological tenets of the communist Socialist Unity Party (SED), and dictatorship ensued. Federalism was abolished in 1952; the parliament rubber-stamped SED policies. The prominent references to one German nationality in the 1949 version were gradually abolished. The revised 1968 constitution declared "a socialist state of the German nation" and paid lip service to eventual unification—under communist auspices. In 1974, the constitution was amended heavily. The GDR was now officially "a socialist state of workers and farmers . . . under the leadership of the working class and its Marxist-Leninist party"; any reference to a German nation was omitted. Perhaps ironically, German unity became reality only sixteen years after the concept was officially swept off the table by East German politicians. In contrast to the West German constitution, the East German document was mostly rhetorical and symbolic. Alterations reflected the changing identity of the GDR, but the rule of law was not a living principle, and none of its provisions allowed citizens to claim their rights against the powerful communist state. SED rulings always superseded constitutional rights.

After the peaceful revolution of 1989, in the east, roundtables, a metaphor suggesting the equal status of participants, brought together major opposition groups and newly founded parties, citizen's associations, and representatives of the ruling communist party. The Central Roundtable convened in East Berlin from December 1989 to March 1990; modeling arrangements in Poland and Hungary, participants negotiated the transition from communist rule to democracy and the first free elections. The democratic election in March 1990 resulted in a landslide victory for pro-unification parties, and the topic of how and when Germany would unify could no longer be delayed. Roundtable members had drafted a new GDR constitution; concurrently, the existing eastern constitution was so heavily amended, it was almost unrecognizable. The draft, particularly its emphasis on plebiscitary elements, influenced the constitutions of the newly established Länder in the former GDR.

Article 5 of the Unification Treaty (1990) recommended that members of the newly elected all-German parliament review and propose amendments to the Basic Law. A joint commission of Bundestag and Bundesrat representatives formed at the beginning of 1992. Their work was controversial, but the momentum for a new constitution was lost, and the asymmetric power relations between west and east allowed only minor changes, which included the promotion of equal basic rights for men and women and amendments for environmental protection. Thus, the constitutional order of the united Germany shows a high degree of path dependence. Institutional choices that had proven quite successful in bolstering democratic development in West Germany proved remarkably durable, even in the face of the sweeping changes that followed the peaceful revolution in the east.

Timing was another factor. The commission's work took place during the adoption of the Maastricht Treaty, which influenced subsequent constitutional adaptations (Quint 1997). The original Article 23 was revoked and replaced by a commitment to European integration, in accord with the intent to create a political union in Europe. Some of the most far-reaching changes to the Basic Law, such as the revision of asylum rights (Art. 16 a), were linked directly to the push for a common European approach. German unification had less impact on constitutional changes than Europeanization.

Although the amendment process requires a two-thirds majority of the Bundestag and Bundesrat, many of the constitution's 146 articles have been amended, deleted, or added. Between 1990 and 2013 alone, more than ninety changes were logged ("Datenhandbuch zur Geschichte des Bundestages seit 1990" 2014). This record contrasts sharply with the thirty-three attempted and twenty-seven realized amendments to the comparatively short US constitution.

On the sixty-fifth anniversary commemoration of the Basic Law, Parliament President Norbert Lammert (CDU) called it one of the "strokes of luck" in German history. Most German citizens agree; they consider the Basic Law one of Germany's greatest achievements. Scholars praise its adaptability and inclusiveness. Some, like political philosopher Jürgen Habermas, emphasize the population's trust in the Basic Law's legitimacy, which he calls "constitutional patriotism" (*Verfassungspatriotismus*) (Müller 2006). Not bad for a constitution that was supposed to be only transitory.

IN DEFENSE OF DEMOCRACY

Lessons from the past did not apply only to power distribution and structures. After World War II, widespread sentiment held that lingering undemocratic attitudes, a polarized political culture, and antidemocratic militancy contributed to the failure of democracy after 1919. In light of this history and the uncertain postwar political climate, newly appointed and elected politicians and the Western allies wondered how to defend the new democracy against its enemies on the left and right to avoid the pitfalls of the Weimar Republic. How could and should the performance of political institutions be strengthened to convince citizens of their legitimacy (Ullrich 2009)? The answers were manifold. Some constitutional principles are inviolable. For example, the federal organization and the bill of rights (Arts. 1 and 19) are exempt from changes. Article 1 protects human dignity. Article 20, 4, reinforces the basic constitutional principles and allows individuals to resist attempts to undermine the democratic order if no other option exists.

The new democracy was built to be resilient; memories of the Weimar Republic and the Third Reich inspired efforts to contain antidemocratic forces. Defensive or militant democracy, as it is often called in the English-language literature, refers to the use of legal means to protect against those who might undermine it. Its tools include civic education, party bans to combat extremism, surveillance of "enemies of the state," the criminalization of propaganda against the state, and restrictions on free speech (Downs 2012; Müller 2006). Freedom of assembly, speech, press, opinion, and religion are guaranteed, but it is a criminal offense to deny the Holocaust and to show Nazi symbols; inciting popular hatred incurs penalties.

In the same vein, social groups can be prohibited should they intend or act to undermine the constitutional order (Art. 9). Upon the recommendation of the Bundestag, the Federal Constitutional Court can ban political parties that threaten to undercut the democratic principles upon which the Federal Republic was built (Art. 21, 2). In 1952, the Socialist Reich Party of Germany (*Sozialistische Reichspartei Deutschlands*) was declared illegal due to its open Nazi sympathies and Holocaust denial. Four years later, the

Constitutional Court acted against the Communist party of Germany (*Kommunistische Partei Deutschlands*). Since then, the threat of elimination has hovered over various parties, especially the right-wing extremist National-Democratic Party of Germany (NPD). Plans to ban it failed in 2003 and again in 2017. The constitutional court argued in its 2017 ruling that the party, despite similarities to the Nazi party, was too feeble to endanger democracy. Defeating a party at the voting booth is preferred to outlawing it.

The concept of defensive democracy also applies to civil service employees, who are sworn to defend the constitution (Art. 33). This provision was put to test when leftist terrorists, the Red Army Faction, openly and violently challenged the existing democracy. Fearful of potential sympathizers, in 1972, the "Anti-Radical Decree" was passed to keep radicals, in particular teachers, out of civil service professions. Highly controversial from the beginning, it was applied unevenly and has since been revoked in most German Länder. In the interim, according to one study, 3.5 million people had been scrutinized, and about 10,000 lost their jobs or were denied entry into public service (Hofmann 2013). After 1990, aspiring public service employees were again vetted for ties to the former GDR state security service, or the *Stasi*. The practice mixed retributive elements with protection of the constitutional order, and, once again, it was applied inconsistently across the federation. Screening for past affiliation with the secret police can still be applied in certain circumstances, but, as before, it does not automatically lead to loss of position.

In Germany, protecting the constitutional order means favoring representative democracy and restricting elements of direct democracy. This preference responds to Nazi ideology's manipulation of the "masses." Public referenda are reserved for two extraordinary occasions. One is revising Länder borders, which requires the assent of the population in the affected Land or Länder (Art. 29, 2). Territorial reform is a topic with staying power but little public support. For example, the governments of the two neighboring Länder, Berlin and Brandenburg, agreed to form one state; the 1996 public referendum failed, but the idea of closer administrative and legal cooperation survived. Other proposals—for example, merging different northern states—were unpopular with citizens and state governments and never succeeded. The second instance that calls for a referendum is the adoption of a new constitution (Art. 146), but even with unification, it did not happen.

National referenda to decide questions of domestic importance and EU involvement have become common in many other European countries, and pressure to implement them in Germany is mounting. In the past, demands for more participatory rights were mostly advanced by Alliance 90/The Greens; that is, a left-leaning party. Now, right-wing parties, such as the Alternative for Germany (AfD), advance the idea of public referenda as a way to represent what they perceive as the will of the people. This usurpation of direct democracy by the populist right as well as the outcomes of recent referenda, including the British vote to leave the EU, have opened a debate on the pros and cons of this approach.

The history of Nazi and communist dictatorships has strengthened the institutional and legal features of defensive democracy in Germany to ensure democratic stability, but they require the active support of civil society, as we will explain in chapter 4.

PARLIAMENTARY SYSTEMS

Forms of horizontal power distribution are classified as parliamentary, presidential, and semi-presidential (hybrid). Great Britain is the model majoritarian parliamentary system; the United States is the model for presidential systems, and France is the model of a semi-presidential system. Parliamentary systems remain dominant in Europe. Their patterns of global diffusion reflect geographic proximity, historical evolution from monarchies to democracies, and legacies of colonialism. The presidential system, created by the United States, is strong throughout the Americas but practiced around the world. In Europe, semi-presidential systems have become more common in recent decades, but the powers of the president vis-à-vis the prime minister vary considerably, muddling definition. In this section, we provide a primer on presidential and parliamentary systems and omit discussion of the semi-presidential system; table 2.1 illustrates the ideal types of executives in presidential and parliamentary systems, although systems vary from country to country.

At first glance, this scheme suggests that presidents play a more powerful role than prime ministers (in Austria and Germany, the term *chancellor* is used). It also points to a weak separation of power between the executive

Table 2.1. Executives in Presidential and Parliamentary Political Systems

Presidential	*Parliamentary*
One-person executive (head of state and head of government)	Prime minister = head of government
	President/monarch = head of state (figurehead)
Popular election	Prime minister: elected by parliament/appointed by president/monarch
	President: popular election or electoral assembly
Fixed term limits	Prime minister: no term limits
	President: term limits
Noncollegial executive	Collegial executive/cabinet government
Strict separation of executive and legislative branches	Interdependence of executive and legislative branches

and legislature in parliamentary systems and relative ease of decision making since the prime minister usually can count on a parliamentary majority to get things done. How do these features work in practice?

Prime Minister vs. President

The list of powers of the chief executive in presidential systems is impressive. Sitting presidents have a popular mandate and cannot be removed from office unless impeached. They are the commander in chief of the armed forces and set the policy agenda. They cannot introduce legislation, but their veto power and the right to issue executive orders can be powerful tools. In contrast, prime ministers' tenure depends on the support of the parliament, to which they are accountable. Still, prime ministers can be authoritative executives through functions assigned by the constitution and political practice, especially when they also lead the strongest party. For example, they appoint their cabinet independent of parliament, and the executive branch introduces most bills. Some can also build influence over time because they do not have term limits.

The pathway to office also differs: in parliamentary systems, candidates for the head of government usually have a long affiliation with their party; in presidential systems, it is easier for outsiders and/or independents to seek the highest office. In all political systems, first office holders often play a decisive role in shaping the position.

In practice, generalizations fall short because power is always personal and contextual. Realized power depends very much on the degree of cooperation a prime minister or president receives from the legislature. In contrast to presidents, who may have to deal with a divided government, prime ministers can generally rely on a majority in parliament, but the specific structure still matters. In strong bicameral systems, if the second chamber is ruled by the opposition party/ies, it can impede governance. Majorities assembled as coalitions of two or more parties can weaken the head of government, who must broker compromises among divergent views.

Not only do presidential and parliamentary systems differ substantially; differences hold within the categories. The position of prime minister in Italy and Japan, for example, is generally weak; in contrast, the British and Canadian prime ministers rank among the most powerful. The German chancellor is routinely included in the list of prime ministers with high authority (O'Malley 2007). The term *chancellor democracy* was coined to describe the tenure of Konrad Adenauer (CDU) and his central role (Niclauß 2004, 68–69), and recent trends have further privileged executive power in policy making. The concept of the *presidentialization of parliamentary systems* (Poguntke and Webb 2005) highlights the salience of the mass media and their focus on the chief executive in daily politics, while acknowledging the resources of prime ministers in terms of staff and their central role in European decision making. Hanna Bäck et al. (2009, 229) define presidentialization "as a trend towards (a) more autonomy of the executive vis-à-vis parliamentary parties, (b) increasingly leadership-centred electoral processes and (c) decreasing collegiality/collectivity within the executive." They also point to the concept's shortcomings, including the intrinsic paradox: How can prime ministers become more presidential when some of them are already more powerful than some presidents? The idea of presidentialization also ignores the ways in which MPs and legislatures counter broadening executive authority, a topic discussed below. Strong, independent courts may also counterbalance tendencies toward presidentialization. Finally, personal characteristics, such as weak or strong public appeal, or charisma, consensual or confrontational behavior, and political experience contribute to executive power.

A parliamentary system is characterized by close interdependence between the executive and legislative branches. The prime minister depends on the legislature for support and often comes from its ranks, as do most cabinet members; the executive is accountable to the parliament. This interdependence intentionally weakens but does not obliterate the principle of separation. Both executive and legislature guard their independence and rights while realizing that cooperation is required. The German system is built on a clear-cut separation of powers between the head of state, which is a ceremonial post, and the head of government and between the executive and the judiciary.

All democratic political systems involve a complex, multilevel network of governance, making decision-making processes often lengthy and incremental. First, they all include various veto players; that is, individuals or collective political actors "whose agreement is required for a change in the status quo" (Tsebelis 2002, 17). Germany's system has strong veto players. In coalition governments at the national and almost always at the regional level, the partners must compromise. Germany is also a federal system that allocates the Bundesrat important decision-making power, and, at times, the Constitutional Court has acted as veto player. Organized interests, in particular trade unions and employers' associations, are strong but limited to specific policy arenas. Veto players are relevant not only to national decision making; they influence the process of Europeanization—that is, the national adaptation of European laws.

Typology of Parliamentary Systems

Political scientists have tried to classify the varieties of parliamentary systems. Arend Lijphart (2012) contrasts the *majoritarian* Westminster system of the

United Kingdom, based on executive dominance, a unitary system, a two-party system, and asymmetrical bicameralism, with *consensual* democracies that rely on executive power sharing in broad coalition governments, balance of power between executive and legislature, multiparty systems, proportional representation as the electoral rule, decentralized federal government, strong bicameralism, constitutional rigidity, judicial review, and an independent central bank. Switzerland, Belgium, and the EU are his examples, but many features also ring true for Germany. Manfred Schmidt (2015, 35–36) refined Lijphart's typology, distinguishing among four "worlds of democracy": unitary majoritarian (United Kingdom); federalist majoritarian (United States); unitary consensus (northern Europe and the Benelux countries); and the "antitype to majoritarian systems," the federalist consensus democracies (Germany and Switzerland).

Gerhard Lehmbruch (1976) focused on the characteristics and evolution of *negotiation democracies*. He highlighted the interplay of party competition at the federal level with the constant need for the central and Land governments to calibrate and negotiate. When partisan majorities are divided between the Bundestag and the Bundesrat, passing legislation that requires the consent of both requires negotiation and compromise. The combination of bicameralism and federalism led Schmidt to label Germany a "grand coalition state"; that is, the major parties have to cooperate even when no "grand coalition" is officially in charge (2011, 41–42).

Peter J. Katzenstein (1987) famously coined the term *semisovereign state* to describe three distinct aspects of West German policy networks that acted as checks and balances: the coalition government in which political parties operate, federalism that connects regions and the central government in interlocking ways, and parapublic institutions as a major arena of policy implementation. They fostered an informal policy style meant to overcome resistance by strong veto players. Incremental change was systemic, but the accumulation of incremental change could be transformative.

These analyses have much in common: they emphasize coalition governments, strong federalism, and the resultant need to find common ground for the system to work. The remainder of the chapter will focus on how these features play out in Germany.

THE FEDERAL PRESIDENT

In republican parliamentary systems, the prime minister, or chancellor in Austria and Germany, is the head of government, while the president acts as head of state. In constitutional monarchies, such as the United Kingdom or Denmark, the king or queen is head of state. The West German constitution deliberately reduced the powers of the president and increased those of the chancellor in response to developments in the Weimar Republic. Under its system, the president was elected by the people for seven-year terms, held the role of commander in chief, and had sweeping emergency powers at his disposal. In the polarized political climate of the interwar years, chancellors came and went; in the fourteen years of the Weimar Republic, twelve chancellors served, allowing the popularly elected president (Friedrich Ebert, 1919–25 and Paul von Hindenburg, 1925–33) to consolidate and usurp power. As a consequence, the Federal Republic clipped the president's power to prevent battles over authority.

Election and Tenure

The presidential term is five years and can be renewed once. So far, all officeholders have been men. The president is elected by a convention of the members of the Bundestag and an equal number of representatives chosen from and by the sixteen states. The major parties determine the choice, and the chancellor has an important voice in the decision. Apart from Joachim Gauck (2012–17), presidents belong to political parties but are expected to be above politics once in office. Gauck's path deviated from the usual recruitment and career channels. A pastor and dissident in communist East Germany, he owes national and international name recognition to his role as the first federal commissioner of an agency responsible for the preservation of, and research into, the records of the infamous state security, the *Stasi*. Under his leadership, the agency was the first of its kind to open its extensive files to those who had been spied upon, a practice now common in many postcommunist countries. Current Federal President Frank-Walter Steinmeier (SPD), on the other hand, had a more typical career path: he twice served as Minister for Foreign Affairs before assuming his new office in March 2017.

Functions and Authority

The division of labor between the chancellor and the president tilts the distribution of power decidedly in favor of the chancellor. The president's duties are largely ceremonial or formal and symbolic. For example, the president receives foreign dignitaries, formally appoints the members of government, and signs legislative decisions into law; his office checks whether the formal procedures of law making have been followed but does not challenge the content of the laws.

The president is nevertheless more than a figurehead. He can act as the "conscience of the nation" and use his soft power to call attention to pressing policy concerns. His main tools are public support, diplomatic acumen, and rhetorical eloquence. Famous speeches by presidents can have lasting influence, maybe none more than the words of Richard von Weizsäcker, in office from 1984 to 1994, at the fortieth commemoration of the end of World War II. He referred to May 8, 1945, as a day of liberation, not capitulation, opening and setting the tone for a renewed confrontation with the legacy of World War II and the Holocaust. Other speeches also made important contributions to the national discourse. For example, Roman Herzog's Berlin Speech in 1997 challenged fellow citizens and politicians to address economic challenges with determination instead of clinging to entitlements. He proposed that a "jolt" had to go through society. His words became a reference point in the debate about reforming major aspects of Germany's economic and social systems at the turn of the century.

THE FEDERAL CHANCELLOR

Election and Tenure

Germany's chancellors enjoy longevity in office, with some exceptions (see table 2.2). The longest serving chancellors in the Federal Republic have been Konrad Adenauer (1949–63), Helmut Kohl (1982–98), and now Angela Merkel (2005–). She has currently served longer than the leaders of any other European democracy, and her role in various EU crises has catapulted her to global status. She is routinely ranked as one of the most, if not the most, powerful women in the world. Compared to her predecessors, her background, professional career, and leadership style are atypical. She is the first female officeholder and one of the few top politicians raised in East Germany. She holds a PhD in physics with a specialization in quantum chemistry. Her father was a pastor, and her upbringing in a Lutheran household in a communist system as well as her work as natural scientist have shaped her values and leadership style. After the Berlin Wall fell, she switched from research to politics; she is said to approach politics as a science project. Her leadership style is described variously as pragmatic, methodological, cautious, highly informed, and detail oriented. Her demeanor is modest. Commentators have called her "the quiet German" (e.g., Packer 2014) only to elaborate on her remarkable rise to, and handling of, power. One noted succinctly, "She doesn't put on a show, except by attempting to impress with this lack of showmanship—an attempt that no one is supposed to notice" (Bannas 2006). Remarkably, she has remained true to this style throughout her chancellorship. She is a consummate politician, having shown her acumen as minister of different portfolios, as chair of the CDU, and as chancellor. Along the way, she has modernized the CDU and successfully co-opted topics to weaken the opposition. In 2017, for the fourth time she successfully led her party as candidate for chancellor in the national election.

Prime ministers/chancellors are not elected by a nationwide electoral vote but stand for office in their home constituency. Normally, the election result settles which party will lead the government, and the prime minister is officially appointed by the president or, in constitutional monarchies, the monarch. In Germany and most other parliamentary systems, the head of government is officially elected by a parliamentary majority (50 percent plus one vote, also called a "chancellor majority") before being confirmed by the head of state. Chancellors do not have to be MPs, although many have been.

Table 2.2. Federal Elections, Coalition Governments, and Chancellors, 1949–2013

Election Year	Coalition Parties	Chancellor
1949	CDU/CSU, FDP, and DP (German Party)	Konrad Adenauer (CDU)
1953	CDU/CSU, FDP, DP, and GB/BHE (All-German Bloc/Federation of Expellees and Displaced Persons)	Konrad Adenauer (CDU)
1957	CDU/CSU and DP	Konrad Adenauer (CDU)
1961	CDU/CSU and FDP ·	Konrad Adenauer (CDU) October 1963: Ludwig Erhard (CDU)
1965	CDU/CSU and FDP	Ludwig Erhard (CDU)
	December 1966: CDU/CSU and SPD	Kurt Georg Kiesinger (CDU)
1969	SPD and FDP	Willy Brandt (SPD)
1972	SPD and FDP	Willy Brandt (SPD) May 1974: Helmut Schmidt (SPD)
1976	SPD and FDP	Helmut Schmidt (SPD)
1980	SPD and FDP	Helmut Schmidt (SPD)
	September 1982: SPD	Helmut Schmidt (SPD)
	October 1982: CDU/CSU and FDP	Helmut Kohl (CDU)
1983	CDU/CSU and FDP	Helmut Kohl (CDU)
1987	CDU/CSU and FDP	Helmut Kohl (CDU)
1990	CDU/CSU and FDP	Helmut Kohl (CDU)
1994	CDU/CSU and FDP	Helmut Kohl (CDU)
1998	SPD and Alliance 90/The Greens	Gerhard Schröder (SPD)
2002	SPD and Alliance 90/The Greens	Gerhard Schröder (SPD)
2005	CDU/CSU and SPD	Angela Merkel (CDU)
2009	CDU/CSU and FDP	Angela Merkel (CDU)
2013	CDU/CSU and SPD	Angela Merkel (CDU)

Source: Adapted from Forschungsgruppe Wahlen e.V., *Bundestagswahl. Eine Analyse der Wahl vom 22. September 2013*. Berichte der Forschungsgruppe Wahlen e.V., 154 (Mannheim: Forschungsgruppe Wahlen, October 2013), 72; own source.

Once appointed, chancellors stay in power until the next election. However, should they lose the support of the majority they can be replaced. In Germany, a principle called *constructive vote of no-confidence* requires an alternate candidate, usually from the main opposition party, to stand in an election for chancellor; that is, MPs have to agree on a successor before they can force out the sitting office holder. It complicates ousting the chancellor while assuring a swift transition should it be necessary. It marks another important difference from the Weimar constitution, which allowed the parliament to dismiss the chancellor without agreeing on a replacement, producing a power vacuum that allowed the president to strengthen his powers. The history of the Federal Republic has witnessed only two attempts: one, in 1972, when Willy Brandt (SPD) was in power, failed; another, ten years later, succeeded because the smaller coalition partner, the FDP, switched sides, allowing Helmut Kohl (CDU) to assume the chancellorship from Helmut Schmidt (SPD).

With few exceptions, Germany follows the British tradition of combining the chief executive position with party leadership. It aims to prevent disruptive struggles within the majority party and allows chancellors to shape the party's profile. It also signifies that their power depends on the support of their party.

Powers of the Chancellor and Cabinet Government

Chancellors are central to the institutional design of German democracy. They form and lead the government (Art. 65); that is, they are in charge of determining general policy outlines and responsible for their implementation (*Richtlinienkompetenz*). They appoint or dismiss their cabinets in an important difference from the Weimar constitution, which allowed *Reichstag* parliamentarians to discharge cabinet members. As discussed below, German national governments are always coalitions, and the portfolio distribution, based on party affiliation, is agreed upon in the so-called coalition treaty. In the spirit of cooperation, the vice-chancellor is appointed from the ranks of the smaller partner—usually the foreign minister—and chancellors and foreign ministers both cooperate and compete for influence over foreign policy. The balance of power matters since the two positions have been in the hands of different parties since 1966; chancellors belong to the major coalition party, and foreign ministers to the smaller coalition partner. Not unlike presidential systems, the chancellor's legacy is often judged by foreign policy successes. In European affairs, the chancellor is seen to be in the driver's seat.

Usually, the chancellor meets with the cabinet on Wednesdays to set out the political agenda, discuss draft bills, and so forth. The cabinet is a collegiate body, but chancellors are first among equals (*primus inter pares*; hence, the term *prime minister* in other parliamentary settings). Should opinions diverge, they act as the main mediator; in the end, the majority decides. Chancellors also have the authority to call a parliamentary vote, or motion of confidence, to unite coalition MPs behind a controversial government position and, if they lose, to call new elections. This mechanism has been used five times— twice to rally the members of coalition government to support the chancellor (Helmut Schmidt in 1982 and Gerhard Schröder in 2001) and three times to deliberately lose a motion of confidence to pave the way for new elections (Willy Brandt in 1972, Helmut Kohl in 1982, and Gerhard Schröder in 2005).

Chancellors have always been prominent, but the ubiquitous reach of traditional and digital media has reinforced the personalization of politics, catapulting the chief executive into the spotlight. Social media also have an equalizing effect; politicians of all ranks use them. In Germany and Europe generally, reporting focuses much more on public than private affairs. For example, most Germans would not recognize Angela Merkel's husband on the street and many do not even know his name.

In sum, German chancellors enjoy relative longevity in office, always act as the head of a coalition government, occupy a leading, if not the leadership position in the major coalition party, and have important powers at their disposal. Nonetheless, the essence of a parliamentary system is the interplay of the national legislature with the executive. The next section focuses on the extent to which a strong executive has weakened parliament's influence and whether and how the parliament uses its powers.

THE BUNDESTAG

The literature on legislatures is replete with references to the dwindling of parliamentary influence, even, or maybe especially, in parliamentary systems. In media-driven societies, the argument runs, the executive is at the center of national and international politics. Europeanization is supposed to have weakened the significance and authority of national legislatures as negotiations fall largely into the hands of the government and its administration. However, dismissing the significance of legislatures in general, and the Bundestag in particular, would be a mistake. Its power derives from the constitution and measures its members take to balance relations with the executive; parliaments are not passive bystanders but movers and shakers. The Bundestag offers a valuable example of a strong legislature among parliamentary systems. It ranked among the highest in a comparative, quantitative study of formal legislative powers (Fish and Kroenig 2009), although they are tempered by such veto players as the Bundesrat, a strong executive, an influential constitutional court, and powerful interest groups.

Election and Organization

The electoral system combines a list-proportional system with single-member district voting (for details, see chapter 3). Unification increased the number of representatives to more than 620; the minimum is 598. The total fluctuates slightly and depends on election results; in 2013, with 630 MPs, it was one of the largest democratically elected parliaments. Besides work in the constituencies, plenary sessions are the public face of the parliament. Attendance is often sparse, and the public shows little interest in watching plenary debates; for the most part, legislative work takes place in two bodies, the parliamentary groups (*Fraktionen*) and the permanent committees.

Parliamentary groups are formed when one party musters at least 5 percent of MPs; since 1949, CDU/CSU have always formed one parliamentary group. At times called "parties in parliament," these groups subdivide into specialized working groups. They discuss bills and form opinions that are subsequently presented in the committees and plenary sessions of the Bundestag. Parliamentary rules confer a number of additional rights, among them the right to initiate bills and table motions.

Once a party decides on a course of action, all parliamentary group members are expected to vote accordingly. This party discipline is not enjoined legally. Indeed, MPs are not bound by instructions from anyone—party, constituency, or otherwise—and should decide according to their conscience (Art. 34). They cannot be forced to vote with their parliamentary group, and, in delicate matters, parliamentary groups explicitly abstain from party discipline, usually when moral and/or religious concerns are at play—for example, abortion, euthanasia, and same-sex marriage—but also for political reasons. Party discipline was not deployed in the decision to move the seat of government from Bonn to Berlin. However, it is overwhelmingly the rule and for good reasons: in a parliamentary system, the government's fate is closely tied to the majority vote of the parties in power, and although more generous in Germany than in many other European parliaments, limited staffing means not every MP will have the expertise necessary to vote independently. Maybe most important, in parliamentary systems, voters tend to vote for the party, not the candidate, so they expect elected officials to adhere to party lines.

The second major parliamentary work arena is comprised of the *permanent committees*. They are a "microcosm of the plenary" since their composition reflects party strength in the Bundestag, but they also align with the different cabinet portfolios of the federal government, although the Basic Law requires some; for example, the Foreign Affairs Committee, Defense Committee, and the Committee on the Affairs of the European Union. When the parliament is in session, they meet every Wednesday. The more than twenty permanent committees (2013–17: 23) are "responsible for preparing the decisions of the Bundestag" and are powerful in their own right (Linn and Sobolewski 2015).

Functions and Authority

The powers of the Bundestag fall into three major categories: elections, lawmaking, and scrutiny of the government. It elects the main executive, the federal chancellor. All MPs, together with an equal number of representatives from the Länder, elect the federal president. They also elect one-half of all judges to the Federal Constitutional Court. Although the executive generally initiates laws (on average, about two-thirds of bills), the lawmaking process rests with the Bundestag, and, in matters that concern the Länder, it acts with the Bundesrat.

It uses several mechanisms to hold the executive accountable. The executive must respond to written questions by MPs, and parliamentary groups can demand written information on bills that are being discussed. Between 2009 and 2013, the government had to respond to 20,141 written and 6,057 oral questions ("Facts: The Bundestag at a Glance" 2016). Another effective method of scrutiny is the commission of inquiry. According to Article 44 of the Basic Law, "the Bundestag shall have the right, and on the motion of one quarter of its Members the duty, to establish a committee of inquiry, which shall take the requisite evidence at public hearings." Commissions can be appointed when at least 120 MPs demand it; government representatives must provide information and be available for questioning. They investigate possible misconduct by the government, the larger bureaucracy, and individual politicians, among other things. They are common and have been part of every legislative period since the founding of the Federal Republic. Some of the most recent commissions have dealt with spying by foreign intelligence services, child pornography, and German automakers' emissions practices, sometimes dubbed "dieselgate."

Enquete commissions conduct a different form of inquiry. They address complicated topics of long-term relevance, include an equal number of MPs and outside experts, and convene for a limited period. Beyond their fact-finding mission, they are also intended as a counterweight to the executive. The result is a lengthy report, which often includes concrete policy recommendations and becomes a reference point in policy discourses. They have been convened on such topics as "The Internet and Digital Society," "Growth, Prosperity, and Quality of Life," and "Law and Ethics in Modern Medicine."

Europeanization has complicated consequences for the work of national governments, beginning with the question of how to measure its legislative impact, which varies not only by policy area but, as Thomas König and Lars

Mäder (2008) show, between regular and important legislation. The latter is less affected than the former. Their longitudinal study estimated degree of Europeanization, based on national responses to EU directives, EU laws, and judgments by the Court of Justice of the European Union (CJEU). They rated European impact on important German legislation at around 25 percent, far below the average of 50–70 percent usually cited when the legislative impact of EU legislation on individual member states is assessed. However, the findings are controversial and numbers vary with measurement criteria.

An important aspect of Europeanization is the transfer of sovereignty to the supranational level. Interactions with European institutions tend to favor the executive and the national bureaucracy at the expense of the legislature since both are always present in negotiations, particularly in situations when decision making in Brussels is urgent. However, the ratification of the Maastricht and Lisbon Treaties, with their expansion of powers to the EU level, called the Bundestag and the Bundesrat to action (see below). They have found an important ally in the Federal Constitutional Court, whose decisions regarding these treaties and euro rescue mechanisms have increased parliamentary scrutiny, access to information, and consultation (Art. 23). Now the government must inform the Bundestag about EU matters early and continuously.

The Bundestag and Bundesrat have also created their own connections to the EU. In the Bundestag, members of the Committee on the Affairs of the European Union maintain close ties to the European Parliament and the European Commission, the institution that initiates EU legislation. The Bundestag must consult and deliberate on European legislative proposals. It and the Bundesrat can challenge EU legislation that impinges on their rights and take the matter to the CJEU (Art. 23, 1a). The Committee on the Affairs of the European Union, one of the few committees mandated by the Basic Law, coordinates the Bundestag's response to European policy initiatives (Art. 45) and maintains connections with similar bodies in other EU member parliaments.

The German parliament has guarded its role in representing the will of the people and in legislation; other important powers include the right to draft and pass the budget and the right to determine German use of military force abroad. Decision making is shared across the national, regional, and European levels; any shifts in authority or jurisdiction are closely monitored by the German parliament.

CENTRALITY OF COALITION GOVERNMENTS

In multiparty systems, one party can rarely muster a parliamentary majority. Thus, coalition governments, which are alliances between two or more parties, are the norm in most multiparty parliamentary systems and the key to understanding how German politics works. Coalitions are normally classified as minimal-winning, minority, and majority-winning (surplus) or grand coalitions.

- *Minimal-winning coalitions* include as many parties as necessary to gain the majority of votes in the parliament.
- *Minority governments* or *coalitions* must gather votes on a case-by-case basis to pass legislation. Germany's strong preference for stable government explains why they have never been attempted at the national level and are rare at the Land level.
- *Maximum-winning coalitions* include a range of parties and are generally reserved for extraordinary circumstances when unity is crucial; for example, during severe economic crises. *Grand coalition governments* are a special form of maximum-winning coalitions. They link the parties with the most seats in parliament; in Germany, they are CDU/CSU and SPD.

Since the Federal Republic's inception in 1949, all national governments have been coalition governments between two parties, if we count CDU/CSU as one party. Grand coalitions were once exceptional. Until 2005, there had been only one (1966–69), and it was formed with the explicit understanding that it would last a short time. Since 2005, they have ruled Germany twice (2005–9 and 2013–17), and at the Land level, they have become common. There, novel coalition scenarios have implications for national politics; they influence the vote distribution in the Bundesrat, and inclusion in a coalition at the regional level also elevates a party's profile.

What are the pros and cons of coalitions? The most common concern is the potential for instability when coalitions repeatedly break apart due to irreconcilable programmatic differences, a prominent factor during the Weimar Republic. This scenario has not played out in the Federal Republic, mostly because coalitions have been limited to two parties (again counting CDU/CSU as one) since 1957 on the national level and a consensual political culture prevails (see chapter 3). In addition, some institutional safeguards to avoid deadlock have been implemented. They include lengthy coalition "treaties" that outline common policy position. These carefully drafted documents set out the policy guidelines for the coming four years. Policy conflicts between the coalition parties still occur regularly, and to counter their potentially divisive impact, regular and ad hoc meetings are attended by the coalition committee, a subset of coalition government members, to discuss common concerns and/or disagreements.

Other arguments against coalition governance focus on policy output. Minor parties that are needed as coalition partners gain influence far beyond their electoral support; the inclusion of a second party potentially dilutes the programmatic goals of the winning party. A final concern is coalition formation. Coalition arithmetic is a favorite among pundits prior to the election; once the votes have been tallied, the party with the most seats takes the initiative in forming a coalition, but if it cannot, the second-ranked party can build an alliance with other parties. Such a scenario played out in 1969 when the second-ranked SPD entered a coalition with the FDP. Party elites make the final call on which coalition arrangement will move forward.

On the positive side, coalitions have fostered a consensual political culture in Germany since compatible programs and people are a prerequisite for cooperation. Different voices are represented, which can moderate and widen the appeal of the government. While these advantages may seem minor compared to the potential drawbacks, they are crucial. At least in Germany's case, they are key to a negotiation democracy that permeates the political system.

Entering a coalition is a double-edged sword; both the major and minor parties risk losing their distinct programmatic profile. Still, every coalition government has its own dynamic, and generalizations are bound to fall short. At the next election, the voters can reprimand a party for not adequately representing its election campaign pledges, or the minor coalition partner can prove its competence and be rewarded. The SPD joined its first coalition in 1966 and reaped the rewards in a successful electoral outcome in 1969. By 2013, in a first for Germany, it invited its members to vote on whether it should join yet another coalition with CDU/CSU, which it did. The move was propelled by greater demand for intraparty democracy but also the outcome of the 2009 general election. The CDU/CSU reaped most of the credit for what most considered years of successful grand coalition governance (2005–9), but the SPD suffered heavy losses. A similar fate befell the FDP. It governed with CDU/CSU from 2009 to 2013 but failed to deliver on its promises, and its fall from power was drastic; it failed to gain seats in the 2013–17 Bundestag.

Particularly controversial are grand coalition governments. They can advance policy change since the major political players form the government, and parliamentary opposition is minor. At the same time, since the coalition partners want to maintain ideological distinctiveness, political outcomes often result in the least common denominator. Grand coalitions are often criticized from a democratic perspective because they limit the voice of the minor opposition parties. Political observers have also asked to what extent grand coalitions negatively influence voter turnout or strengthen parties on the political fringe. At least in the past, most German voters seem to have had fewer reservations and, in pre-election polls, routinely endorsed these arrangements (Forschungsgruppe Wahlen 2016).

FEDERALISM

Typology of Federal Systems

In addition to the parliamentary system and coalition governance, Germany's federal system both enforces and slows consensual decision making. At the most basic level, federalism refers to institutional arrangements between federal and subnational units that allow shared and self-rule (Elazar 1987). A simple dichotomy distinguishing unitary from federal systems no longer adequately captures the multiplicity of arrangements. Both systems are dynamic, and theory often does not match reality. The United Kingdom remains unitary, but devolution of powers to Northern Ireland, Wales, and Scotland has introduced elements of federalism. Indeed, in most unitary states, demand for greater local and regional participation has led to a redistribution of powers; political scientists speak of a "decentralist" turn in modern democracies (Hooghe, Marks, and Schakel 2008).

To place Germany's federalism, we adopt César Colino's typology of balanced, segmented, accommodation, and unitary federalism (2013, 56–60).

- *Balanced federalism* evolves from confederal arrangements and, as the name implies, aims to balance rights and responsibilities while controlling "possible abuse of the central power." The United States and the EU are examples.
- *Segmented federalism* is commonly found in settings with distinct cultural communities, such as Belgium and Switzerland. The aim is to preserve the country's unity while guaranteeing substantial autonomy to the subnational units.
- *Accommodation federalism*, like segmented federalism, allocates autonomy to subnational units, particularly in cultural affairs; decision-making styles combine features of cooperation with competition, but the national government controls the devolution agenda. Colino's study cites Spain as an example of accommodation federation although officially the country is a unitary state. Spain and the United Kingdom illustrate the blurring of unitary and federal elements.
- Germany and Austria are prime examples of *unitary federalism*. Its main objective is cooperation among the different units; it is the least competitive, most hierarchical and solidarity-oriented form of federalism. Other terms used to describe this kind of federalism are cooperative, consensual, and interlocking. Unitary federalism reflects a political culture that favors regional diversity in culture and traditions but common rules and standards of living across the federation. The equalization of living conditions, which includes infrastructure, socioeconomic conditions, general guidelines in education, and gender equality is an important feature of German federalism.

History and Structure

Rejecting the centralized structure of the Third Reich, the federal arrangement agreed upon in 1948 found a middle ground between the highly decentralized structure of the German Empire founded in 1871 and the greater centralization of power that characterized the Weimar Republic (Heun 2011, 14). When the framers of the Basic Law convened in 1948–49, only the eleven states in the western part of the country participated. Of those, only three, Bavaria and the small city-states Hamburg and Bremen, existed before 1945; the others reflected new territorial arrangements. In the east, a federal structure was initially established but unceremoniously abandoned in 1952. With unification in October 1990, the five Länder in the east were reinstated, increasing the total from eleven to sixteen (see table 2.3). Newly built missions for each in Berlin showcase their regional and cultural diversity through distinct architecture, cultural symbols, and interior design.

National- and Land-level powers are divided across four categories (Arts. 70–74):

1. The federal government has *exclusive power* over foreign affairs, citizenship laws, customs, and tariffs.

Table 2.3. Vote Distribution in Bundesrat, Länder Population, and GDP per Capita

	Federal Länder Statistics		
Federal State	*Vote Distribution in Federal Council*	*Population (in millions)*	*GDP per Capita (2013 in euros)*
Bavaria	6	12.74	39,700
Berlin	4	3.48	31,500
Mecklenburg-West Pomerania	3	1.60	23,000
Saarland	3	0.99	32,300
Saxony	4	4.06	25,400
Saxony-Anhalt	4	2.23	23,900
Baden-Württemberg	6	10.77	38,700
Brandenburg	4	2.46	24,200
Bremen	3	0.66	44,300
Hamburg	3	1.77	54,600
Hesse	5	6.12	39,600
Lower Saxony	6	7.68	31,100
North Rhine-Westphalia	6	17.68	33,900
Rhineland-Palatinate	4	4.02	31,100
Schleswig-Holstein	4	2.84	28,600
Thuringia	4	2.15	23,900

Source: http://www.bundesrat.de/DE/bundesrat/laender/laender-node.html; http://ec.europa.eu/eurostat/documents/2995521/6839731/1-21052015-AP-EN.pdf/c3f5f43b-397c-40fd-a0a4-7e68e3bea8cd

2. The Land governments have *exclusive power* over cultural affairs, including education.
3. They share *concurrent power* over refugee and expellee matters, public health, and welfare.
4. *Framework legislation* establishes federal guidelines and guarantees federal cooperation and consultation even in areas where exclusive power is allotted to the Land governments.

These categories veil considerable battles over power distribution, and most constitutional changes have been related to them, first restoring power at the federal level and then increasing institutions at both the Land and federal levels (Gress 2010). After much discussion, the most comprehensive of these reforms took place in 2006; twenty-five articles in the Basic Law and twenty-one federal laws were altered to reflect a redistribution of responsibilities. Länder influence on federal decision making would be curtailed, but they would benefit from greater competencies in selected legislative areas.

Recent research finds that the German system mirrors the "two faces of federalism" that are visible, not only in policies, but also in public sentiments. The unitary impulse toward coordination and similar policies across the federation competes with impulses toward decentralization and greater Land autonomy and differentiation (Jeffery and Pamphilis 2016, 190). Many are skeptical of reforms that address the distribution of authority, suggesting that even when instituted, political reality reinforces old patterns but a gap between capabilities and expectations keeps reform of intergovernmental relations on the political agenda (Scheller 2015).

A focal point in the ongoing reform dispute is the constitutionally prescribed "equivalence of living conditions" ("uniformity of living conditions" prior to 1994) and its interpretation (Art. 72). As in all federal systems, the subnational units have their own revenue-raising powers, but they vary greatly according to economic strength. Germany's tax distribution system is complex and includes federal payments to poorer states (*vertical equalization*) and from richer to poorer states (*horizontal equalization*), with the expected grumbling from the richer states in the south. Last but not least, special projects often rely on intergovernmental grants and subsidies.

At first, unification did not seem to have a dramatic effect on federalism, but later it exposed disparities in the economic strength of the Länder and reignited long-standing battles over power distribution and revenue sharing. The redistribution of finances remained a problem; the economically "rich" states, in particular, Bavaria, Baden-Württemberg, and Hesse, have been the major contributors, while most other Länder have been net beneficiaries.

Critics contend that the system failed since instead of equalization, further differentiation has taken place.

The recalibration of the fiscal equalization scheme acquired increased urgency since the current arrangement ends in 2019. A major reform package, leading to thirteen changes in the Basic Law, received the necessary two-thirds majorities in Bundestag and Bundesrat in June 2017. The new policies will go into effect in 2020; among others, horizontal equalization will be abolished. Significantly, some of the new provisions increase the federal government's monetary contributions; concomitantly, its authority over spending increases as well. Critics worry about a further hollowing of the federal principle and the erosion of solidarity among the Länder.

The Bundesrat

As one of the five permanent constitutional bodies, the Bundesrat represents the interests of the Länder at the federal level and intentionally tempers the majority-based system of competition in the Bundestag with the "administrative-bureaucratic expertise of the Länder" (Gress 2010, 181). Article 50 of the Basic Law states that "the Länder shall participate through the Bundesrat in the legislation and administration of the Federation and in matters concerning the European Union." The Bundesrat's involvement in legislation varies: in some areas, a bill can only pass with its express consent; in others, it can object, but a majority in the Bundestag can overturn it.

Although sometimes referred to as the upper house or second chamber, the terms are technically inaccurate since the Bundesrat's history does not mirror the slow devolution of power from the upper to the lower house in Great Britain's parliamentary system. It is not a second house of parliament in the traditional sense since popular vote does not elect its members. Delegates are chosen from members of the Land governments, and, once the Bundesrat is constituted, votes are cast in blocs; that is, states cannot split their vote. Their very different population sizes, varying from 0.657 million in the city-state Bremen to 17.68 million in North Rhine-Westphalia, are reflected in their relative voting weight. Every Land has at least three and at most six votes for a total of sixty-nine votes. For these reasons, its official website describes the Bundesrat as "entirely unique."

The transfer of power to the EU spurred the regional governments to action, and the Maastricht Treaty introduced the subsidiarity principle, subsequently reformed in the Lisbon Treaty, which decrees that decisions that can be made on the regional or national levels should not be transferred to the European level. The subsidiarity principle was incorporated into the revised Article 23 of the Basic Law, which also stipulates that any transfer of sovereignty to the EU level requires Bundesrat consent: "It was the 'price' the Federation (Bund) had to pay for the Bundesrat's consent to the Maastricht treaty law." (Dette-Koch 2003, 184).

This complex, multilevel network of governance lengthens or stalls decision making when the Bundestag and Bundesrat are governed by different party majorities. When a bill requires the consent of the Bundesrat, but its members object, a special thirty-two-member *mediation committee* convenes. One member represents each Land; the sixteen Bundestag delegates are chosen based on their party's strength in the Bundestag. The committee can submit proposals to amend the bill but cannot adopt it; it must be confirmed by Bundestag and Bundesrat. The frequency of mediation committee action has varied greatly; it peaked between 2002 and 2005 when it acted on 100 legislative drafts. Since then, its involvement has declined considerably, due partly to the prevalence of grand coalition governments but also to the reform of the federal system, which curtailed the number of areas in which Bundesrat consent is required, underscoring its relative loss of power.

However, the involvement of the Länder governments in decision making is not limited to the Bundesrat. For example, Land minister presidents and representatives of the federal government meet regularly to discuss important policies and related guidelines. In 2016, federal and Länder interior ministers met to discuss measures to limit refugee immigration, such as stricter border controls; improvements in police training and equipment upgrades; and closer cooperation with other European countries.

The German states participate in EU affairs at different levels. For example, the federal government is obliged to inform Länder parliaments about EU activities. Each of the sixteen Länder maintains an official representative in Brussels, the capital of the EU, to lobby and to represent its interests. At the request of the Bundesrat, Länder representatives can take part in the Council of the European Union and Commission meetings, and when their exclusive competencies, such as education and cultural affairs, are on the agenda, they lead negotiations. The Bundesrat's Committee on European Affairs examines EU documents of interest to the Länder. The separate Chamber of European Affairs convenes only on special occasions when questions emerge that require immediate attention and response. In addition, Länder bureaucracies and parliaments train their staff in European law and disperse knowledge and expertise on EU decision making. All states have a Ministry for European Affairs, and its ministers normally meet three times a year to coordinate their positions.

Federalism is a cherished principle, but it is not immutable. The resource scarcity in many Länder necessitates national funding, which has structural and political consequences. It gives the national government "golden reins" to steer the debate and initiate policies. In addition, the vastly different economic strengths of the Länder contribute to both a north-south and a new east-west divide.

THE FEDERAL CONSTITUTIONAL COURT

Evolution of Constitutional Courts

The evolution of democracy in Europe shifted powers from monarchs to parliaments and established the principle of parliamentary supremacy. In contrast to the United States, where the separation of executive, legislative, and judicial powers has deep historical roots, in parliamentary systems, the judiciary upheld parliamentary supremacy. This evolution explains why the model UK parliamentary system created an independent judicial branch only in 2005 (in place since 2009) but the newly established Supreme Court is still without judicial review powers. Judicial review examines acts of parliament or government and can declare them unconstitutional.

In the US political system, the Supreme Court, established in 1803, combines the functions of an appellate court and a constitutional court. This model became popular in parts of the British Commonwealth, Scandinavia, and most of Latin America. The Austrian Constitutional Court (1920) set the example for an independent constitutional court; a special tribunal whose jurisdiction is limited to constitutional matters, it guards against unconstitutional legislation. It became the model in European countries (Schwartz 1999).

In Germany, the Weimar Republic established a constitutional court, but it was limited to adjudicating disputes between and among organs of the state. After 1945, reflecting upon the failure of parliamentary democracy in much of interwar Europe and the political abuse of the judiciary during the Third Reich, new democracies allotted an independent judiciary a major role. Austria reconstituted its constitutional court in 1945; Italy (1948–49) and West Germany were among the first to institute new independent constitutional courts. In 1948, time ran out during constitutional talks, and the members of the first democratically elected West German parliament were left to make critical decisions about the court, which was established in 1951 in Karlsruhe. The geographic separation between government and court was meant to demonstrate the separation of powers and the independence of the highest judiciary. Over time, the role of the Constitutional Court as independent arbitrator between different and sometimes highly polarized political viewpoints has grown.

Praise for Germany's constitution as "one of the world's most celebrated" is often related to its Federal Constitutional Court, which, along with the US Supreme Court and the Austrian court, has served as a paradigm (Kommers and Miller 2012). The US Supreme Court has a special place in pioneering judicial review; the Austrian court set the example for independent special constitutional courts, while the German court is known for its wide jurisdiction and sweeping powers, using both abstract and concrete review as well as constitutional complaints launched by citizens (Sweet 2012). Its protection of rights, including human rights, made it appealing to many countries that abandoned dictatorial rule and introduced democracy. From Spain and Portugal to South Africa and in many of the former communist countries in Central and Eastern Europe, the German Constitutional Court was a frequent reference point in discussing the proposed institutional structures of the new judiciaries.

Election and Tenure

Since 1963, the court has served in two senates, independent in jurisdiction and personnel. The eight judges in each serve for a nonrenewable term of twelve years. They must be at least forty years old, meet specific legal qualifications, be eligible for election to public office, but not hold any electoral office. The mandatory retirement age is sixty-eight. These provisions are intended to attract highly qualified judges and to minimize politicization while guaranteeing regular but limited turnover.

Until 2015, half of its members were selected by a special committee of the Bundestag, the other half by the Bundesrat. Now, the Bundestag committee presents its list of candidates to the full house, which then elects the judges without prior plenary debate. This adjustment intends to introduce greater transparency without politicizing the election procedure. The process in the Bundesrat remains unchanged. A two-thirds majority (until 1956, a three-quarters majority) is required in both cases, necessitating that the major parties, CDU/CSU and SPD, reach a consensus on the candidates. Informally, CDU/CSU and SPD share equally in the nomination of judges, a privilege that they, at times, transfer partly to coalition partners. The need to compromise and the lack of public debates on the candidates depoliticizes the selection process.

Structure and Proceedings

By far the most common proceedings involve individual or legal persons who feel that their constitutional rights have been violated. They can lodge a *constitutional complaint*; the caseload now routinely exceeds 5,000 constitutional complaints filed annually. From 1951 to 2015, constitutional complaints made up nearly 97 percent of the court's caseload. About 99 percent have no constitutional significance and are handled by three-person chambers of one of the senates. Only selected cases are deliberated by one of the full senates. Most visibly and most importantly in terms of impact, the court is responsible for *abstract* and *concrete judicial* reviews. Abstract review affirms or denies the constitutionality of a statute and can be initiated by the federal government, one of the Land governments, or one-quarter of MPs. In cases of concrete judicial review, launched by courts, the court in Karlsruhe is asked to rule on the constitutionality of specific laws. For a vote to pass in one of the two chambers, five of the eight judges must approve (Kneip 2015, 275–77). Additional court proceedings involve disputes between the federal government and the Länder and among federal bodies (*Organstreit*), electoral complaints, and the prohibition of political parties.

The Constitutional Court is independent from other European courts, in particular the CJEU and the European Court of Human Rights. They complement each other and deal with different aspects of the law. Citizens can appeal to the European Court of Human Rights if they believe their rights have been infringed, and national courts have not been able to settle the dispute. The CJEU is an organ of the EU and rules on questions related to EU treaties; its rulings have precedence over national law. Judges in the national court usually have expertise in both national and European law.

The supremacy of European law over national law in some areas has undermined the power of the German Constitutional Court, but deepening European integration has also allowed it to shape European politics. In 1993, it declared the Maastricht Treaty constitutional but stipulated that any sovereignty transfer requires the consent of the parliament. Consequently, the German parliament voted on the introduction of the euro. In 2009, the Treaty of Lisbon came under scrutiny; in a landmark decision, the court ruled the treaty constitutional but criticized the lack of involvement of the German parliament (Dyevre 2011). The court demanded more time to deliberate on European legislation. The Lisbon Treaty could be ratified only after passage of legislation that gave the Bundestag greater oversight of European affairs. In 2014, the German Constitutional Court confirmed the legality of the euro bailout fund and in 2016 ruled in favor of the bond-buying program of the European Central Bank (ECB). It has evolved into one of the most important institutions shaping European policy (Bulmer and Paterson 2013).

Security and defense policy is another area in which the Constitutional Court has established a crucial role. In a highly polarized 1994 debate, it ruled that, despite their constitutionally prescribed defensive character, the German

Armed Forces (*Bundeswehr*) could participate in military actions outside of NATO territory. At the same time, the court reaffirmed parliamentary control and jurisdiction over military actions (*Parlamentsarmee*). The Bundeswehr's Afghanistan mission as part of NATO, for example, required an annual parliamentary vote for renewal. These highly publicized debates kept the war in the public eye. Some critics view this procedure as too complex and lengthy, while others praise parliament's involvement in security questions.

Several times, the Constitutional Court has settled highly controversial social issues. For example, in 1995, it annulled legislation that required the display of the cross in Bavarian public school classrooms. In 2013, the court handed down two decisions involving the rights of same-sex partnerships, which included tax benefits and the right to adopt the partner's child. The court favored inclusive and nondiscriminatory social practices, but some critics argue that the rulings did not go far enough in establishing equality. Legislation in 2017 gave same-sex couples the right to marry.

In most Western democracies, we can observe a trend toward what has been called the *judicialization* of politics. The term is often used loosely but benefits from closer scrutiny since it refers to more than the increase in constitutional review proceedings, which is an important prerequisite. It has been attributed to various factors, among them "explicit provisions for judicial review in constitutions adopted after 1945, the prevalence of rights discourse, the appointment of less deferential judges, the decline in public support for elected political institutions, the desire to depoliticize some sensitive issues, and the instrumental or strategic use of courts by interest groups and other policy entrepreneurs" (Tolley 2012, 67). The cross-border influence of European courts should be added to this list, in particular, the directives of the CJEU and the European Court of Human Rights. What matters ultimately is whether the constitutional judges see their role as actively shaping policies according to a political agenda (active judicialization) or whether their rulings act as a passive restraint on governments and political parties (passive judicialization) (Kneip 2011).

This debate is highly relevant in Germany. Its Constitutional Court protects and interprets the constitution, but its decisions have raised questions about its reach as a veto player or even an alternate government (*Gegenregierung*). "Going to Karlsruhe" has emerged as an important opposition tool since individual party members outside the government, political parties in general, and Land governments use it to challenge policies. Based on a longitudinal study of rulings from 1951 to 2005, Sascha Kneip (2011) challenges the notion that the judges act predominantly as veto players, although they do occasionally. Rather, he sees them as legitimate political team players, yet not driven by their own political agenda (passive judicialization). The public widely shares this affirmative perception. The court enjoys high legitimacy because the elites and the populace do not perceive it as a politicized body but one that adjudicates important constitutional questions and mediates political controversies.

POWER DISTRIBUTION REVISITED

Political structures provide the formal frame by which powers are distributed; how these powers are enacted varies from country to country. Classification schemes facilitate quick orientation, basic understanding, comparison, and identification of broader trends across the political world but remain a shortcut that glosses over important within-system differences. For example, parliamentary systems are classified as majoritarian or consensual, but Germany is widely seen as both. Federal systems differ greatly in how they decentralize power and fiscal authority, and Germany illustrates a layering of centralizing and decentralizing trends. Actual power distribution is notoriously difficult to gauge. The authority of the main German institutions is high compared to those of many other democracies. International observers routinely rank its chancellor, Bundestag, and Federal Constitutional Court as powerful institutions in their own right.

The multilevel German governance system is particularly adept at responding to the many levels of EU governance because they share many features. Overall, EU developments have influenced German institutional structure more than unification, although the merger strained certain aspects—in particular, the federal system—forcing adaptations. Dispersion of power at home and at the supranational level makes decision processes more complex and lengthy, but national institutions have adjusted their structures accordingly.

History shaped the peculiar features of the German political system. Their high level of legitimacy guaranteed that unification did not alter the basic features of West German structures even when presented with new policy challenges. The experience of merging two different political systems confirmed the logic of institutionalism: the path chosen for institutional arrangements and the choices made at critical junctures profoundly reflect past experiences. In response to major domestic and international challenges, the political structures of the unified Germany have proved remarkably resilient and adaptable.

Chapter 3

Political Actors, Parties, and Elections

KEY TERMS

cleavages	party state
dealignment	party system
electoral campaigns	political elites
electoral system	quota systems
gender and politics	realignment
members of parliament	representation
party membership	voter turnout

Each year, the Society for the German Language selects a "word of the year," coined in the preceding months to capture a prevailing mood or trend. *Politikverdrossenheit* was chosen in 1992; it loosely translates to disenchantment with politics, although many thought it really meant disillusionment with political parties. The timing was no coincidence—Germany was in the midst of the unification crisis—yet the phenomenon was not new, nor has it vanished. In the opinion of many citizens in Germany and other Western democracies, political parties cannot be trusted. Regardless of whether voters like them or not, political systems in general and parliamentary systems in particular are party systems, and political parties perform important functions. They are socialization agents; they articulate and aggregate interests; they organize elections and mobilize voters; they recruit politicians, who, once elected, are the decision makers. In Germany, the parties' principal role in all areas of politics and polity soon led to its characterization as a party state (*Parteienstaat*) or party democracy.

Party systems are dynamic, and since the 1980s, major reconfigurations have been under way in Western Europe. The party landscapes have become

more diversified; the major parties are losing seats to new parties; voter turnout and membership in the established parties, but not necessarily the minor
parties, have declined. These developments can be interpreted as either the
normal byproduct of societal and political change or a warning signal about
the health of representative democracy.

In most democracies, political parties are the gatekeepers to political office, while electoral systems structure political competition. The mix of candidate selection, voters' choices, and the electoral system frame Germany's
moderate multiparty system. National parliamentary elections are conducted
with a mixed-member electoral system, in place since 1953. A rarity at the
time, it combines single-member districts with proportional representation
(restricted by a 5 percent threshold). Interactions among political parties also
reflect the role perceptions, values, backgrounds, and career characteristics
of their elites. We outline three aspects of mostly descriptive representation: elite turnover in East Germany and the representation of East Germans
in today's political system; the composition of the national parliament, the
Bundestag; and the role of gender in political life.

In what follows, we illustrate trends and challenges associated with political representation that are common to Western democracies but emphasize
their specific expression in Germany. We analyze the party system and the
main parties but not their inner workings. Our focus is on national parties,
elections, and elites and only occasionally do we refer to the European or
Land levels.

BACKGROUND

Once the occupying powers gave political activity the green light after World
War II, historical political parties reorganized, while others started with new
programs and cross-cutting alliances. The parties on the left, SPD and KPD,
built on old structures and programs, but FDP, CDU, and, in Bavaria, CSU
bridged old political and confessional divisions to create entirely new organizations. A broad spectrum of smaller historical and new parties also emerged.
Some party functionaries had been politically active prior to the takeover by
Adolf Hitler; some had survived the concentration camps; others returned
from internal or external exile or engaged in politics for the first time. For
example, the first postwar chancellor, Konrad Adenauer (CDU), was replaced
as the longtime mayor of Cologne and briefly imprisoned when Hitler came
to power and again in 1944. He was one of those who withdrew from politics
to reemerge in 1945. His major political opponent, Kurt Schumacher (SPD),
had spent more than ten years in concentration camps. Willy Brandt (SPD),

chancellor from 1969 to 1974, was forced to flee from the Gestapo, change his name, and survive in exile in Norway and later Sweden.

In the Soviet Zone of Occupation, the forced merger of the SPD and KPD established the Socialist Unity Party (SED), which dominated political life in the GDR until the end of 1989. Its two leaders, Walter Ulbricht (1950–71) and Erich Honecker (1971–89), had the working-class backgrounds typical among postwar communist functionaries. One was a cabinetmaker, the other a slater. Ulbricht returned to Berlin after exile in Spain and the Soviet Union, whereas Honecker reentered politics after nearly ten years in prison. Four so-called bloc parties gave the illusion of a multiparty system, but they all had to adhere to the Marxist-Leninist principles of the SED.

Fourteen parties competed in the 1949 election to the newly established West German parliament, the Bundestag. Ten were elected, and the pattern was repeated in 1953. Unusual among constitutions, the Basic Law specifically addressed the role of political parties without defining them: "Political parties shall participate in the formation of the political will of the people. They may be freely established. Their internal organization must conform to democratic principles. They must publicly account for their assets and for the sources and use of their funds" (Art. 21, 1). Only in 1967 did the Party Act, revised several times since, define political parties as permanently organized associations of citizens that take part in national and regional elections but does not regulate municipal parties. The Länder governments set the rules that govern them.

At first glance, unification would seem to have had no effect on the party landscape, as long-established western parties dominated the first all-German election in December 1990. Some eastern German parties were incorporated into CDU and FDP, although the SPD refused membership to former communist party members, and many newly founded eastern parties failed to pass the 5 percent threshold, although for this time only, it was applied separately in east and west and not nationally, as is the rule.

However, below the surface, important and long-lasting change was brewing. The successor party to the SED, the PDS, now the Left Party, garnered a sufficient number of votes in the eastern part of Germany in 1990 and has been a fixture in every Bundestag since. Alliance 90, a group of former dissidents, also passed the electoral threshold; in 1993, it joined the West German Green party, which had failed entry into the Bundestag in 1990 but recovered thereafter. Electoral behavior then and now has moved toward regional variations and asymmetries in electoral outcomes. Except for the CDU, the major parties' vote share is lower in the east than the west (see table 3.1). In recent years, populist right-wing parties have found a more appreciative sounding board in the east than the west.

Table 3.1. Percentage of Second Votes in Bundestag Elections, 1990–2017

Year	Voter Turnout (%)	CDU/ CSU	SPD	FDP	Alliance 90/ The Greens	Left Party	AfD	Others
1990	77.8	43.8	33.5	11.0	3.8	2.4	—	5.4
1994	79.0	41.4	36.4	6.9	7.3	4.4	—	3.6
1998	82.2	35.1	40.9	6.2	6.7	5.1	—	5.9
2002	79.1	38.5	38.5	7.4	8.6	4.0	—	3.0
2005	77.7	35.2	34.2	9.8	8.1	8.7	—	4.0
2009	70.8	33.8	23.0	14.6	10.7	11.9	—	6.0
2013	71.5	41.5	25.7	4.8	8.4	8.6	4.7	6.3
2017	76.2	33.0	20.5	10.7	8.9	9.2	12.6	5.0

Source: *Bundestagswahl: Eine Analyse der Wahl vom 22. September 2013*, Forschungsgruppe Wahlen e.V., Mannheim, September 2013; 2017 provisional result: https://www.bundeswahlleiter.de.

Unification's impact has been relatively straightforward, but Europeanization's effect on political parties is more difficult to assess. It requires differentiating Western political parties from those in Central and Eastern Europe. The postcommunist setting remains characterized by electoral volatility; exposure to, and membership in, the EU has left deep marks. Robert Ladrech (2009, 7–9) sums up the relationship between Europeanization and Western European political parties: "Europe does not 'hit' parties in a direct manner." In contrast, "direct impact is on the domestic political environment in which parties operate, not on parties *per se*." Indirect impact can be seen in programmatic and organizational change, patterns of party competition, and other areas. All political parties had to respond to European integration by adjusting their programs and stating their general position on European unity and on specific policies. They created new positions to deal with EU matters and established channels to recruit and fund their representatives in the European Parliament (EP). The integration process has opened spaces for ideological competition among political parties, which has been fierce and polarizing in some member states but hardly in Germany. In chapter 7, we will explore the relationship between European and German politics in detail.

Convinced that the failure of the Weimar Republic was due to the lack of democratic attitudes among elites and the public, the Western Allies wasted no time in reeducating Germans after World War II. German institutions followed suit. In addition to the usual civic education channels in schools, universities, and adult education venues, special offices were established at the national and regional level to promote political education (Roberts 2002). What sets Germany apart from other Western democracies is the special role political parties played in this endeavor. All major parties maintain political foundations (*Politische Stiftungen*) to advance democracy at home and abroad. Government agencies supply most of the operating funds but cannot interfere with the now six independent foundations. They are strongly linked to their political party organization but enjoy a certain degree of freedom from them as well. Their activities reach worldwide. They have their own research institutes, publish educational and academic material, and organize field trips and conferences, among other actions.

CONFIGURING PARTY SYSTEMS AND POLITICAL PARTIES

A *party system* is characterized by the number of political parties represented in political offices, their relationship to each other, their competitiveness, and their programmatic differences. On the other hand, parties themselves are grouped according to their origins, ideologies, links to transnational federations (for example, membership in EU parliamentary groups), and name (Mair and Mudde 1998). The most prominent ideological linkages are between conservatives/Christian Democrats; social democrats/socialists; green/environmentalists; and the right-wing/radical right. Each party's programmatic stance and success is shaped by historical trajectories, socioeconomic changes, and electoral laws, including the electoral system but also party financing and voter registration rules. Consider the emergence of the so-called catch-all party, a concept introduced by Otto Kirchheimer (1966). According to him, catch-all parties emerged with the expansion of the middle class after World War II and try to attract as many votes as possible across the ideological spectrum. The resultant decline in the importance of social milieu, which had provided social and political solidity and reliable voters, led to decline in ideological differences. The German concept of a people's party (*Volkspartei*) differs from the catch-all party in one salient aspect: cognizant of the history of political polarization during the Weimar Republic, West German political leaders aimed to avoid polarization and actively promoted the inclusion of different clientele (Zolleis and Wertheimer 2013).

The structural transformation of the electorate has continued across Europe. Citizens are better educated, more secular, and mostly employed in the service sector. Old cleavages based on economic distribution, welfare, and religion are still relevant but now compete with new divisions that coalesce around immigration, European integration, environmental concerns, and regionalism. Disenchantment with the established political parties has grown; they are often seen as corrupt, elitist, and out of touch with the electorate. New right- and left-wing parties voice resentment against the political elites, or what is often called the establishment, and their perceived lack of concern for "our" worries; these parties claim to speak for the common people.

In southern Europe, parties to the left are the primary beneficiaries of this frustration and alienation, while parties to the right benefit in the northern and western European countries. The proliferation of new parties, electoral volatility, and, some argue, the decline of catch-all parties are results of these developments. Traditional left/right attributes are no longer a clear dividing line but merely an orientation.

Whether some of these new parties should be labeled populist is a matter of debate. Cas Mudde (2016, 25–26) defines populism as "an ideology that separates society into two homogenous and antagonistic groups, 'the pure people' and 'the corrupt elite,' and that holds that politics should be an expression of the 'general will' of the people." Jan-Werner Müller (2016a, 28) adds an important distinction. Not all critics of the political establishment should go into one category; after all, democracy should welcome critical input. Populists claim that they alone represent the will of the people and consequently view other parties and their supporters as illegitimate. Usually they embrace sharp distinctions between "insiders" and "outsiders" in society. Pappas (2016) emphasizes the need to distinguish among antidemocratic, nativist, and populist parties, although the dividing lines are often muddled. He finds populist parties democratic since they take part in competitive elections and claim allegiance to representative democracy. However, they pursue illiberal means, among them undermining the rule of law, free discourse, and minority rights to hollow out democratic institutions.

The terms *dealignment* and *realignment* capture the changed relationship between the electorate and the established parties. *Dealigned* voters are no longer tied to one party but decide at election time. *Realigned* voters have abandoned their old party identification for a new one. These processes started in the 1970s and 1980s, when new social movements, some of which turned into incubators for political parties, set out new political agendas focused on environmental concerns, individual liberties, and political participation, especially for women and minorities. Voters favoring these goals gravitated to parties like the Greens in Germany. Partly in response to this "new left," a "new right" with a nativist agenda and populist rhetoric emerged in the 1980s and 1990s.

THE GERMAN PARTY SYSTEM

Main Characteristics of the Party System

The German party system is considered consensual, since the mainstream political parties generally avoid polarization though not competition, which can be fierce, and moderate, since the number of parties in the national parliament fluctuates between three and six. CDU/CSU form one parliamentary group and govern together at the national level but remain two distinct entities that operate in different areas of Germany; we count them here as one. From 1961 to 1983, CDU/CSU, SPD, and FDP were the only parties represented in the Bundestag. In 1983, they reluctantly welcomed a newcomer, the Greens, and in 1990, the PDS. However, this accounting disguises myriad political parties. For example, in 2013, thirty parties were on the ballot for election to the Bundestag, but only CDU, CSU, SPD, Alliance 90/The Greens, and the Left Party gained seats. Parties regularly come and go; many are local or regional. The Land level provides a testing ground for possible success at the national level; the mortality rate of the many "flash parties" is high.

Traditionally, the major political parties are associated with colors: CDU/CSU = black; SPD = red (now in competition with the Left Party, which also uses red); FDP = yellow; Alliance 90/The Greens = guess what? Green! Indeed, coalition scenarios are customarily color-coded: black-red (CDU/CSU and SPD); red-green (SPD and Alliance 90/The Greens). Color attributes are so pervasive that a special blue was designed for the Bundestag seat covers to avoid any suggestion of party favoritism.

Like other Western European countries, Germany has seen a steep decline in the electoral share for the major parties. In the 1970s, CDU/CSU and SPD routinely garnered over 90 percent of the vote, but their share fell to 66.8 percent in 2009 and decreased drastically to 53.5 percent in 2017. Parties to the left—Alliance 90/The Greens, the PDS, and now the Left Party—have benefited from this shift, and several small parties have increased their vote share but without being able to pass the 5 percent threshold required for representation in the Bundestag. Prior to unification, government coalitions were negotiated routinely between CDU/CSU, SPD, and FDP. However, the diversification of the party landscape as well as the convergence of some ideological positions on the center has widened the potential pool (see figure 3.1).

In European party systems, joining a party is a formal act and comes with rights and duties, including paying dues, which are a substantial funding source. They are usually structured according to income, and those in political office pay considerably more. With the weakening of lifelong party identification, however, the inclination to join has waned. Since 1990, CDU and SPD have lost more than 40 percent of their membership, hovering around 440,000 each. Alliance 90/The Greens has bucked the trend but only in the western part of the country (see table 3.2). In 2014, 2 percent of the population were political party members as compared to 3.8 percent in 1990 (Weßels 2016, 406).

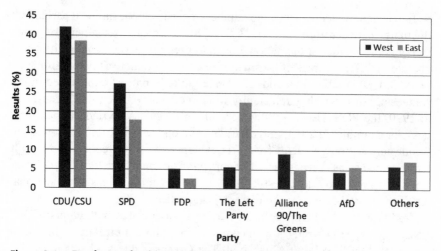

Figure 3.1. Bundestag Election Results 2013: West vs. East

Source: Bundestagswahl. *Eine Analyse der Wahl vom 22.* September 2013, Forschungsgruppe Wahlen e.V., Mannheim, September 2013.

Party Profiles

Christian Democratic Union of Germany (CDU)

In 2015, the CDU celebrated its seventieth anniversary. It is by far the most successful post–World War II party; together with its sister party, CSU, it collected the highest number of votes in sixteen out of the nineteen national elections. As of 2017, a CDU chancellor has governed for forty-eight of the sixty-eight years of the Federal Republic's existence. Of the twelve federal presidents, six were CDU members.

In 1945, it was a genuinely new party, formed mainly to overcome traditional cleavages between Protestants and Catholics. In combining the words conservative, liberal, social, and Christian under one umbrella, it is often considered the first example of a *Volkspartei*. Its early loose organization has been centralized, but it still grants state and local party organizations considerable freedom. Its success has been rooted in pragmatism, gradual change, and integrating diverse voters. The core members are Catholic, over sixty years of age, and self-employed. The party is strongest in southern Germany, both east and west, and weakest in large cities.

The CDU's conservative profile is tied to social values, family, and religion. It champions a free-market economy tempered by social responsibility. Its considerable electoral weight draws on its reputation for economic competence. It has also favored stricter enforcement of law and order principles. Angela Merkel is credited widely for having moved the CDU toward the center

Table 3.2. Party Membership, 1990–2015, and Percentage of Female Membership*

Year	CDU Total	CDU Women (%)	SPD Total	SPD Women (%)	CSU Total	CSU Women (%)	FDP Total	FDP Women (%)	Alliance 90/The Greens Total	Alliance 90/The Greens Women (%)	Left Party Total	Left Party Women (%)	AfD Total	AfD Women (%)
1990	789,609	—	943,402	—	186,198	—	168,217	—	41,316	—	280,882	—	—	—
1995	657,643	—	817,650	—	179,647	—	80,431	—	46,410	—	114,940	—	—	—
2000	616,722	25.2	734,667	29.4	181,021	17.4	62,721	24.4	46,631	37.4**	83,475	45.6	—	—
2005	571,881	25.3	590,485	30.4	170,117	18.2	65,022	23.2	45,105	37.1	61,270	44.9	—	—
2010	505,314	25.6	502,062	31.3	153,890	19.1	68,541	22.8	52,991	37.1	73,658	37.3	—	—
2015	444,400	25.9	442,814	32.0	144,360	20.1	53,197	22.8	59,418	38.6	58,989	37.2	16,385	16.0

*Data availability prior to 2000 is inconsistent across parties, so we omit them here.
**Data are for 2001.

Source: Oskar Niedermayer, *Parteimitglieder in Deutschland*, version 2016 (working paper no. 26, Otto-Stammer Center, Free University Berlin, 2016).

of the political spectrum in terms of labor and social policies, family, immigration, and even nuclear energy policy. Her followers view these policy shifts as pragmatic; they have modernized the party and usurped votes from the SPD. Programmatic updating also aimed to increase the CDU's appeal among young voters and women, two groups among whom the CDU had lost support since the 1980s. Critics lament the loss of a conservative nucleus and programmatic leadership. Some emphasize that these policy adjustments opened space on the right of the political spectrum, which the AfD has taken up.

Christian Social Union (CSU)

The CSU is an anomaly in the party system for three reasons. First, it is a regional party that exists only in Bavaria, where the CDU is not on the ballot. Second, in Bavaria, it has governed alone and only occasionally in a coalition since 1957. Third, CDU/CSU are coupled at the national level and in the Bundestag, giving the CSU considerable national veto power, which it uses regularly. For example, CDU and CSU leaders routinely dispute immigration, family, and European integration policies, with the CSU claiming to be the champion of conservative ideals. Its dissident role started early, when its representatives failed to support the ratification of the Basic Law because they considered its federalist elements too weak.

Its dominant position in Bavaria rests on a strong regional identity (Hepburn 2008), rooted in folklore (beer festivals and traditional dances), dress (lederhosen and dirndls), cuisine (beer, pork, dumplings, and apple strudel), dialect, religion (Catholicism), and a long history of state autonomy. Visitors crossing into Bavaria by car may notice colorful road signs inscribed *Free State of Bavaria*; the only other Land using this designation is Saxony. The import of this self-characterization should not be underestimated. Many Bavarians attest a strong element of self-determination, if not defiance, which the CSU can use to its advantage in relations with the central government. Under CSU leadership, this once mostly agricultural region in the south has become one of the most prosperous nationwide; the economic success story has worked in the party's favor. Having been in power for so long, the party's infrastructure is both deep and wide across the region. The CSU has lost about 40,000 members since 1990 but despite its regional character, it is still the third-largest party in terms of membership.

Social Democratic Party of Germany

The CDU/CSU's main competitor, the SPD, is by far the oldest existing party. Its origins can be traced to the mid-nineteenth century, when it represented the interests of the emerging working class by propagating a socialist ideology. The name SPD was adopted in 1890, and although harassed by authorities and politically marginalized, it became a major electoral force before World War I. During the Weimar period, it routinely joined coalition governments, but its leaders were handicapped by lack of allies and expertise. The SPD also battled the KPD for members and voters. After Hitler's ascent to power in 1933, the NSDAP quickly became the only party. All others were banned and their members harassed, but KPD and SPD functionaries were special targets of Nazi repression; many ended up in concentration camps or in exile. After World War II, the SPD was the first party to organize in all four zones of occupation. Soon SPD and CDU/CSU were battling for dominance in the West by presenting quite different worldviews: CDU/CSU advocated close relations with the West, NATO membership, and a social market economy, while the SPD favored massive economic intervention, workers' rights, and unification of East and West Germany, even at the cost of neutrality.

The rivalry between CDU/CSU and SPD continues, but the parameters have changed. The 1959 reform of the SPD's program to make it a more pluralistic and market-oriented party was a turning point that opened new opportunities, and in 1966, it emerged as the junior partner in a Grand Coalition with CDU/CSU. In 1969, for the first time, it entered a coalition government with the FDP under the leadership of Chancellor Willy Brandt. It had become a *Volkspartei* like the CDU and CSU. Peaking in the 1970s, its electoral fortunes have since wavered, although it is still strong in some northern and western states.

Today, three parties on the political left—the SPD, Alliance 90/The Greens, and the PDS/Left Party—vie for similar clienteles, and their competition has splintered the vote. At the same time, most European leftist parties are experiencing an identity crisis. The SPD's traditional voter base, the working class, has shrunk along with membership in labor unions that provided loyal support and voters. In the aftermath of the collapse of communism in Europe, shifting demographics, global competition, and sporadic financial crises forced many center-left parties to sign on to a leaner, meaner welfare state. Slogans about social justice and protecting working-class interests started to sound hollow to the many voters who feel threatened by globalization and, most recently, immigration. These developments increased the appeal of fringe parties on the left and right.

In Germany, these forces arose during and in the aftermath of SPD Chancellor Gerhard Schröder's tenure in office (1998–2005). Under his leadership, the party moved closer to the center in the mid-1990s, gaining electoral success and, later, initiating policies that some credit with the revival of the German economy and others with the dismantling of the welfare state. They divided the

SPD, and ultimately, a new party, further to the left, aptly called the Left Party or The Left (*Die Linke*), emerged. On the other side of the political spectrum, feelings of uncertainty about the future and xenophobia fed votes to rightist parties. The CDU's usurpation of traditional leftist issues, such as gender equality and education, siphoned off some of the social-democratic voter base. SPD feels competition from many directions.

The selection of Martin Schulz, president of the European Parliament from 2012 to 2017, as the designated SPD chancellor candidate in the 2017 Bundestag election briefly improved the standing of the party in the polls, but this positive effect quickly dissipated. Among others, any SPD-led government coalition needs the votes of both Alliance 90/The Greens and the Left Party, and the inclusion of the latter in a national coalition government remains an obstacle.

Free Democratic Party of Germany (FDP)

The FDP, sometimes called the Liberal Party, promotes a policy agenda informed by classical economics and political liberalism with an emphasis on free markets, less government interference, and individual freedom. Formed in 1948, this centrist-liberal ideology positioned the party firmly between CDU/CSU and SPD, and until the 1990s, it was crucial to the formation of stable coalition governments. Traditionally, it attracted entrepreneurial middle-class voters with secular views, but its increasingly neoliberal economic policy never found many adherents in the eastern part, where the demand is for greater state involvement. In 2009, promising steep tax cuts, it garnered the highest number of votes in its history, but only four years later, for the first time, the party did not pass the threshold required for representation in the Bundestag. In a political environment in which liberal principles prevail, a centrist party finds it hard to carve out a distinct political profile. The FDP's fate in 2013 also shows the pitfall of close association with a dominant party; for many, the FDP was just the junior partner of the CDU/CSU. Strategic voters who preferred a CDU/CSU coalition with the FDP often allotted their vote to the FDP even if their party identification was closer to the CDU/CSU. After its disappointing performance as a junior partner from 2009 to 2013, fewer voters opted for a "vote on loan." In addition, some FDP leaders voiced Euroskeptic positions that alienated its traditional business-oriented, liberal, pro-market base. However, most recent Land elections have evidenced a partial revival of its electoral fortunes; in 2017, it was represented in nine of the Land parliaments, all located in the old Federal Republic and Berlin. The September 2017 election resulted in the party's return to the national parliament based on new leadership, a revamped party program, and a changed political environment in Germany and Europe.

Alliance 90/The Greens

The Green party emerged from various social movements in West Germany and entered the Bundestag in 1983. Initially, its founders emphasized antiparty and antiestablishment views, challenging not only conventional policy positions but also organizational principles of party hierarchy and demeanor. Leadership positions were shared, and parliamentary representation rotated biannually; that is, MPs vacated their seats after two years to make place for a fellow party member. Rather than donning suits and ties, representatives favored jeans and T-shirts and arrived on bicycles rather than in fancy official cars.

From these rebellious beginnings, only the principle of dual leadership survives. Until the mid-1990s, intrafactional struggles between the Realists (*Realos*) and Fundamentalists (*Fundis*) threatened to tear the party apart. While *Realos* advocated pragmatism and cooperation with other parties to advance their policy agenda, the hardcore *Fundis* rejected both in favor of opposition and strict adherence to their more radical goals. In a drawn-out process, the Realists gained the upper hand. In 1993, the party merged with the East German Alliance 90, mostly former dissidents, and the name changed to *Alliance 90/The Greens*, although in common parlance, it is simply called the Greens.

Many of the party's messages—sustainability, environmental protection, closing nuclear power plants, greater participation of women and minorities—have become mainstream, and carving out a distinct programmatic niche has become more difficult. Originally, the party drew its voters predominantly from the young and educated; university towns were its centers of support. Today, its voters are predominantly in the west; they are still better educated with above-average incomes, and many are self-employed. Some early voters remain loyal, leading to a "graying" of the Greens. The party is represented in most Länder parliaments, and from 1998 to 2005, it formed a national-level coalition with the SPD; one of its leaders, Joschka Fischer, held the influential position of foreign minister.

Once an outlier, shunned by the political establishment, Alliance 90/The Greens is now a sought-after coalition partner. In 2016, it participated in ten of the fifteen Länder coalition governments (in Bavaria, the CSU governs alone). These alliances spanned the ideological spectrum: it had coalitions in place with the CDU in Hesse and Baden Württemberg and with SPD and the Left Party in Thuringia, but most followed the traditional SPD-Green trajectory. No other Green party in Europe can match Alliance 90/The Greens in terms of influence and government participation.

PDS/The Left Party

The PDS originated with the collapse of communism in East Germany and subsequent unification. As the successor of the disbanded SED, it decried the economic and social costs of unification and established itself as the champion of eastern interests. It divided the electorate, but it was particularly disparaged in the west, where it never gained more than 1 percent of the vote, and many thought it was doomed to fail. However, it quickly garnered a large majority of eastern votes. This imbalance changed in 2004, when disgruntled western SPD members founded a new party, the Electoral Alliance of Labor and Social Justice (WASG). The catalyst was Chancellor Gerhard Schröder's controversial labor and social policies, which, many felt, undermined the programmatic goals of his party—in particular, protection of the welfare state. Officially, the Left Party formed in 2007, after PDS and WASG ran successfully as an alliance in the 2005 federal election.

Its electoral strength remains in the east: in the 2013 federal election, it achieved 5.6 percent of the vote in the west and 22.7 percent in the east. Left Party voters share a socioeconomic background, leading Peter Doerschler (2015, 398) to suggest that "the Left Party has bridged some of the persistent regional divides within the Federal Republic and now appears to be as much a source of unity as division between the two regions." Still, many differences linger; it is a regional party in the east and a protest party in the west (Patton 2011), and infighting continues among its many factions.

In the east and the city-state Berlin, the Left Party is represented in Land governments routinely, and in 2014, for the first time, it took the lead in forming a government in Thuringia. It has not been included in a national coalition government. Nevertheless, even as the party's communist origins fade, many voters still reject some of its policy positions. Particularly in the western part of the country, its critical attitude toward NATO and the EU disqualify it for participation in a left-of-center government with the SPD and Alliance 90/The Greens. To many, the Left Party, like the AfD (see below), remains a pariah.

Alternative for Germany (AfD)

Until recently, Germany seemed immune to the draw of extreme right-wing parties seen in other Western European countries, at least on the national level, as protest votes favored parties on the left, not the right. This lack of support was mainly attributed to Germany's Nazi past, which makes association with extreme rightist parties taboo for many. In addition, the media erect a strong front against their functionaries, limiting their exposure, while highlighting their intraparty quarrels and extreme positions. The parties themselves—in particular, the Republikaner and the National Democratic Party of Germany (NPD)—contributed their share of ineptitude; plagued by factional struggles and lacking charismatic leaders, often seen as a prerequisite for their success, they quickly faltered at the regional level.

The AfD formed in March 2013 during the eurozone crisis and in time for the upcoming Bundestag election. Six months later, it garnered 4.7 percent of the vote and narrowly missed entry into the Bundestag. It was successful in the 2014 EP election, gaining seven seats with 7.1 percent of the votes. Its founders, mostly economists, including some university professors, espoused a particular brand of soft Euroskepticism—approval of European integration but opposition to the euro, specifically, Germany's membership in the euro—but from the beginning, many members and voters supported a more radical Euroskepticism coupled with strong anti-immigration sentiments. Tensions within the leadership and the diverse expectations of its voters could not be contained. The neoliberal and more moderate party founders quickly distanced themselves and formed the Alliance for Progress and Renewal (ALFA) in 2015. The AfD group in the EP broke apart, with five members joining ALFA, although this party has little chance of survival.

The split facilitated a right-wing shift by the AfD toward more open populism while maintaining its neoliberal economic positions. Just as the eurozone crisis provided a window of opportunity in the 2013 Bundestag elections, the refugee crisis of 2015–16 offered another electoral opening. By spring 2017, after the terrorist attacks in Paris in November 2015, sexual attacks on women by mostly North African immigrants in Cologne during the 2015–16 New Year's celebration, and a general sense of anxiety about the challenges of integrating more than one million refugees, the AfD had representatives in thirteen of the sixteen Land parliaments, a first for a right-wing party in the history of the Federal Republic. In two states, the party achieved the second-highest percentage, behind the CDU in Saxony-Anhalt and SPD in Mecklenburg-West Pomerania. Its voter clientele comes from diverse backgrounds; it draws support from all other parties and mobilizes nonvoters. It attracts many workers—men in particular—but shared values, not social class, drive the party's growth (Decker 2016, 10–11). They include strong nationalism, nativism, and law-and-order views. Its rapid rise also illustrates the appeal of antiestablishment politics. Its members and supporters protest, not just government policies and the other parties, but what they see as the mainstream media's collusion in portraying them. With the flow of refugees into Germany stemmed, the party's move to the extreme right and continued factional infighting and scandals With the flow of refugees stemmed, the party's move to the extreme right and continued factional infighting and scandals seemed to dampen its appeal, but by the September 2017 election, it had sufficiently rebounded to receive 12.6 percent of the vote.

ELECTIONS AND POLITICAL PARTIES

Electoral procedures are among the most consequential features of any political system: they influence the number of parties represented in parliament, who is chosen to run in elections, and the ease or difficulty of gaining seats. As a result, they influence the building of governments, the behavior of politicians seeking election, and even voting behavior. The basic distinction between plurality/majority systems, in which a constituency is represented by one candidate, and systems with proportional representation and multimember districts, seems straightforward, but it veils many possible alternatives within and across them based on district magnitude, electoral thresholds, the choice of mathematical formulas to calculate electoral outcomes, quota systems, and open- versus closed-list systems. Depending on the election, several electoral systems are usually in place even within one country. European nations have a dizzying variety of electoral rules, although most favor some form of proportional representation.

German residents have to register with local authorities when they move to a new address, but no additional voter registration is required. All elections take place on Sunday, normally every four years for national elections, and every five years for EP elections and most Land parliamentary elections and municipal elections. Land election outcomes are often interpreted as a gauge of the national government's popularity and a test run for national elections. They also influence Bundesrat composition since its members are not elected by citizens but appointed from the ranks of the different Land governments.

The electoral system for the Bundestag combines proportional with plurality, or first-past-the-post, features, termed a mixed-member proportional system (MMP) or personalized proportional system (see figure 3.2). In other words, it combines a personal vote for a candidate on the first ballot with a vote for a party (closed-list proportional system) on the second ballot.

What is unusual in the German system is the vote distribution. The so-called second vote (since it is second on the ballot) determines the number of seats a party holds in the Bundestag, presuming the party can jump the 5-percent threshold, which was established in 1953 for Land and subsequently national elections to reduce the number of political parties represented in the Bundestag. The policy is a response to the political turmoil in the Weimar Republic, where the plethora of parties contributed to democracy's demise. If a party wins three seats based on the first ballot, the 5-percent threshold does not apply. Parties can secure reelection of many incumbents by putting their names on both ballots.

Ballot

For the election to the German Bundestag
in electoral district ——
24 September 2017

You have 2 votes

One vote here
for the election of
a district representative

One vote here
for the election of the Party List
(determines the overall distribution of
seats for the individual parties)

First vote Second vote

	First vote			Second vote	
1	**Last name,** First name Occupation **SPD** Social Democratic Place of residence Party of Germany	◯	◯	**CDU** Christian Democratic Union Names of top-ranking party candidates listed	**1**
2	**Last name,** First name Occupation **CDU** Christian Place of residence Democratic Union	◯	◯	**SPD** Social Democratic Union Names of top-ranking party candidates listed	**2**
3	**Last name,** First name Occupation **GREENS** Alliance 90/The Place of residence Greens	◯	◯	**GREENS** Alliance 90/The Greens Names of top-ranking party candidates listed	**3**
4	**Last name,** First name Occupation **LEFT** The Left Party Place of residence **PARTY**	◯	◯	**LEFT PARTY** The Left Party Names of top-ranking party candidates listed	**4**
5	**Last name,** First name Occupation **FDP** Free Democratic Place of residence Party	◯	◯	**FDP** Free Democratic Party Names of top-ranking party candidates listed	**5**
6	**Last name,** First name Occupation **AfD** Alternative for Place of residence Germany	◯	◯	**AfD** Alternative for Germany Names of top-ranking party candidates listed	**6**

Figure 3.2. Sample Ballot for the Elections to the Bundestag

Note: This is an abbreviated ballot; in reality, many more parties are listed. The order in which the parties appear is determined by the outcome of the last election in the district in which the ballot is used.

There are no primaries; the parties decide on the nominees and the ranking of candidates on the closed-party list. Placement is influenced mostly by position in the party, gender, region, and membership in special organizations, such as unions. This electoral system encourages strategic voting; that is, voters whose political sympathies tend toward smaller parties less likely to win a district vote may cast their personalized vote for one of the candidates of the major parties, but the second and more decisive vote to one of the smaller parties.

With its short campaigns tightly orchestrated by electoral rules and political parties, Germany's elections are typical of European parliamentary systems. The "heated" phase of the campaign lasts no longer than six weeks. Campaigns are organized and paid for by the candidates' parties. Campaign financing is integral to party financing overall and draws from three sources: party membership contributions, public financing, and donations from sponsors. Membership dues make up the largest share (around 40–50 percent), followed by public funds (around 25 percent), which are based on the number of votes a party receives in European, federal, and Land elections, provided that it gains 0.5 percent of the vote in European or national elections or 1 percent in Land elections. Parties also receive 0.38 euro for each euro raised through dues or donations. The upper limit for public funds to all parties was 156.7 million euro in 2014. Private party donations are not restricted but must be disclosed if they exceed 10,000 euro. Overall, private donations play a minor role in Germany, notwithstanding occasional financial scandals (Niedermayer 2015a). Compared to the United States, electoral campaigns are cheap. For example, in 2013, the overall campaign cost for the national election and three Land elections amounted to 151.4 million euro (Niedermayer 2015b).

In all Western democracies, declining voter turnout is a fact of life. In Germany, national election turnout is higher than that for Land and municipal elections; overall, turnout is lower in the east. In the former West Germany, the highest level was reached in 1972 with 91.1 percent and the lowest, in unified Germany, in 2009 with 70.8 percent. To explain this phenomenon, observers cite loss of trust in political parties, declining party identification, and a shift toward other forms of civic engagement; for example, grassroots initiatives and protest movements. Abstention can also signal satisfaction with the current political situation. Voter turnout alone is not a sign of political crisis.

POLITICAL ELITES

In democracies, political elites represent the will of the people. They are defined as those who aspire to or hold political office—in particular, elected politicians and senior civil servants—but also journalists and lobbyists.

Political scientists differentiate various forms of representation by the questions they pose. *Descriptive representation* asks to what extent political elites should reflect the characteristics of those for whom they act. *Substantive representation* asks whether and how elites advance the interest of voters. *Symbolic representation* asks how descriptive and substantive representation affect the public legitimacy of the political system.

East and West: Halting Integration

When the communist regimes collapsed in Central and Eastern Europe, many expected thorough elite replacement. However, considerable elite continuity tempered the purge, except in East Germany. The newly formed successor party, the PDS, was built almost completely by young, uncompromised former SED members; the old guard was ousted. In other parties, newly recruited East German politicians came mostly from the small dissident community or apolitical sectors of society; they advanced to new political roles without much administrative and even less political experience. West Germans seized on the resulting new political opportunities; they had the know-how and the party connections. Partnerships between western and eastern states encouraged intra-German personnel transfer with lasting consequences; many westerners stayed and still occupy elite positions.

From 2012 to 2017 both the head of state, Joachim Gauck, and the head of government, Angela Merkel, hailed from the east, and their professional backgrounds reflected the career paths typical of the first-generation political elite after unification: Merkel was a physical chemist; Gauck a pastor. Neither had played an active political role during communism but became politically active once the regime loosened its grip. For example, Merkel joined a small, mostly church-based opposition group that, in 1989, formed the party Democratic Awakening, which later merged with the CDU. In March 1990, she became deputy speaker for the new GDR government and, after Germany's unification on October 3, 1990, a close associate of former chancellor Helmut Kohl (CDU), who became her mentor (Mushaben 2017). Jennifer Yoder (2010, 554) identifies several factors that helped East Germans advance to leadership positions. Considering their apolitical background, most were "accidental politicians"; freedom from communist ties was a sine qua non. Their advancement was facilitated by the efforts of western elites, political scandals or party infighting that allowed them to climb the career ladder, and pragmatism and willingness to adjust quickly to Western norms and behavior.

Despite these obvious success stories, the overall integration of East Germans into the political establishment has been halting. Eastern Germans constitute only 14.6 percent of the national Members of Parliament (MPs) (Kintz

2014, 19), slightly less than their proportion of the population. The east-west split is much more pronounced when measured by those holding top positions in the civil service, business, the justice sector, the military, and the media. In these sectors, eastern Germans make up less than 3 percent. Even in institutions located in the former GDR, eastern Germans constitute a meager 23 percent of the elite. For example, in the five eastern Land governments (without Berlin) in 2016, 70 percent of political elites (2004: 75 percent) were born in East Germany. In a small sign of progress, eastern Germans now occupy 46 percent of undersecretary of state positions in eastern governments, a substantial increase from 26 percent in 2004 (Lukas and Reinhard 2016). The connection between the underrepresentation of eastern Germans and their alienation from, and disappointment with, politics—measured by, for example, lower voter turnout, greater electoral volatility, and greater willingness to vote for extreme right parties—is hard to gauge, but it recalls the early days of unification when many easterners felt like second-class citizens.

Members of the German Bundestag

Asymmetric representation among elites, however, is not limited to east-west differences. In all democratic political systems, the background characteristics of elected politicians do not mirror the population: in general, they are mostly men and better educated; few are workers. The German Bundestag fits this pattern. The 630 members in session between 2013 and 2017 held over 100 different occupations, but two groups dominate as they have in the past: tenured civil servants (*Beamte*), including jurists, and the self-employed. For civil servants, a return to their job is guaranteed should a political career not pan out. Workers were a tiny minority (2 percent), whereas professionals with tertiary education were in the majority (about two-thirds), and about 20 percent of them held a doctorate. The great majority of MPs was born between 1951 and 1970 (average age: fifty years). Their religious composition reflected the almost even divide between Catholics and Protestants in the population at large: 202 were Protestant and 205 Catholic; 194 left the section on religious background blank; 23 were of no religious persuasion. Not indicating a denomination does not necessarily mean no religious affiliation since MPs can choose not to reveal it. Three MPs were Muslims, far fewer than the approximately 5 percent in the population. The number of MPs with immigrant backgrounds has increased from 21 (2009) to 35 (2013).

German incumbency rates are high (about 70 percent) but not quite as high as in the United States (Edinger 2009, 203). The ousting of the FDP from the Bundestag in 2013 provided opportunities for more newcomers. Almost a third were first-time MPs; another 139 were serving only their second stint in the national parliament. These figures attest to continued elite replacement amid stability. On average, MPs can claim about twenty-five years of party membership, which demonstrates the lengthy career paths in parliamentary systems and the limited opportunities for outsiders (Kintz 2014). Political careers start at the local level, and even without institutional hurdles, aspiring politicians chose distinct career paths that tie them to the Land, national, or EP level; their upward mobility is limited by choice (Borchert and Stolz 2011, 219). Many consider it a side effect of professionalization; electoral officials are offered few monetary incentives to move from one assembly to another. Indeed, compared to other OECD countries, German MPs fare well in terms of staff and remuneration; only members of the US Congress did better (Edinger 2009, 189).

Gender and Political Representation

Socioeconomic, cultural, and institutional factors explain the political underrepresentation of women around the world (Norris and Inglehart 2001). Socioeconomic variables determine women's level of education and professional qualifications; cultural values reflect religion and egalitarian as opposed to paternalistic attitudes. Institutional factors are related to the nature of the party system, electoral rules, and the use of a quota system. In a multiparty setting, leftist parties often advance the idea of gender parity; other parties are under pressure to follow suit. Proportional closed-list electoral systems in multimember districts facilitate the election of women more than single-member districts. They allow the strategic positioning of women in top slots or even the alternation between male and female party members on party lists. Quotas can supply the needed additional push, but they vary in form. They can be constitutional or legal acts to reserve seats for women or guarantee a minimum number of positions on party lists for women. Their institutionalization should not be equated with automatic implementation; parties find loopholes and/or pay fines when quotas are not met. Voluntary quotas are left to party statutes.

Nordic countries, known for their egalitarian political culture, have pioneered political gender equality, but in the rest of the European countries, the journey toward more descriptive representation has been long and remains incomplete. The adoption of quota systems has made a difference. Germany illustrates the interplay of the variables noted above. Men still make up the majority of Bundestag members; the women's proportion was among the highest in the world from 2013 to 2017 before it dropped to 30.7 percent in the 2017 election. Until the 1980s, women's political careers were held back by cultural factors, as well as power dynamics within political parties, not their level of education or professional accomplishments. Institutional factors helped to remedy this situation. Once the left-libertarian Green party championed the idea of parity between men and women, it diffused to other parties, and the electoral system of mixed member proportional representation facilitated implementation. Quotas still differ substantially among political parties, and some have not introduced them. The CSU, reluctantly and after much debate, instituted a 40 percent quota for women in top leadership positions at the party and district levels but has no legislative quota. The FDP still abstains from quotas (see table 3.3). Nevertheless, even parties without gender quotas are not immune to pressure to increase recruitment of women; in all political parties, women are now represented in much higher numbers (see tables 3.4 and 3.5).

Table 3.3.   Voluntary Legislative Party Quotas

Party	Quota Size (%)	Implementation Year
Alliance 90/The Greens	50	1986
Left Party	50	1990
CDU	33	1996
SPD	40	1988
CSU	no quota	—
FDP	no quota	—

Source: Quota Project, Global Database of Quotas for Women, http://www.quota project.org; Wendy Stokes, *Women in Contemporary Politics* (Cambridge, UK: Polity, 2005), 89.

Table 3.4.   Percentage of Women in the Bundestag, 1949–2016 (selected years)

1949	6.8
1980	8.5
1983	9.8
1994	26.2
2009	32.9
2013	36.5
2016	37.1

Source: http://www.bpb.de/lernen/grafstat/grafstat-bundestagswahl-2013/147348/ mw-04-06-frauenanteil-im-deutschen-bundestag-1949-2009; http://www.bun destag.de/bundestag/abgeordnete18/mdb_zahlen/frauen_maenner/260128.

Table 3.5.   Gender Distribution in the Bundestag, June 2016

Party	Women	Men	Women (%)
CDU/CSU	80	230	25.8
SPD	85	108	44.0
Left Party	35	29	54.7
Alliance 90/The Greens	34	29	54.0
Total Bundestag	234	396	36.8

Source: http://www.bundestag.de/bundestag/abgeordnete18/mdb_zahlen/frauen _maenner/260128.

After analyzing the impact of gender quotas on political participation, Louise Davidson-Schmich (2016, 220–25) concludes that, despite considerable advancement of women in German politics, the glass still remains half empty. She carefully weighs the pros and cons. Women have not achieved parity, and while impressive increases in descriptive representation have taken place in the EP, Bundestag, and Land parliaments, quotas in municipalities are often unenforced. Furthermore, women still make up a small proportion of political party members, which reduces the pool of eligible candidates. On a left-to-right political scale, the percentage of women slides downward (table 3.3 above). Women still have to shoulder both housework and professional responsibilities, and they remain the primary caregivers for children and elders; party cultures have not completely reversed centuries-long male dominance. On the flip side, the success of voluntary party quotas goes beyond the increase in parliamentary representation. They have dispelled any notion that women are less capable than men in running for and gaining political office. Their acceptance is undisputed and has spawned other policies working toward gender equality, including mentoring networks and female quotas on executive boards (see chapter 4). Substantive and symbolic representation have benefited from the increase of women in political positions. Long gone are the days when politics was firmly a male bastion with women tolerated only as outsiders.

COMMON TRENDS AND NATIONAL VARIATIONS

All Western democracies have a broad array of political actors. Here, we focused on political parties and certain aspects of elite composition. In Germany and elsewhere in Europe, parties are at the heart of politics and policy making, and when challenged by societal, economic, and global changes, they adapted their programs. The loss of support for established parties and the emergence of new parties—in particular, the strengthening of fringe parties on the right and left—signal a shift. Many of the challenges that beleaguer the established political parties are homegrown; others are linked to globalization. Migration flows are harder to control; immigrant populations are increasing; economic developments are global, not just national or regional. How political parties and their elites respond will influence the future of European democracy decisively.

Germany illustrates these European trends, but the national imprint is strong. The legacy of the failed Weimar Republic set the foundation for a moderate and consensual multiparty system, electoral rules that safeguard against the proliferation of parties, and constitutional proscriptions of antidemocratic parties (discussed in chapter 2). Unification did not alter these basic structural arrangements, but lasting east-west distinctions in voter turnout, party preferences, party identification, and party and union membership have developed. Alliance 90/The Greens has consolidated its place as the most successful green party in Europe.

The AfD erased Germany's distinction as the one country where right-wing parties could not achieve widespread success; the 2017 national election was the turning point. Following national elections in the United Kingdom, France, and the Netherlands, it was expected to reinforce Germany's stability at a moment of international instability and change. Overall, forty-two parties competed for seats, although many were represented only in certain districts. The CDU/CSU were sure to garner the most votes, and a grand coalition between them and SPD loomed large, but despite four years of successful governance, the public seemed restless. The electoral campaigns were described as lackluster and sidestepped contentious foreign and domestic policy questions. Increasingly, attention shifted to the minor parties.

Election night carried a number of surprises. The two major parties earned fewer seats than ever before in the history of the Federal Republic; the result was the worst in the postwar history for the SPD and second-worst for CDU/CSU (see table 3.1). As anticipated, the right-wing party AfD entered the Bundestag, but few had predicted it would shatter the 10 percent barrier and become the third-largest party, followed by FDP, Alliance 90/The Greens, and the Left Party. The 2013 revision of the electoral law, intended to make outcomes fairer by making them more representative, also ballooned the number of MPs to 709, the highest ever.

The 2017 election outcome may lead to the first three-party (four if the CSU is counted separately) national coalition, bringing together CDU/CSU, FDP, and Alliance 90/The Greens under the chancellorship of Angela Merkel. This arrangement is called a *Jamaica coalition* since the parties' colors—black, yellow, and green—are the colors of the Jamaican flag. Other scenarios include a minority government, new elections, or even a return to a grand coalition government. German politics is about to enter uncharted waters; the smooth sailing of the last few years may have come to end.

The direct impact of European integration on parties can be seen in the creation of new positions, adjustment of programs, and development of supranational connections. In many European countries, party programs reflect rising Euroskepticism, and, in some, EU membership constitutes a main cleavage. Germany was the outsider with its cross-party consensus for EU membership. Although membership is still strongly supported by a great majority of citizens, soft Euroskepticism has grown.

Chapter 4

Citizens and Politics

KEY TERMS

civil society
demography
direct democracy
gender
grassroots initiatives
family policy
interest groups

labor unions
political culture
political participation
protest
religion and religious communities
social movements

Parties and elites are central political actors. In a representative democracy, they act on behalf of the citizenry, who are also political players; their participation is prerequisite to democracy's stability, legitimacy, and vitality. Scholars have long differentiated between conventional forms of political participation, such as voting or joining political groups, and unconventional forms, such as staging demonstrations or engaging in active protest. The distinction between these forms has become blurred as protests, however unconventional, are part of the normal repertoire of citizen involvement.

This chapter first analyzes various and shifting practices of political participation and attitudes toward the political system. We introduce general methods of citizen participation followed by illustrative, contemporary case studies. These include labor unions, citizens' groups in East and West Germany, and recent examples of collective action. Two protests, Stuttgart 21 and Pegida (Patriotic Europeans against the Islamization of the Occident), were chosen because they do not fit simple categorizations of social movements. Finally, the protest against TTIP (Transatlantic Trade and Investment Partnership) is part of a left-leaning, transnational, antiglobalization movement but exhibits distinct national features. We conclude this section with an exploration of political culture, asking to what extent eastern and western Germans have come to share values and viewpoints.

The second part of the chapter examines two areas in which tradition contests transformation: gender and religion. In a long, drawn-out process, the traditional role of women as mothers and housewives has been expanded without completely erasing some engrained attitudes. One side effect is Germany's consistently low birth rate, which, coupled with the population's aging, has created a demographic conundrum.

Religion in contemporary German society is experiencing a similar struggle between tradition and change. Judeo-Christian traditions, deeply rooted in the German (and European) political, cultural, and social fabric, are now complemented and, at times, challenged by secularization and the influx of Muslims. Unification and Europeanization are background variables that, at times, reinforce and accelerate these evolutionary developments common to most Western societies. The chapter highlights both transnational trends and German variations.

BACKGROUND

Any effort to understand and to measure the relevance of political participation in a particular society must address a complex web of concepts, organizations, and activities. In democratic theory, *civil society* refers to diverse societal networks, such as voluntary associations, nongovernmental organizations (NGOs), and advocacy groups that perform public functions for either specific interests or the collective good. The modern origins of the term go back to the early Enlightenment philosophers, and contemporary social scientists and politicians still argue its significance for a functioning democracy. It experienced a renaissance when mass public protest challenged the entrenched communist regimes and helped to drive the transition toward democracy (Ekiert and Kubik 1999). An active civil society is the foundation of *social capital*; that is, a network of social relations built on trust and cooperation. However, civil society also shows two sides: one democratic and inclusive; the other more authoritarian and closed. In other words, the values that civic organizations promote matter. Simone Chambers and Jeffrey Kopstein differentiate between particularistic and democratic civility. In the former, the values of "trust, public spiritedness, self-sacrifice" are shared by members of a particular group but do not extend to outsiders, often promoting intolerance and, worse, xenophobia and antidemocratic values. "Democratic civility, in contrast, extends the goods learned in participation to all citizens regardless of group membership" (2001, 841).

Over the past fifty years, the number of civil society organizations in Germany has skyrocketed from 86,000 in 1960 to 589,000 in 2014; the most substantial jump came after unification in 1990. While the curve has flattened, more citizens are volunteering their time to promote the interests of civil society organizations (Alscher and Priller 2016, 383). Furthermore, activism in a global civil society has been facilitated by modern mass communications media (Keane 2003). Many civil society groups are linked to similar groups across European or international borders.

Interest groups have an often-disputed place in civil society due to their relatively high level of organization and membership. Occupation-based interest groups, such as labor unions and employers' associations, as well as advocacy groups lobby nationally and, in some cases, internationally for specific rights and benefits. According to the European Transparency Register, 8,572 lobbying organizations operated across Europe in 2015. About one thousand are headquartered in Germany, and one-fifth of the largest also maintain offices in Brussels (von Winter 2016, 190).

In contrast to interest groups, *social movements* are amorphous, often composed of several overlapping and/or competing organizations. Relations among members are informal, based on shared values and goals, and political participation often takes the form of protest, using unusual techniques to make interests heard. Protests are most often linked to public demonstrations but also include boycotts, civil disobedience, strikes, marches, street theater, sit-ins, and road blockages. The term *new social movement* is usually applied to collective action to contest social and cultural policies, including organizations representing women's rights or environmental protection. These "new" movements are distinguished from traditional social movements, such as the nineteenth- and early-twentieth-century labor movement, that sought material, or bread and butter, remedies. In the past, most scholarship on social movements conceptualized them within the framework of the nation-state. New social movements, however, challenge this notion. Today, political opportunities for participation and opposition extend beyond national borders. Such cross-border cooperation is particularly strong in Europe due to physical proximity and the spillover effects of European integration. Movements that exist in several countries can reinforce each other.

Modern democracies are representative, but all have witnessed demands for more *direct democracy*. Ballot initiatives and public referenda have increased in most European countries with some surprising and even bewildering results, such as the United Kingdom's referendum to exit the EU in June 2016. In Germany, forms reflecting direct democracy are confined to the state and local level. The Basic Law allows referenda only to restructure state territories, and only citizens in the affected locales can vote. In contrast, at the Land level, direct democracy initiatives have become common, although only some are binding. They have sought, and at times succeeded, to modify state constitutions, school policies, and various energy and transportation policies, and have introduced voting-age regulations and a smoking ban in public places.

Political culture, commonly defined as values and attitudes toward the political system, is a slippery concept, crucial for understanding regime satisfaction, stability, and aspects of political participation, but measured largely by surveys that may be skewed by the questions asked. Assessments often favor the dominant culture and downplay minority positions. While political culture is in flux, the perception of a country's values often remains firm, and stereotypes tend to linger. In addition, values and attitudes may not coincide with actual political behavior. Still, surveys conducted over longer time spans and across countries provide an important barometer of citizens' attitudes about the political system.

German experiences highlight both the usefulness of the concept and the inherent difficulties in applying it. After World War II, West Germany proved that an authoritarian political culture can become democratic. In 1990, unification raised a new question: Can we speak of one political culture when two groups of citizens with common aspirations but different political socializations merge into one political community? Most scholarly work postulates a dominant national political culture, but citizens' attitudes and values vary. In Germany and elsewhere, regional identities, shaped by historical experiences, dialects, and religious affiliations, remain strong. Traditional north-south divides now crisscross east-west differences. Germany is also a good test case to explore what impact over sixty years of European integration might have on citizens' identity.

INTEREST AND ADVOCACY GROUPS

Function and Organization

Democratic legitimacy depends on a system for including interest groups. Membership size, goals, and organization vary, but they usually finance their activities through membership fees or donations. They try to influence public opinion by framing a specific question and lobbying rather than running for elective office or participating in government; their goals are narrowly focused, while political parties need broad platforms to gain voter support in elections. Since World War II, interest-group representation has shifted in three phases, according to Annette Zimmer and Rudolf Speth (2015). In West Germany, during the first phase, organized interest groups were often portrayed as antagonistic, undermining state authority. This narrow view soon gave way to a hierarchical, yet cooperative relationship between major interest groups and state institutions, generating the concept of *neocorporatism* (see chapter 6). Today, market forces prevail. State institutions no longer rely predominantly on the input of organized interests but can choose among advising agencies or create their own expert bodies; professional lobbyists have become more influential; and civil society organizations rely on expert marketing and social media, among other avenues, to effect policy outcomes. Zimmer and Speth conclude that lobbying now consists of "public affairs agencies, freelance lobbyists, public relations agencies, large law firms as well as professionally led NGOs" (2015, 43; our translation). Membership strength, they argue, no longer guides interest-group representation since they too are now professionally managed and respond to opportunities with greater flexibility. We illustrate some of these trends in our discussion of interest groups and civil society organizations.

All major German interest groups, including advocacy groups, operate on two levels, the national and the European. With the Maastricht Treaty (1993) and the Lisbon Treaty (2009), policies are increasingly debated and decided at the European level. To promote their agendas and to navigate multilevel European governance systems, national interest groups and NGOs build coalitions and promote their agendas by joining European-level federations. For example, the German Trade Federation (DGB) is a member of the European Trade Federation; the Federation of German Industry (BDI) and the Confederation of German Employers' Association (BDA) belong to an organization called BUSINESSEUROPE. German interest-group lobbying often targets governmental institutions at home and their representation in Brussels, particularly in the European Commission or the European Parliament. Many also maintain an office in Brussels as well as departments or portfolios for European affairs at home.

Programmatically, groups position themselves as either advocates for deeper integration or critics of European initiatives. Typically, they bring their own agendas to the table by promoting, for example, social policies to counterbalance market liberalization. As public institutions, the German Social Welfare Federations (*Wohlfahrtsverbände*) provide national welfare services but also communicate their "social Europe" agenda to protect the socially disadvantaged or marginalized across the EU (von Winter 2016, 200).

The Changing Face of Labor Unions

In Germany, stretching back to the nineteenth century, industrial relations, particularly in mining, steel, and metal work, were built on strong unions. After World War II, West German unions were organized on the principle "one firm, one union" and played an important role in labor relations, wage bargaining, and modernization. Their influence was elevated by the system of codetermination that grants union representatives decision-making rights on the boards of major companies. This arrangement not only empowers unions but benefits employers by alleviating class conflict and averting strikes. In 1950, about 5.4 million employees were organized in the DGB. This number increased steadily to reach a high of about 7.9 million in 1990.

In East Germany, membership in the Free German Trade Union Federation (FDGB) was officially voluntary but actually mandatory and encompassed roughly 98 percent of the workforce. The different unions within the system transmitted the will of the ruling SED party to the labor force but also fulfilled social roles. For example, they organized vacations, including the provision of vacation homes, and were responsible for running the social insurance scheme. In 1990, West German unions started to recruit members in the east; the FDGB soon dissolved, and not surprisingly, by 1991, the unified German trade unions swelled to 11.8 million members, or about 40 percent of the labor force. Since then, membership has been in steady decline to 6.1 million in 2015, or roughly 20 percent of all workers (see figure 4.1). In particular, eastern labor union membership shrank 43 percent between 1991 and 1995, reinforced by growing unemployment (Fichter 1997, 90).

Union membership has dropped across Europe. Globalization plays into changing labor organization and collective bargaining conditions, primarily

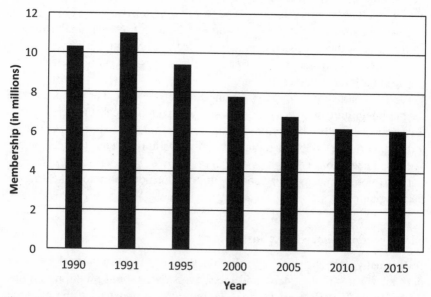

Figure 4.1. Membership in German Labor Unions, 1990–2015
Source: http://www.dgb.de/uber-uns/dgb-heute/mitgliederzahlen.

based on outsourcing, increased cross-border competition, smaller industries, and a larger and more diverse service sector. Different work patterns and labor contracts and competition from new, often smaller labor unions challenged the traditional union model.

Labor unions may have lost members and clout, but they are still crucial to collective bargaining. Workers' councils, mostly run by union members, are the backbone of shop-floor social organization. Union representatives "on the ground" fulfill important functions in improving workplace security, addressing grievances, and managing social problems, such as the integration of the many foreign-born workers. In postunification East Germany, most protests were organized by unions (Lemke 1997). Public-service unions, including those for teachers, nurses, and other healthcare workers, organized strikes and public actions aimed at raising wages and securing jobs after the dismantling of the extensive state-run public sector. Other large union protests included the metal-workers union, miners, and, in some cases, even farmers. Strikes designed to disrupt public life in support of wage-bargaining demands remain a powerful bargaining tool. In the early 2000s, union-organized protests against social reforms (such as Hartz IV, see chapter 6) spread throughout Germany. In 2014 and 2015, the locomotive engineers' union organized a wave of strikes, which affected many commuters on their way to work. In 2015–16, a months-long strike of preschool teachers (*Kita Streik*) rattled the German public; following years of wage restraint during the economic recession, they demanded higher pay and workplace improvements in childcare facilities.

Social Movements and Contentious Politics

Germans experience fewer strikes than France, Greece, and Italy, but public protest is a common means of political participation to voice concerns and to mobilize support. Comparative studies class the frequency of protest activities in Germany as moderate (Della Porta, Kriesi, and Rucht 1999). Many West German social movements emerged in the 1970s and peaked in the 1980s, leaving a deep imprint on the party system, political discourse, and policies (Karapin 2007; Roth and Rucht 2008). In the past two decades, movement concerns and strategies have altered along with their social bases. We first outline the history of social movements in West and East Germany before introducing selected case studies to illustrate new trends in movement activity.

West German New Social Movements

In the 1970s, a growing environmental movement protested air and water pollution and the use of nuclear energy. The peace movement strengthened in the late 1970s and peaked in the 1980s, when it protested NATO's "dual track" decision spearheaded by the West German government and the United States. This policy aimed to modernize weapons systems within NATO-member countries in response to the military buildup in the Soviet-led Warsaw Pact countries, while offering arms-control negotiations to build confidence and suggest improved relations. Most controversial, new, middle-range missiles would be stationed on West German soil but under US control. The decision led to a heated debate and to countrywide protests. On October 10, 1981, the peace movement drew hundreds of thousands of citizens to major demonstrations; 350,000 alone took to the streets of the capital, Bonn, in the largest public protest in the history of the Federal Republic to date.

As in many other Western countries, a new wave of the women's movement formed. German women organized in the early twentieth century to attain social rights and the right to vote, but in the 1970s, the approach to the right of self-determination was more radical. Feminist activity addressed reproductive rights, women's health, domestic violence, and other concerns previously considered "private" or even taboo. Looking toward the United States, Italy, France, and the United Kingdom for support and inspiration, women's, peace, and environmental groups increasingly organized as transnational movements. They attracted citizens from different walks of life, although strategies to achieve shared goals often differed.

These political activities and grassroots initiatives led to the founding of the Green party in 1980; the protest party's followers came mainly from the educated middle class, were often (but not exclusively) urban activists, and criticized the major parties for ignoring key questions pertaining to quality of life and democratic participation. Public attitudes shifted from material to quality-of-life concerns, especially among younger people, in what Ronald Inglehart (1977) called the "silent revolution." Intergenerational differences in values, he argued, can be explained by the relative affluence and security of post–World War II generations. Other scholars, such as Herbert Kitschelt (1989), who conducted one of the first studies about the rise of the Greens in West Germany, linked the quest for political participation to the emergence of a new and important cleavage based on quality of life concerns.

The East German Civic Movement

Across Central and Eastern Europe, discontent with the ruling communist elites was tightly monitored by the state security services and controlled by state agencies. The East German state was particularly paranoiac about dissent. The ruling elite instituted a dense and wide network of informers who spied on citizens to detect any alteration from the ideologically prescribed path; any contact with the West was potentially subversive. Those who took action often lost their jobs and served prison terms. By the 1980s, communist ideology still dominated official rhetoric but was slowly accommodating opportunism and criticism, provided they did not confront the SED or the Soviet Union directly. A major turning point was the emergence of the Polish independent union movement *Solidarność* in the early 1980s, which soon evolved into a broader social movement. At its height, approximately ten million workers, farmers, and intellectuals were members; in comparison, the communist Polish United Workers' Party had only two million members. At around the same time, small oppositional groups in East Germany formed under the umbrella of local Protestant churches. They questioned large-scale rearmament in Western and Eastern Europe, criticized environmental degradation, and advocated women's and human rights (Lemke 1991). Churches were the only independent social organizations, and by the late 1980s, some church-based communities had started to organize protest activities. In the Zion Church in East Berlin, for example, activists founded a small basement library and printed an underground newsletter called *Umweltblätter* (environmental gazette) to document and analyze environmental degradation. They were watched closely by the Stasi, the East German Ministry for State Security; raids and arrests followed, and publicity even reached the west. In fall 1989, several pastors were active in organizing new opposition groups and parties, such as the re-founded Social Democratic Party in the GDR, the New Forum, and Democratic Awakening. After the opening of the Berlin Wall in November 1989, citizens occupied Stasi headquarters to prevent destruction of approximately sixty-nine kilometers of material, mostly files on GDR residents, as an important witness to SED rule.

Church-affiliated activities were one side of the peaceful protest against the regime. Encouraged by democratic developments in Poland and Hungary and enraged by obvious voter fraud in summer 1989, increasing numbers of East German citizens left through newly opened emigration channels in Hungary and, later, Czechoslovakia in September and October. At home, protests erupted. In the terminology of economist Albert Hirschman, citizens used both "exit" and "voice" to show their discontent with the status quo. Although his theory describes consumer behavior, it applies readily to political dissent in the GDR since citizens voted with their feet (exited the country) or voiced their demands in demonstrations (Pfaff and Kim 2003). The resignation of Communist Party leader Erich Honecker on October 18, 1989 only exacerbated protest. By November 4, 1989, about half a million people protested in East Berlin. After the Monday evening prayer in the Nikolai Church in Leipzig in fall 1989, Monday demonstrations challenging SED rule continued well into the 1990s. The courage and resilience of this civic movement generated the peaceful revolution against the SED regime, paving the way to unification.

Contemporary Forms of Contentious Politics

After unification, citizens resorted to unusual forms of participation but with important differences. Their profile became more varied; east-west patterns diverged; globalization and Europeanization added new concerns and calls for direct citizen participation; and the ubiquitous use of social media expanded the repertoire of mobilization. Recent social movements include antiglobalization protesters, transnational consumer rights organizations, human rights advocates, and LGBT rights groups. Some operate within the EU; others, like the antiglobalization and LGBT rights movements, also reach out internationally. Some protests are local with cross-national ties; others mobilize broad segments of society in a single location; yet others mobilize only particular segments of society. We present three examples of these new social movements: Stuttgart 21, Pegida, and the opposition to TTIP.

Stuttgart 21

Protests began almost immediately after plans to link Stuttgart, the capital of Baden Württemberg, to cities across Germany and Europe via high-speed rail became public in the mid-1990s. Grievances included the enormous cost, the destruction of inner city green spaces, including an old park, and the restructuring of the train station into an eight-track through station. Critics targeted the inadequate official communication and lack of citizen inclusion in the planning process. Expanding protests peaked in 2010, when police used tear gas and other violent tactics to disperse a crowd of several thousand at the site. National media coverage and the ensuing political crisis led to the victory of Alliance 90/The Greens in the 2011 Baden-Württemberg parliamentary election and the first Green-led coalition government in the history of the Federal Republic. A November 2011 referendum to halt the new train station was defeated, but negotiations to appease the protesters led to some alterations of the original plan. Construction of the tunnel officially started in 2016, although lawsuits linger, and costs are well above budget projections.

Protesters came from all age groups. According to one study, 62 percent were between forty and sixty-four years old; new social movement protesters are usually younger. Half held a university degree, and many worked in the public service sector (Rucht, Baumgarten, and Teune 2010). They included conservationists—one group called itself the "park protectors" (*Parkschützer*)—and a broad assembly of environmental and antinuclear energy activists. They also established connections with similar protests against large urban infrastructure projects in France, Italy, and Romania.

Because of its broad social base, the movement was called a middle-class protest (*bürgerlicher Protest*), and some of the German media framed participants as *Wutbürger*—angry citizens—which quickly circulated and became the 2010 "Word of the Year." However, the protesters felt they were not simply angry about any decision perceived as top-down and a waste of taxpayers' money but had precise demands. They proposed modernizing the current rail system without building a tunnel and restructuring green spaces based on citizen input. In a democratic polity, critics argued, seeking inclusion should not be denigrated as anger.

Anti-Immigration Protests

Right-wing rallies against asylum seekers, mostly from Eastern Europe, and refugees from war-torn regions in the former Yugoslavia began in 1992 and 1993 and also affected long-standing Turkish residents of Germany. Xenophobia and violence increased and led to the burning of some homes. Protests abated in the late 1990s but resurged in 2015 and 2016 during the refugee crisis, when hundreds of thousands, primarily from Syria, Afghanistan, and Iraq, crossed EU borders; in Germany, asylum applications from Albanians and Kosovars also remained high. The primarily east German group Pegida strongly opposes immigration in general and Muslim immigration in particular. Demonstrations and rallies were first organized in Dresden in winter 2014 and spread to other cities in Saxony and throughout the country, although in several German cities, especially in the west, counterdemonstrations uniting civil society organizations, unions, and churches were common. The number of participants in Pegida marches peaked in 2015 and abated as fewer refugees entered Germany. In spring 2017, some drew fewer than fifty participants in such cities as Leipzig, leading organizers to cease calls for rallies. In other cities, such as Dresden, marches continue.

The movement claims that German society is increasingly shaped by Muslim culture and religion; this theme draws on fears articulated in Oswald Spengler's *Decline of the West* (*Der Untergang des Abendlandes*, 1922). Even though most participants are not church members, religion is their defining marker. They do not distinguish the Muslim faith from radical Islam. Pegida tends to attract people with little trust in political institutions; many are employed and relatively well educated. A survey of Dresden Pegida participants in 2015 found that they were mostly middle-class men with higher-than-average incomes, and two-thirds had no party affiliation (Vorländer, Herold, and Schäller 2016). While only a small percentage approached at the demonstrations responded to the questionnaire, other studies confirm this social composition (Reuband 2015). They are united by their resentment of the political elite and the media. They refer to print media as *"Lügenpresse,"* or a press that disseminates lies, indifferent to the term's use by the Nazis. All mainstream parties condemn their xenophobic and anti-immigrant rhetoric; only the new right-wing populist party, AfD, keeps close ties. Pegida leadership maintains connections to neo-Nazis and the new right. Criminal procedures were opened against some of them, including the founder, Lutz Bachmann, who is accused of hate speech; other activists have been tried for displaying Nazi symbols or membership in illegal neo-Nazi organizations. Pegida organizers have reached out to other European anti-Islamic and anti-immigration movements and parties—Dutch right-wing populist Geert Wilders, for example, was invited to one of its rallies—but the movement is mostly confined to eastern Germany.

According to a federal government report, the protests against refugees showed that "the borders between citizens' protests and right-wing forms of agitation have become increasingly blurry" (Die Beauftragte für die neuen Bundesländer 2016, 11; our translation). Protests against Islam in reaction to the influx of refugees are accompanied by an increase in violent attacks on asylum applicants and refugees; some mayors and politicians received death threats for housing refugees in their communities. Right-wing verbal attacks, propaganda on the Internet, and physical attacks on buildings and homes for refugees exacerbated in 2015 and 2016 and were far higher in the eastern than the western states. Measured in violent acts per one million residents, the Federal Office for the Protection of the Constitution, the domestic intelligence service, reported the highest number of offenses in Mecklenburg-West Pomerania (58.7), Brandenburg (51.9), Saxony (42.6), Berlin (37.9), and Thuringia (33.9). The average in the western states was 10.5 (Die Beauftragte für die neuen Bundesländer 2016, 10–11). Many people in the new Länder share antiforeigner sentiment with citizens in Central and Eastern Europe. Under communism, they were isolated from the flow of in-migration and, except for international students and workers, encountered few non-Europeans. According to Croatian writer Slavenka Drakulic (2016), those who suffered under communism now see refugees as "competition for victimhood" and resent the arrival of even small numbers. Material insecurity may also play a role, although seemingly not for most Pegida participants, who wield nationalist rhetoric as a weapon against immigration.

TTIP and Globalization

For some time, global social justice movements and antiglobalization groups, such as Attac, formed in France but also active in Germany and other European countries, have protested free trade agreements at such meetings as the G7 summits held in Europe. These organizations usually operate transnationally and use the Internet as a networking tool. Supported mainly by well-educated young people, the protests embody their ambivalence about transnational market liberalization trends; for many, EU neoliberal policies pay insufficient attention to social consequences. The controversy over TTIP illustrates how globalization protests can spread across European countries and affect decisions on the EU level.

TTIP negotiations between the US Department of Commerce and the European Commission began in 2013. Proponents cited the mutual advantages of a free trade agreement between the two largest economic players in the world—more jobs, more trade, more investment—as well as its geopolitical significance (Hamilton 2015). Civil society organizations soon joined forces to protest three elements: the secrecy of the negotiations; the establishment of special courts to settle trade disputes outside of normal jurisdictions; and the potential weakening of food safety standards, such as lifting the ban on genetically modified foods (GMOs), which are strongly opposed by many Europeans, particularly Germans.

Based on public opinion polls, citizens in Austria, Germany, and France were more opposed to the free trade agreement than citizens in other EU countries. Protest actions were organized, and German groups were particularly vocal due to "institutional thickness": consumer-rights, anticapitalist, and environmental groups are well established. A coalition of NGOs called *Unfairhandelbar* (which inserts the English word *unfair* into the German word for nonnegotiable) registered criticism of TTIP on the Internet and through social media, pointing out potential risks to consumers with catchy phrases like "chlorine chicken" and other perceived shortcomings of the agreement.

Access to documentation about TTIP was initially restricted, and by the time the EU changed its information policy in response to outside criticism, public opinion in major countries had shifted toward rejection. The future of TTIP is now in doubt. EU leaders no longer push for talks to continue, and with the United Kingdom's exit, a key advocate will be gone. Meanwhile, resentment against free trade has been growing in the United States. Negotiations were put on hold in 2016 with the election of Donald Trump, who opposed the agreement during the election campaign, to the presidency.

POLITICAL CULTURE

While social movements capture political participation as a societal actor-centered concept, *political culture* refers to values and attitudes that may or may not spark political action. Socialization processes as well as dramatic political and economic changes influence how citizens view their political system. The ravages of World War II forced a break with authoritarian values, but remembering the Weimar Republic, some observers feared that support for democracy in West Germany would collapse with the first major economic crisis. These concerns underestimated the change in political culture. Already in the late 1950s, "the original 'fair weather' democracy was changing into a 'rain or shine' democracy." Support for democratic values and institutions has only deepened; while Germans took pride in the economic success symbolized by the Deutschmark, today they rank the constitution as the greatest source of national pride (Conradt 2015, 252, 261).

Constitutional Patriotism

History burdens what citizens in most societies consider normal national pride. German atrocities during World War II barred flag waving or singing the national anthem with gusto. West Germany had no nonreligious holidays, except for a day commemorating the June 17, 1953, uprising in the east, until 1990, when October 3 was declared a national holiday. It still does not evoke the same feelings as Bastille Day parades in France or Fourth of July celebrations in the United States. This mundane date in the crowded holiday calendar, when a few politicians give fair-weather speeches, was picked instead of November 9, the day the Berlin Wall opened, because on November 9, 1938, anti-Jewish pogroms swept the nation on what was called *Kristallnacht*, night of broken glass.

When pride was measured, most West Germans referred to economic and scientific achievements or the constitution. Coined by Dolf Sternberger and elaborated by Jürgen Habermas, the term *constitutional patriotism* suited West Germany well. In a divided country, pride and allegiance were not based on nationhood but rather the principles of a liberal democracy, which were expressed in the constitution. Even unification did not evoke nationalism; it was more or less a business affair.

Not until Germany hosted the 2006 Soccer World Cup did more citizens wave the colors of the flag—black, red, and gold—with pride. Many now produce the flag at major international soccer festivals and dutifully roll it up afterward. This rather circumspect behavior represents a broader change, most visible in the younger generation. In one study, 62 percent of citizens aged twelve to twenty-five said they are proud to be German (Shell 2015). While this number is high for Germany, in the United States, 85 percent of the population routinely claims to be "extremely/very proud" to be American (Newport 2013).

Nonetheless, aside from far-right groups, nationalist sentiment is still shunned and carefully distinguished from patriotism. The positive and negative sides of patriotism, the role patriotism can and should play, and how Germany's neighbors deal with its new expressions of national consciousness are still debated. Is nationalism on the rise? Will Germany's influence in the EU be tamed and tempered by its loyalty to the idea of Europe? Should Germany be feared?

Europeanization has remolded national consciousness, and even though many younger Germans are proud of the accomplishments of their country, their pride is embedded in a wider sense of belonging. Citizens can attest many identities, and Europe is an important frame of reference. Eurobarometer data show that 59 percent of Germans feel they are German *and* European citizens, and only 27 percent see themselves as German only. According to the same survey, 12 percent of Germans see themselves as European and German. More educated and younger people are more likely to subscribe to various identities (European Commission 2014, 11).

Support for Democracy and Trust in Institutions

Political culture studies focus on support for democracy and distinguish between procedural and outcome-oriented democracy. In 1991, 86 percent of West Germans agreed that democracy is the best form of government; in 2014, 90 percent did. In East Germany, contrary to expectations, 70 percent found democracy the best form of government immediately after unification in 1991; in 2014, 82 percent did. East-west differences defied simplistic characterizations. Russell J. Dalton and Steven Weldon (2010) found strong support for democracy in both parts of unified Germany, but citizens in the east were more critical of how it functions; among other caveats, they favored a greater state role in addressing inequality. Arnold, Freier, and Kroh (2015) found that eastern and western Germans share a similar interest in politics but disagree on the efficacy of individual political engagement. Specific measures of political participation, such as voting and party membership, remain lower in the east.

Trust in institutions is another important feature of a country's political culture. Although trust in political parties and parliament is relatively low in most advanced democracies, Germany fares quite well. Not surprisingly, trust in the armed forces is higher in the United States, and trust in unions is higher in Germany. Support for the courts is almost the same. In both countries, the percentage of those saying they don't trust political parties is high, but more Germans than Americans say they trust them (see table 4.1)

Table 4.1. Trust in Institutions: Germany and the United States Compared*

	Federal Army		Labor Unions		Police		Courts		Federal Government		Parties		Bundestag/Congress	
	DEU	US	DEU	US	DEU	US	DEU	US	DEU	US	DEU	US	DEU	US
A great deal	11.5	35.1	5.5	3.1	22.3	16.5	17.0	8.9	5.5	3.7	2.6	1.2	5.0	1.7
Quite a lot	52.1	46.5	40.0	21.5	59.4	51.8	54.3	44.9	38.9	28.9	21.3	11.3	38.5	18.5
Not very much	27.5	12.8	38.4	49.5	13.6	24.3	21.6	37.6	43.6	51.2	57.8	64.9	44.7	57.1
Not at all	5.5	3.7	9.1	23.8	3.6	5.7	4.8	6.5	10.4	14.1	15.8	20.4	9.1	19.6
Missing	0.1	—	0.9	—	—	—	—	—	—	—	0.1	—	0.1	—
No answer	0.3	1.9	0.4	2.1	0.2	1.7	0.2	2.1	0.3	2.1	0.4	2.1	0.5	3.1
Don't know	3.0	—	5.8	—	0.9	—	2.1	—	1.3	—	2.0	—	2.1	—

*The surveys were conducted in 2011 (US) and 2013 (DEU).

Source: World Values Survey Wave 6, 2010–2014, Official Aggregate v.20150418. World Values Survey Association (http://www.worldvaluessurvey.org). Aggregate file producer: Asep/JDS, Madrid, Spain.

Gender Roles and Family Policy

In the late nineteenth century, the traditional role of women was captured by the phrase *Kinder* (children), *Küche* (kitchen), and *Kirche* (church), or the three Ks. Emancipatory trends during the Weimar Republic were quashed during the Nazi era, which strongly reinforced the traditional maternal role of women. Motherhood was encouraged and workforce participation discouraged, although labor shortages increasingly forced women to work. Women who returned to work after childbirth were often labeled "raven mothers," comparing them to birds who abandon their nests. After World War II, two different social conceptions prevailed in the divided Germany. In West Germany, traditional role expectations lasted well into the second half of the twentieth century and shaped the conservative welfare system. This model was pioneered by Gøsta Esping-Andersen (1990), who delineated a liberal, conservative, and social democratic model. In the conservative welfare system, men's wages provide for the family; women provide important social services by supporting working men and caring for children and the elderly. Women's work outside the home should be an exception, not the rule. Until the late 1950s, legal provisions required West German wives to seek their husband's consent if they wanted to work outside the home, and pregnant women were banned from certain public-sector jobs, such as teaching. Social policies and the tax system favored the model of male breadwinner with dependent spouse.

This patriarchal system prevailed well into the 1970s and was only gradually replaced by more modern conceptions of gender relations based on equality. As more women qualified for, and enrolled in, professional schools, their outlook on life changed. As in other European countries and the United States, a new women's movement emerged in the 1970s, demanding more rights and an equal share in society (Ferree 2012). Its proponents targeted violence against women, reproductive rights, and more self-determination in career patterns. A substantial reform of the marriage and divorce laws in 1977 gave women better rights and entitlements to social security support in case of divorce. Later, the new women's movement influenced party platforms and the political culture of institutions. Educational opportunities, child-rearing options, and social activities should no longer be defined by gender but reflect the inclusive philosophy of modern democracies. As political parties introduced gender quotas in representation, women became more visible in politics. Their share in the Bundestag and cabinet rose continuously (see chapter 3).

In contrast, policies in East Germany promoted the socialist ideal of gender equality by enrolling women in the workforce but, more concretely, responded to the chronic labor shortage, which worsened with westward migration in the 1950s. Women working was an economic necessity supported by generous investment in public childcare. However, gender equality did not extend to the political arena; women's representation was based on a quota system and gave them no voice in modeling policies to meet their needs. Feminism was shunned as a "Western" ideology, although some women engaged in feminist groups, at least in East Berlin. Propaganda and workforce participation still made their mark. At the time of unification, East German women had one of the highest employment rates in Europe, a high birth rate, and one of the highest proportions of single parents.

Women in the Workforce and Education

Today, Germany mirrors EU trends in promoting gender equality in the workplace. The ratio of women attending institutions of higher education and their overall level of education have increased over the past two decades to equal those of men, but women are still greatly underrepresented in top-tier academic positions. In 2013, 50.8 percent of all graduates in the tertiary sector were women, and 44.2 percent of all PhDs were granted to women. However, career prospects still differ. Women held only 21.3 percent of professorships and only 11.3 percent of the most prestigious and better-paid professorial positions. The percentage of women in tenured professorships is increasing at a snail's pace (Kahlert 2015, 60–61).

Women are also entering the labor force in larger numbers (see figure 4.2), but, as in other EU countries, a gender pay gap persists. It ranges from less than 10 percent in Slovenia, Malta, Poland, Italy, Luxembourg, and Romania to over 20 percent in Hungary, Slovakia, the Czech Republic, Germany, and Austria to 30 percent in Estonia (2012 Eurostat data). The rather significant gender pay gap in Germany and Austria is due to the high percentage of women working part-time (European Commission 2016). Part-time work must also be considered when interpreting overall female labor-force participation. It has grown, but many women still combine housework and child rearing with part-time employment.

By the mid-1990s, all Länder had enacted equal opportunity laws (*Gleichstellungsgesetze*) for women working in the public service sector. Public institutions, such as universities, state and local administrations, and state agencies, established so-called equality offices to advance and monitor gender equality. The federal structure enables some states to set trends, while others lag, but comparative studies show that the overall effect on women's hiring and promotion has been limited (von Wahl 2011). The situation in the corporate world is worse. Women are still vastly underrepresented on company boards and as top managers; in 2016, they held only 22 percent of leadership

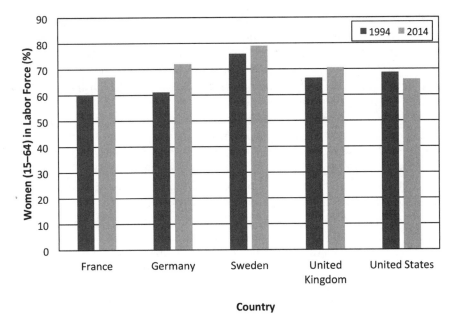

Figure 4.2. Female Labor Force Participation Rate, 1994 and 2014
Source: http://data.worldbank.org/indicator/SL.TLF.ACTI.FE.ZS/countries.

positions. A law in force since January 1, 2016, requires the boards of about 100 larger firms to include 30 percent women. If no women are identified, the positions remain open.

Progress in gender equality notwithstanding, childcare and household duties are still very much a woman's domain. Public daycare and elementary and secondary schools normally release their charges at midday, requiring an adult, mostly mothers, to provide afternoon supervision and meals. The availability of all-day programs is growing but remains limited, and capacities for after-school care depend on state funding. Therefore, many women must choose between part-time work and abandoning the workforce altogether. In rural areas and small cities, traditional notions of women's place result in peer and family pressure to stay at home and raise children. The tension between women's expectations about work opportunities and a work environment often inimical to combining work with childcare and other family responsibilities creates many problems, among them a particularly low birth rate.

Modernizing Gender Relations

Today's family law is modern and respects gender diversity. The UN's Gender Inequality Index (2015) ranks Germany among the most equal (http://

hdr.undp.org/en/composite/GII); the index reflects disparities between women and men in terms of empowerment and economic status based on measures of health, education, political representation, and labor-force participation. While women trail men in leadership positions, domestic policies initiated before, and pushed after, unification as well as EU influence have moved Germany closer to gender equality.

Abortion rights contrasted substantially in East and West Germany. In 1972, East Germany legalized abortion in the first trimester. A similar law was passed in West Germany in 1974, but the Federal Constitutional Court declared it unconstitutional in the following year. The new policy allowed abortion only in cases of rape, for medical reasons, or "social distress," the definition of which remained controversial. Not surprisingly, when the Unification Treaty was negotiated, opinions about reproductive rights differed greatly among political elites. An agreement was not reached until 1993, and once again, the new law was challenged in the Federal Constitutional Court, which upheld the more restrictive West German model but gave women the freedom to choose, provided they sought mandatory counseling in the first trimester of pregnancy. Thus, while abortion is illegal, it is not punished.

In 1997, rape within marriage became a criminal offense. Several reforms addressed childcare and equal opportunities at work. Surveys also show a significant change in attitudes and behaviors, although east-west differences persist. By 2012, three-fourths of western Germans had egalitarian views, up from slightly over 50 percent in 1991; in the east, the figure was 86 percent (Blohm and Walter 2016, 426).

As in most European countries, awareness of gender identity and diversity has increased, but the road was long and obstructed by various forms of discrimination. Same-sex activities were criminal based on Paragraph 175 of the criminal code (in place from 1871 to 1994), but in the 1920s in cities like Berlin, gays and lesbians were generally tolerated and enjoyed a vibrant culture. During the Nazi period, laws became repressive; homosexual citizens (mostly men) were persecuted, incarcerated, and murdered, and many perished in concentration camps. In 1950, the Nazi laws were repealed; in 1968 and 1969, sexual activity between adult men was decriminalized in East and West Germany, respectively, but Paragraph 175 was not formally eliminated until 1994. In 2002, convictions of homosexuals during the Third Reich were annulled, but not until March 2017 was a bill introduced promising compensation for gay men who had been jailed according to Paragraph 175 after World War II and into the 1970s; their criminal records would be cleared. Legislation passed three months later. A small but emotionally powerful memorial in Berlin, built in 2008, remembers and honors homosexual victims of Nazi persecution.

Opposition by conservative groups, the CDU/CSU, and the churches has prevented passage of a same-sex marriage act until 2017. Registered partnerships for same-sex couples have been legal since 2001, supported by most Germans. Subsequent reforms provided most, though not all, of the same rights and benefits to same-sex couples as to married heterosexual couples, including taxation schemes, social and healthcare benefits, and, in 2005, adoption of the children of a partner (but no general adoption). Almost by coincidence, in response to Chancellor Merkel's statement during an interview that she would welcome an open discussion about same-sex marriage and that MPs should be allowed to vote freely and not according to party lines, the situation changed. Her coalition partner, the SPD, seized the time—some say by ignoring the coalition treaty—to introduce a bill that passed easily in June 2017. Support came from the three left-center parties and some members of the CDU/CSU. With this act, Germany joined most Western European countries in giving equal rights to same-sex couples. In 2015, Germany became the first country in Europe to enact a law that allows citizens to identify as neither male nor female on their birth certificates.

The public gender-reform discourse has been shaped by different ideological and political concepts. The conservative political parties, such as CDU and CSU, have tended to favor traditional role models and opposed same-sex partnerships for a long time; parties left of center embraced social change. Social Democrats in particular have pushed for equal pay legislation, while the Greens favor an inclusive policy regarding gender identities. The Left argues for equal pay and against discrimination in the workplace. However, legal changes have not been clear-cut along party lines, and some of the most progressive policy changes occurred when the CDU/CSU were in power in a coalition government with the SPD. Important legislation regarding public childcare, same-sex partnerships and later same-sex marriage, and women's representation on corporate boards passed under Chancellor Merkel, showing that the CDU has modernized in many of these areas.

Demographic Trends

In contrast to other European countries, such as the United Kingdom, France, and Italy, the German population is predicted to decrease dramatically by the year 2060, based on the consistently low birth rate and, in the past, low immigration rates. The data presented in table 4.2 do not account for the most recent surge in immigration, although its long-term implications are not yet clear.

For over four decades, the birth rate has held at less than 1.5 (the replacement rate is 2.1), which is unparalleled in any other country (Bujard 2015). In 2014, the fertility rate of 1.47 births per woman was the highest since

Table 4.2. Demographic Trends in Comparison

Country	2015 Population (millions)	2060 Population Forecast (millions)	2014 Foreign Residents (%)	Fertility Rate (no.)	2013 Life Expectancy	
					Women	Men
Germany	81.2	71.0	8.7	1.40	83.2	78.6
France	66.4	75.6	6.3	1.99	85.6	79.0
Italy	60.8	66.3	8.1	1.39	85.2	80.3
Poland	38.0	33.3	0.3	1.29	81.2	73.0
Spain	46.4	46.1	10.1	1.27	86.1	80.2
United Kingdom	64.8	80.0	7.8	1.83	82.9	79.2

Source: https://www.destatis.de/Europa/DE/Staat/Vergleich/DEUVergleich/html.

unification but still low compared to France (2.0) and the United States, Sweden, and the United Kingdom (1.9). At the time of unification, the rate in eastern Germany was significantly higher than that in western Germany, but it has adjusted to the lower western level.

Persistent low fertility coupled with an aging population has raised concerns about Germany's future economic competitiveness, labor market, the financing of its comprehensive welfare state policies, and, consequently, its international standing. For example, the social welfare system can only be sustained if the active workforce outnumbers retirees. How exactly to accomplish the goal of increasing the birth rate is a cause of disagreement. While some conservative commentators worry that women's increasing participation in the labor force will erode traditional family values, others argue that changing work patterns and a social environment that frowns on combining work and family life discourage young couples from having children.

Reversing the low birth rate is a key goal of political elites, which partially explains the more open policy toward recent immigrants. Long-standing policies grant generous maternity benefits during and after pregnancy, including paid leave from work. Significant reform packages passed in 2007, 2008, and 2015 aim to encourage young couples to have children and to better combine work and family responsibilities.

The first policy to protect pregnant women, introduced as far back as 1878, has been extended and revised throughout the twentieth century. Now, pregnant women are given a mandatory leave of absence at full pay six weeks before and eight weeks after childbirth; they enjoy protection from job loss until four months after childbirth. Until 2007, only mothers could claim tax-funded state subsidies after the maternity benefits expired; now, following an approach introduced in Sweden, an income-dependent parental allowance (*Elterngeld*) provides up to 67 percent of the previous salary (up to 1,800 euro per month) for twelve to fourteen months after a child's birth. It was hailed as a major departure from the traditional male-breadwinner model in recognizing women's roles in the workforce and fathers' roles in raising a child. Parents can split the allowance, but usually, one is the designated recipient, and the other is granted an eight-week leave to share in childcare.

In 2015, new legislation (*Elterngeld Plus*) went into effect, extending the allowance to parents who work part-time from twelve to twenty-four months. The time can be split between the parents until the child turns eight. In 2012, the CSU insisted on introducing a childcare subsidy (*Betreuungsgeld*) for mothers who stay at home until their children reach the age of three. In 2015, it was declared unconstitutional on the grounds that such policies are the prerogative of the Länder and cannot be enforced nationally. Now it is in force only in Bavaria.

Families also receive tax breaks and a monthly child allowance until the child is eighteen years old. Under certain circumstances—for example, if the child is in school—the allowance is paid until age twenty-five. Child allowances were introduced under the Nazis in 1936 for mothers with five or more children and reintroduced in West Germany in 1954 for women with three or more children. Since then, the benefits were altered and extended to the current form. After World War II, child allowances were introduced in many Western European countries. They are tied to the number of children, but in some countries, the benefits are means-tested. In Germany, all families, regardless of income, are eligible; payments are high compared to other countries worldwide (in 2017, 192 euro for the first and second child, 198 for the third child, and 223 euro for each additional child).

Childcare is under the jurisdiction of the Länder and largely financed from state coffers. It was always more readily available in the eastern part of the country than the west, where parents struggle to find adequate public childcare. Options are limited by the assumption that a mother would give up her job to care for her children at home at least until they reached the age of three, when they are eligible to enter kindergarten (preschool). Attendance is not mandatory but highly sought after. In 1996, for the first time, children three years of age or older were entitled to a place legally, but available childcare facilities could not meet demand. A major 2008 reform package contributed federal funds to help the Länder expand them and introduced a legal claim to childcare for toddlers between the age of twelve months (the end of parental leave) and kindergarten entry at age three. This law brought Germany in line with EU goals to support parenting, and as yet another measure to reverse the negative demographic trend, it aims both to improve conditions for women's employment and career building and to provide children, independent of social background, with opportunities to learn at an early age.

Despite progress, the ambitious 2013 deadline was not met. In March 2016, about one-third of children had access to a publicly funded childcare facility. The east-west gap persists: in the eastern part of the country, 51.8 percent of children were in childcare facilities; in the western part, 28.1 percent (Press Release no. 345, 2016). Private daycare supplements public institutions, but, in contrast to the United States, German parents consider the state responsible for providing educational opportunities for children.

When Domestic Agents Find Support Elsewhere

Political actors, such as unions and women's rights groups, frequently refer to EU policies. Equal pay provisions in the Treaty of Rome (1958), antidiscrimination provisions in the Amsterdam Treaty (1999), and the equal opportunity goal in the Lisbon Treaty (2009) informed reform policies in areas as diverse as equal pay, gender-based violence, LGBT legislation, and female representation on company boards. In addition to the European Treaties, EU-commissioned reports on discrimination in the workplace, sexual harassment, gender-based violence, and human trafficking have all sparked initiatives to change and improve gender relations.

In response to the 1975 and 1976 European Community directives calling for equal pay for work of equal value and equal access, training, promotion, and working conditions for women and men, the EC finally passed antidiscrimination legislation, the Adaptation Act, in 1980. Germany was among the countries that did not comply with the equal pay rules and was criticized in a ruling by the European Court of Justice (ECJ) in 1984. In 1985 and again in 1990 and 1994, the federal government revised the guidelines to promote women's recruitment, training, continuing education, and employment.

In 1996, the EU Commission formally adopted *gender mainstreaming*, which recommends that member states review all policies for gender inequality, not just gender-related policies like family policy. EU institutions use gender mainstreaming to monitor the implications and effects for men and women of existing and proposed policies; projects supported financially by the EU in member states are evaluated according to the gender mainstreaming guidelines. Its effectiveness is still debated. Some research shows that gender mainstreaming sparked national reviews of different employment strategies but rarely extended into other policy areas (Cooke 2011). In Germany, the discourse pitted advocates of gender mainstreaming against advocates of affirmative action for women. Should state equality offices focus on improving women's professional situation through affirmative action programs or develop and sponsor programs that include men? While both approaches address gender disparities in income and job promotion, they stress different viewpoints and strategies, which affects, for example, how public offices distribute funds. Gender mainstreaming has become an important strategy for promoting equality but may divert funds from women's programs.

Lobbying and networking on the European level are now indispensable for women's rights groups, nondiscrimination activists, and groups addressing gender identities (Lang 2013). In his comprehensive study on LGBT rights, for example, Phillip Ayoub (2016, 8) asserts the influence of European institutions on norm diffusion: "The norm that LGBT people are entitled to fundamental human rights, and deserving of state recognition and protection, is clearly articulated in both the rhetoric and the legal framework of the institutions of the EU and the Council of Europe." He analyzes their impact on several European countries. Under communism, Poland and Slovenia restricted the rights of LGBT people, but afterward, Slovenia developed earlier, deeper, and more transnational ties to the first-mover states in LGBT rights than Poland did. These ties accelerated awareness of LGBT people and facilitated subsequent legal change in Slovenia, while Poland remains a laggard.

Louise Davidson-Schmich (2015) asserts that LGBT politics in Germany profited from a strong, united, national movement as well as the activism of the European branch of the International Lesbian, Gay, Bisexual, Trans and Intersex Organization (ILGA-Europe) and other transnational organizations. Lobbying at the EU level resulted in the passing of European antidiscrimination legislation based on sex, gender orientation, and gender identity. Thus, transnational networks can advance EU norm diffusion, but success still depends on the opportunity structure in receiving countries.

RELIGION AND RELIGIOUS COMMUNITIES

Religion and politics are inseparable in Europe as everywhere. Most European societies are religiously diverse, but the influx of migrants from mostly Muslim countries challenges traditional Christian customs, attitudes, and practices. The history of communism left many countries in Eastern Europe secular, but in Poland, Catholicism remained strong and is part of the national identity. Secularization can be forced, as by communism, or voluntary, propelled by modernization or individual choice or both; for example, large segments of society in Scandinavian countries are not church members. The diversity of religious convictions became evident during the European constitutional debate in 2004–6. Poland, backed by Spain, another predominantly Catholic country, favored a reference to God in the preamble of the proposed European Constitutional Treaty, while northern countries opposed it. With its strong Christian roots but increasing religious diversity and nonaffiliation,

Germany was caught in the middle. Its negotiators worked toward a compromise, and the final draft referred to common humanitarian values. The Constitutional Treaty eventually failed; its substitute, the Lisbon Treaty, uses a broader frame, and its preamble refers to Europe's "cultural, religious and humanistic heritage."

As in many other Western nations, the German constitution, or Basic Law, grants religious freedom and protects the separation of church and state. A majority of Germans are Christians and Christianity has shaped culture, public life, and political orientations. In fact, religious affiliation plays an important role; Christian holidays structure the year-round cycle of activities in schools and public institutions, and shops and businesses observe them. Catholic and Protestant churches also play an important role in social policy. A vast network of church-affiliated hospitals, day-care centers, facilities for the disabled, and retirement homes, organized in large social welfare associations, complement state-funded social programs and are an indispensable part of welfare services in an otherwise increasingly secular society. Two of the major political parties, the CDU and the CSU, rely on constituencies with strong ties to religious communities. The CDU is home to Protestants and Catholics; the Bavarian-based CSU has strong Catholic roots (see chapter 3). Church membership is one of the most decisive indicators of voting behavior. Those who grew up and live in an environment in which church membership, attendance, and activities are important tend to vote for the CDU and CSU in larger margins. Those without church affiliation tend to prefer center-left parties.

Roughly 60 percent of Germans are Christians, according to the 2011 national census. Due to immigration, about 4.2 million residents belong to one of the Muslim denominations, although most are Sunni. Accurate data on Muslim religious affiliations are difficult to acquire; responses vary with source and self-identification, and the recent influx of refugees and asylum seekers has outpaced statistical documentation. Fewer than 1 percent of Germans are Jews, Buddhists, Hindus, or Sikhs. Unlike the United States, in Germany, members of certain denominations pay a so-called church tax to the state that generally amounts to 8 to 9 percent of the payroll tax, depending on the state and the denomination.

Christian Churches

Prior to 1945, the religious composition of Germany heavily favored Protestantism, and Protestants and Catholics were often political and social rivals. After Germany's division into two states, the two major religious denominations almost achieved parity in the west, and their prior antagonism was ameliorated by the conscious decision to form united Christian parties (CDU and CSU). In 1950, almost all West Germans were members of religious organizations.

East Germany was predominantly Protestant, but the state deliberately marginalized the role of the church in accordance with communist ideology. Members faced educational and career disadvantages. After the Berlin Wall was built in 1961, the mostly Protestant churches had to sever ties with their West German counterparts and suffered social and political isolation as well as financial loss. The East German government did not confiscate church property but stopped collecting church taxes, and donations dwindled due to sharply declining membership. Atheist rhetoric prevailed in public, and many church buildings were left to decay. Faced with nearly complete marginalization in the early 1970s, Protestant church leadership entered a new policy of coexistence with the SED, and open hostility ceased. The SED in turn hoped to improve its international standing through this conciliatory gesture. Nevertheless, churches did not play a role in public life and church members kept activities private. This changed during the peaceful revolution of 1989 when churches became a safe haven for the emerging civic opposition. The modest revival of church significance could not reverse the trend toward secularization.

Forty years of communist rule left a lasting imprint on the eastern part of Germany (Pickel 2009). The numbers are striking. In the west, in 1991 and 2012, only 11 or 18 percent respectively were not registered as church members. In the east, 65 percent did not belong to a church in 1991; in 2012, the figure increased to 68 percent (Meulemann 2016, 379). Those who opt to leave a church cite criticism of the leadership, unwillingness to pay church taxes, and, in the Catholic Church more recently, child abuse scandals. Regional differences are pronounced: the north is mostly Protestant; the south, Catholic; the southwest and some other areas are mixed; and in the east, most citizens are unaffiliated.

The constitution (Art. 7, 3) guarantees religious instruction in public schools. It is defined as a joint task of the Länder and the churches; instructors hold a university degree, but they are also certified by the respective church. Since the Länder are responsible for public education, the courses on the curriculum vary accordingly. Most states provide lessons in one of the Christian religions (Protestant or Catholic) or both, depending on the religious composition of the region. Judaism and Islam are on the curriculum in some states (for example, in Lower Saxony and North Rhine-Westphalia), and Buddhism is taught in Berlin. For students who do not wish to participate in religious instruction, the states offer ethics or philosophy courses. These rather powerful structural advantages of churches are somewhat at odds with the trend toward secularization.

Jewish Communities

Since the fall of communism, the Jewish community in Germany has been one of the fastest growing in Europe. Many Jews from the former Soviet Union—mostly Russia, the Ukraine, and the Baltic states—now reside in Germany. The German government upholds a "right of return" policy and generally grants residency and citizenship rights to Jews as one way to atone for the Holocaust. Although in 2014, only about 100,400 Germans were listed as members of Jewish religious communities (Statista 2014), the migration has rejuvenated the mostly aging Jewish communities in cities like Berlin, Frankfurt, and Munich. In some communities, 70 to 80 percent of the new members speak Russian, and many speak neither Hebrew nor Yiddish because communist-ruled governments suppressed Jewish expression. New synagogues have opened, and even some smaller towns have seen a revival of Jewish life.

Secularization has also affected these communities. Many German Jews do not belong to one of the registered religious communities or practice their faith. Jewish students, artists, writers, and intellectuals have made the new and vibrant cultural center of Berlin their temporary home, but not all attend synagogue. Despite encouraging signs of a revival of the once pivotal influence of Jews on German culture and society, continued police protection of synagogues is a sad reminder of the virulent anti-Semitism that persists in a small minority.

Muslim Communities

While fewer Europeans attend churches or believe in God today, the Judeo-Christian tradition is deeply engrained in their cultures and societies. In contrast, most Muslims adhere to their religious beliefs strongly and attend the mosque regularly, although their communities in Germany are diverse, and their practices depend on their country of origin, among other factors. The first mosque in Germany was opened in the 1920s in Berlin, but for decades the Muslim community remained very small. Following the influx of guest workers from Turkey in the 1960s, more were established. Today, about two-thirds of German Muslims are Turkish immigrants and their descendants. Immigrants from Albania, Bosnia, and Kosovo formed mostly small Muslim communities, and now refugees from Syria, Iraq, and other Middle Eastern countries are calling Germany their home (see chapter 5).

Like all other European countries, Germany practices freedom of religion, but in daily life, Muslim and Christian groups rarely intersect, and Germans generally know very little about Islam and its different practices. Regular meetings between state representatives and members of the various Muslim communities, interfaith dialogues, and community initiatives seek to foster mutual understanding. They also contribute to the development of policy guidelines in such areas as education and address concerns about religious freedom in society. Controversies discussed include headscarves worn by teachers in schools, the building of new mosques, and the increasing hostility against Muslims in parts of German society. With Muslim communities becoming more diverse, fears that some promote radicalization increased. Radical Islam is still a fringe phenomenon, but state agencies have stepped up security measures, and police forces are better trained to combat violent Islamic fundamentalists.

AN ENGAGED CITIZENRY

Voter turnout may be declining or stagnating; party membership has lost appeal, but new forms of citizen engagement are blossoming in many Western democracies (Dalton, Scarrow, and Cain 2004). Citizens' initiatives, social movements, and NGOs have widened the repertoire of political action; in some cases, they act as a surrogate for conventional forms, but more often, they complement them. Germany is a particularly good illustration of these developments. Citizens old and young, German and non-German, left and right increasingly pick and choose among avenues of political engagement. To see so many groups actively involved in politics is an encouraging sign of a changing political culture. These shifts are characteristic in most European societies and a litmus test of a civil society's vitality. Citizen participation is more multilayered and crosscutting than before, yet it carries the potential for both democratic enrichment and conflict.

In West Germany, the societal role of women was long confined to wife and mother, while in the east, enforced communist ideals about gender equality moved women into the workplace and changed women's perceptions about their role in society, without freeing them from primary responsibility for household duties. The western, incremental approach to changing women's role in German society prevailed after unification. Today, tradition mixes with modernity. Shattering ingrained attitudes takes time, but the influence of the women's movement, the impact of unification, EU policies specifically and transnational trends more generally, and the demographic crisis have left their mark on the economic and social status of women. Traditional role models still hold power in the west, but mothers who work are no longer considered raven mothers. Gender equality and LGBT rights have improved.

Germans hold both traditional and modern views of the role of religion in society. Church membership has declined, and even most believers do not attend services regularly, yet Christian religious traditions and beliefs remain an important part of social life. Catholicism and Protestantism coexist peacefully. The fall of communism brought an influx of Soviet-bloc Jews, reviving Jewish life in Germany. However, the influx of devout Muslims challenges secular and traditional religious trends, at times in unsettling ways, reviving an age-old mistrust of the "other." In new and unanticipated ways, religion is back on the social and political agenda.

Societal change is most often gradual. Unification did not alter citizen participation and social change dramatically but rather reinforced and deepened them. Europeanization provided a frame for defining citizenship and citizens' rights more inclusively. Transnational political activity, especially within the EU, has complemented national political activity in a two-way process. Citizens draw on EU policies and support to lobby for domestic demands.

Chapter 5

Migration, Immigration, Integration

KEY TERMS

assimilation
asylum seekers and refugees
cultural representation
education
ethnic Germans
EU immigration and asylum policies
integration

jus soli vs. *jus sanguinis*
labor recruits
multiculturalism
Muslim community
naturalization
normal immigration country
Schengen area

Channeling immigration and promoting integration of nonnationals are urgent policy concerns in all advanced democracies. The recent rush of asylum seekers from war-torn and impoverished regions in southern Europe, the Middle East, and Africa call for new political and administrative measures in EU member states and the EU. However, challenges related to immigration and integration are not new. Indeed, under pressure from persistent population streams, German policy makers had to abandon rhetorical posturing to acknowledge that Germany, like other countries, has become "a country of immigration." It exhibits the characteristics of such countries: its immigration politics and policies are interest driven and contested; hence, politicians react to shifting economic and political environments by opening or restricting legal access; as a general rule, political parties to the right tend to restrict and those to the left tend to support open access. Finally, in a Europe with mostly open borders, immigration and citizenship laws remain in the policy jurisdiction of national governments, but member states increasingly search for joint solutions to common problems (Messina 2009).

Citizenship, immigration, and integration are separate yet interconnected topics. The difficulty or ease with which citizenship can be attained influences but does not control migration flows; in turn, citizenship rights and responsibilities influence integration but do not guarantee it. With its conditional introduction of *jus soli* and targeted integration initiatives to turn foreigners into citizens, Germany is a good example of the gradual convergence of West European policy preferences. It is an equally good example of the lingering power of path dependency, as ethnic concepts of citizenship are deeply ingrained in the discourse and parts of the population.

This chapter highlights the major concerns, controversies, and developments associated with immigration and integration, emphasizing the strong continuities flowing through pressures for and realized change. We begin with background information and the recurrent themes in discourse and policies. Next, we trace the development of citizenship practices, analyzing asylum policies in Germany and the EU. Policies to advance nonnationals' social and economic integration are the latest adjustments to address the fact that Germany today is not only multiethnic but also multireligious. We pay special attention to the growing Muslim community.

BACKGROUND

Migration is difficult to control. Push-and-pull factors and wider global trends pose new challenges. Among them, external shocks, such as the fall of the Berlin Wall, the collapse of communism, and, most recently, the war in Syria, test established legal codes and bureaucratic practices intended to channel and to regulate the flow of migration. Until the second half of the twentieth century, Europe was mostly a continent of emigration; migration shifts after World War II and again after 1990 made societies religiously, ethnically, culturally, and linguistically more diverse. Major differences between Eastern and Western Europe persist as most newcomers settle in the West.

Like other European and North American countries, Germany's multiethnic and multireligious reality is embedded in a transnational world with complex migration dynamics and different migrant groups; generalizations about *the* immigrant fall short. Problems in exactly categorizing these groups reflect the difficulties in coming to terms with growing diversity; no one term fits all. Immediately after World War II, the term resettler was applied and a distinction was made between those coming from communist East Germany (*Übersiedler*) and Germans expelled from Central and Eastern Europe (*Aussiedler*). The latter are now commonly referred to as ethnic Germans. Initially, the term guest worker (*Gastarbeiter*) was used for labor migrants from southern

Europe and Turkey, but it became obsolete when many decided to stay. Foreigners (*Ausländer*) is the legal term for non-German nationals. Some prefer the term foreign fellow citizens (*ausländische Mitbürger*), especially when describing migrants who have resided in the country for some time. EU citizens are foreigners with a special status; they have the right to live and work in any member state and vote in local and European Parliament elections.

The category "persons with a migration background" is the most neutral way to denote immigrants and descendants of immigrants. It may sound strange, but it has become the expression of choice in official statistics and political rhetoric to circumvent the simple dichotomy of foreigners vs. nationals based only on citizenship criteria. Its widespread use acknowledges the lingering challenges of integrating second- and third-generation immigrants, and attaching this label to a highly diverse group of people who may have been born in Germany also perpetuates their status as outsiders.

Asylum applicants and refugees are distinct categories, but the terms are often used interchangeably. A refugee's request for asylum has been granted, whereas an asylum seeker's claim still must be evaluated. The 1951 UN Convention on the Status of Refugees defines a refugee as someone who flees his or her country for fear of persecution or even death; it was updated in 1967 and, as of 2015, has been signed by 145 parties. Under German law, a refugee's claim must be considered on an individual basis unless the government designates a certain group of people from a crisis region, like Syria in 2015, as refugees without formal proceedings. These exceptions are rare. The distinction between asylum applicant and refugee has important implications for work and residency permits. Over the years, the term asylum seeker (*Asylbewerber* or, more pejoratively, *Asylant*) has acquired negative connotations due to the large number of people who come to Europe fleeing poverty, not persecution, and seeking a better future.

By the end of 2014, of Germany's 80.9 million residents, 8.2 million were foreigners; overall, nearly one-fifth of the population has a "migration background," and about half of them hold German citizenship. Poles and Italians make up the largest share of EU nationals. Non-EU residents have mostly Turkish roots followed by citizens of the former Yugoslavia (Federal Ministry of the Interior 2014). The multiethnic mix varies greatly between East and West Germany and between urban and rural areas. In the former East Germany, less than 5 percent of the population has foreign origins; in some western Länder, the percentage is between 25 and 30. Some major metropolitan areas (e.g., Berlin and Munich) boast more than 180 nationalities. The east-west divide can be explained by differences in economic well-being but even more by the lingering effects of history. In contrast to the West, where immigration has been constant for decades, in the communist East, leaving aside the resettlement of ethnic Germans after World War II, immigration was tightly controlled and limited to other communist-governed countries. In 1989, if we do not count members of the Soviet Red Army, fewer than 200,000 foreigners resided in the GDR.

Germany remains a primary destination for immigrants in Europe, even if Europe-wide comparisons are muddied by divergent definitions of who counts as a foreigner. Nearly 45 percent of tiny Luxembourg's population is foreign, largely due to the high number of resident EU nationals. When considering overall numbers rather than percentages, Germany ranks first followed by Spain and France, but this view is misleading because, despite liberalization, about 40 percent have lived in Germany for twenty years or more (figures apply to December 2013).

EU migration and asylum policy has evolved slowly but steadily as a result of global migration shifts. Germany has been an important actor in absorbing and shaping these policies, which remain a patchwork and insufficient to address migration flows. EU nationals have special privileges: free movement, residency, employment, and the right to vote in local and European elections. In contrast, the struggle to address the influx of non-European migrants has earned European countries (and the EU) the unflattering nickname Fortress Europe. Immigration policies vary from country to country, and the recent refugee crisis has once again challenged a common and coherent EU policy.

In Germany, postwar division and the legacy of ethnic German settlement in Central and Eastern Europe and the former Soviet Union promulgated adherence to ethnic citizenship principles that allowed the immediate legal inclusion of migrant ethnic Germans and relative exclusion of others. After unification, citizenship began to be defined by residency. Incremental changes in laws and procedures opened to conceptual changes embracing residency (*jus soli*) as a second gate to citizenship next to the traditional *jus sanguinis*.

Migration flows stem from a changeable mix of push-and-pull factors. Push factors—discrimination, human rights abuses, economic misery, and political upheavals such as the fall of communism—drive them. Pull factors—the attraction of particular host countries as a new home—include legal frameworks, the promise of economic opportunities, and location. Despite the absence of a legal residency framework until 2005, Germany's location in the heart of Europe and economic prowess have been compelling; at times, it actively recruited or enticed workers to settle, even when policies were not in place.

Germany's immigration landscape remains tense and paradoxical. Many scholars and politicians advocate immigration due to low birth rates, an aging population, and labor shortages in specialized professions, particularly the IT sector. Germany is once again among the most sought-after places for asylum seekers in the world, but its targeted programs to attract skilled workers have had limited success.

PARTIAL LIBERALIZATION OF CITIZENSHIP RULES

Citizenship Conceptions

For centuries, Germany was a country of emigration. Many citizens left for the United States among other places, and now about forty-six million US citizens claim German ancestry (*Economist* 2015a). However, its geopolitical location in the center of Europe, rapid industrialization at the turn of the twentieth century, and political ruptures, such as the rise of National Socialism, the end of World War II, and east-west division in 1945, created major migration and refugee movements. By the mid-1950s, the balance of outward and inward migration tilted toward immigration, but unlike the United States and many other countries, Germany did not consider itself a country of immigrants mostly because of a narrow ethno-national conception of citizenship that dates to 1913.

The institution of citizenship is closely linked to the rise of nation-states in Europe; it defines an individual's legal and political status within a particular state (Habermas 1994). Thomas Humphrey Marshall (1964) divided the history of citizenship into three consecutive phases: civil rights in the eighteenth century; political rights in the nineteenth century; and social rights in the twentieth century. The gradual extension of democracy granted citizenship status to members of the polity regardless of class, ethnicity, or gender.

Countries vary in apportioning citizenship to newcomers. *Jus sanguinis* (right of blood) allocates citizenship based on descent of one or both parents; *jus soli* (right of soil) grants citizenship based on being born in the country. The naturalization process for newcomers is tied to specific conditions, such as length of residency and language skills. Three critical junctures—the imperial Wilhelmine era, the postwar democratic reconstruction of the Federal Republic of Germany, and German unification in 1990—defined the trajectories of German citizenship. At each, making migrants *German* was a primary objective in defining citizenship and legal immigration, and ethnic and liberal conceptions of citizenship or *Germanness* inevitably clashed.

Belated nation building and regional fragmentation in what became the German nation-state in 1871 put an acute strain on legal and cultural conceptions of citizenship. The acquisition of colonies in Wilhelmine Germany further challenged notions of who was entitled to be German, but while long-term absences from the homeland endangered citizenship, organizations with *völkisch* nationalist orientations, such as the Pan-German League, called for privileges for *Auslandsdeutsche*, or Germans abroad. They also roused anti-foreigner sentiment, suggesting that migrants from the east, especially Poles and Jews, were inundating the Reich. At the same time, rapid industrialization attracted workers; between 1890 and 1910, the number of resident foreigners tripled, from 430,000 to 1,260,000. A citizenship or nationality law was finally codified in 1913. By preserving citizenship for Germans abroad, the law severed citizenship from residence and defined citizenry as a community of descent. This conception defined the modern understanding of German citizenship and still shapes the discourse.

Rogers Brubaker (1992) contrasted the French Republican model of citizenship based on territoriality, which promoted the assimilation of foreigners, with the German ethno-cultural model, which favored exclusion of migrants other than ethnic Germans. By the early 1990s, naturalization rates for migrant workers and their descendants were four to five times higher in France than in Germany. The gap was even greater for second- and third-generation immigrants. In France, assimilation and naturalization were expected, while the German government made naturalization the exception.

More than two decades later, this narrative no longer holds, and the change reflects a wider trend across Europe. Citizenship rules in France have tightened, while Germany now accepts more migrants as citizens and restricts ethnic Germans. As in other liberal democracies, Germany's responses to increased immigration are shaped by the notion of universal rights and have resulted in an increase in *jus soli* provisions for naturalization through birth in the territory and increasing tolerance of dual citizenship (Joppke 2010). The concrete manifestations of this European trend in Germany are the subjects of the following sections.

Privileging Ethnic Ties and Economic Imperatives

Citizenship is least controversial when ethnic ties exist, and many countries privilege them. In post–World War II West Germany, *jus sanguinis* acquired special significance due to the division of the country into west and east and both the expulsion from, and continued residence of, many ethnic Germans in communist Eastern Europe and the Soviet Union. The authors of the West German Constitution followed the ethno-national understanding of community membership; Article 116 of the Basic Law enables admission of people who qualify as nationals based on ancestry (*Aussiedler*). Of the twelve to fourteen million Germans who fled or were expelled by 1950, two-thirds resettled in West Germany. Despite resentment and occasional hostility, their integration was smoothed by the postwar economic boom and comprehensive federal relief legislation that enjoyed broad public support. These immigrants were deemed German by descent, culture, and language, and since they had suffered expulsion or communist repression, they deserved the solidarity and support of German society. They were granted citizenship by an administrative-legal procedure specifically designed for them.

The 1949 division into communist East and democratic West Germany reinforced ethnic ties. West Germany did not recognize the East German government as legitimate, and West German citizenship was granted to immigrating East Germans. Between 1949 and 1961, approximately 2.6 million East Germans took advantage of this opportunity. To designate their special status and to distinguish them from other ethnic Germans, they were referred to as *Übersiedler*. Desperate to stop this exodus, communist authorities erected the Berlin Wall in August 1961. Almost overnight, east-west migration was reduced to a trickle.

The 1972 Basic Treaty between East and West Germany opened official channels of communication under the mantra "two states, one nation," but West German governments insisted that unification remain on the agenda, and its citizenship policy in place. The treaty made the border more porous, allowing increased inter-German travel in the 1970s and 1980s. East German retirees were allowed to resettle permanently in the west, and the East German government tried to mollify domestic unrest by allowing regime critics to leave the country. Migration to the more prosperous west, following the collapse of the communist regime in fall 1989, challenged its labor market, housing, and school accommodations.

Formal unification in October 1990 curbed but did not end the flow of East German migrants as large-scale plant closings dramatically reduced job prospects. The stream was highest in 1990 and 1991 and again at the turn of the century; between 1990 and 2010, about 10 percent of East Germans, mostly young, migrated to the west. Reverse migration (from west to east) was less common and initially limited to professionals hired to support the transition in the postcommunist era; for example, new administrative aides, plant managers, or university teachers. In 2013, for the first time, more people moved east than west. They settled mostly in cities; the bleeding of residents from many rural areas continues. Nevertheless, the normalization of internal migration patterns signals the normalization of east-west German relations.

The crisis and demise of communist rule in Europe in the 1980s and early 1990s renewed migration of ethnic Germans from Central and Eastern Europe as well; they came mostly from Poland and Romania and later from the successor states of the Soviet Union. By 2005, a total of 4.5 million ethnic Germans had settled in Germany, three million of them after 1988. To distinguish them from the postwar wave of ethnic migration, they were categorized as late resettlers, or *Spätaussiedler*, and their right to return proved more contentious. Restrictions were implemented incrementally. Discrimination based on German ethnicity had to be demonstrated, except for those wanting to leave the territory of the former Soviet Union; German language-skill tests were added, and the government instituted programs to encourage ethnic Germans to remain in their home countries. Their arrival in Germany coincided with a surge of asylum seekers, prompting anti-immigration sentiments, xenophobia, and the emergence of new right-wing political parties, which stoked them.

The expanding economy facilitated the influx and incorporation of millions of ethnic Germans after World War II, and when this stream was exhausted, the government invited "guest workers" to serve the automobile, chemical, and construction industries through bilateral agreements with Turkey and several southern European countries, including Greece, Italy, and Spain. Turkish guest workers constituted the largest group; by 1990, 1.78 million resided in Germany. Based on the agreements with sending countries, the government expected these workers to return to their home country after their contracts expired. Moreover, when the Western economies were severely hit by the oil crises of the 1970s, Germany and many of its fellow EC members restricted labor immigration. However, most guest workers had come from poor regions, and many decided to stay despite monetary incentives to return. Humanitarian considerations continued to allow family reunification. By the 1990s, a second and third generation of immigrants flowed through schools, colleges, and work without sharing the rights to political participation and socio-cultural inclusion. Finally, in 1999, a new, modernized citizenship law granted migrants easier access to naturalization and citizenship.

Temporary and strictly regulated labor schemes came and went in the 1980s and 1990s. A population decline coupled with shortages in certain professional occupations led to the adoption of a Green Card program in 2000; it expired in 2005 when a new residency law included similar provisions. The residency law stopped short of overhauling the immigration system but added new exceptions for highly qualified workers, foreign graduates of German universities, and investors (Klusmeyer and Papademetriou 2009). Rather than widening the circle of immigrants substantially, the law focused on the integration of nonnationals.

West Germany's Constitution was written during and immediately after the Nazi period, when memories of war, expulsion, and refugee movements were fresh. Its authors intended to make amends, including special provisions for those persecuted under the Nazi regime. Article 116, 2 of the Basic Law allows the restoration of citizenship to "former German citizens who between 30 January 1933 and 8 May 1945 were deprived of their citizenship on political, racial, or religious grounds, and their descendants." This policy recognizes the citizenship of exiled German Jews and their descendants, among others.

Soviet Jews and their families constitute a special category. Their influx in recent decades made Germany home to the third largest group of Jewish citizens in Europe, altering the composition and reinvigorating Jewish life in many communities (Peck 2006). This special immigration status originated in the last days of the East German government in 1990; after some debate, the practice was extended and revised in the unified Germany. Once the 2005 residency law came into effect, this special status was rescinded. By the end of 2013, more than 214,000 Jewish immigrants and their families had settled in the Federal Republic of Germany.

Updating Citizenship, Naturalization, and Residency

Germany has joined other European countries in promoting civic-republican citizenship values, which emphasize integration by active participation in civic responsibilities. What prompted the policy shift in Germany? Several interrelated developments resulted in legal codes that combine *jus soli* and *jus sanguinis* and changes to naturalization practices. With unification and the end of the Cold War, "protecting" ethnic Germans from communist or dictatorial rule by offering them a safe haven and citizenship in the west was no longer necessary. The failure to integrate millions of foreigners into German society and the rise of xenophobia and violence against foreigners also fueled the quest for a new citizenship model. The introduction of EU citizenship as part of the Treaty on the European Union (Maastricht Treaty)—the free movement of EU residents and the diffusion of republican trends related to citizenship in much of Europe—framed the question beyond the nation-state. Changing party politics, in particular the role of the SPD and Alliance 90/The Greens in pushing for more flexible citizenship applications, also played a role, but enacting a new law still took a decade (Howard 2012).

A revised Aliens Law (*Ausländergesetz*), introduced in 1990, simplified naturalization of second- and third-generation foreigners, but between 1994 and 1998, only about 17 percent of all naturalizations were discretionary; more than three-fourths were granted to ethnic Germans. Citizenship policy quickly became one of the priority reform projects of the coalition government of SPD and Alliance 90/The Greens (1998–2005). The first draft of a new law, presented by the Minister of the Interior in 1999, envisaged a radical departure from existing policies, advocating *jus soli* and a general tolerance of dual citizenship. After the opposition CDU/CSU mounted a successful public campaign against provision of dual citizenship, these ambitious plans were abandoned, but a new law on citizenship (nationality) came into effect on January 1, 2000. While *jus sanguinis* was maintained, for the first time in German history, *jus soli* was granted on conditional grounds.

The citizenship act maintained that, at birth, a child of non-German parents in Germany is a German citizen if one parent (a) has a minimum legal residence period of eight years and (b) has held an unlimited residence permit for at least three years or holds a residence entitlement. A transition arrangement allowed children born in Germany within the previous decade to be naturalized under these conditions by December 30, 2000. A child who obtained German citizenship via *jus soli* (or the transitional arrangement) had to choose between it or foreign citizenship upon reaching legal age or face losing German nationality by the age of twenty-three (option obligation). The new law reduced naturalization requirements from fifteen to eight years of residence, curtailed fees, and made bureaucratic procedures easier (Mushaben 2008).

The law was a remarkable departure from previous practice but still excluded a sizable group of foreigners who did not meet the requirements. The dual citizenship provisions were another obstacle to naturalization. As before, dual citizenship could be granted as an exception at the bureaucracy's discretion but was not a legal right. Exceptions included cases in which the "home country" had no provision for, or hampered release from, citizenship or if the applicant was a legal political refugee. In 2014, the dual citizenship law was reformed to allow children of foreign parents the right to remain dual citizens beyond the age of twenty-three, provided certain conditions, such as length of residency and schooling in Germany, were met. The new requirements still fell short of accepting dual citizenship as a right. Nevertheless, Germany has made significant steps toward a modern, inclusive notion of citizenship. In 2011, about 4.3 million Germans held dual citizenship. At the same time, millions of longtime residents remain foreigners from a legal point of view largely due to bureaucratic obstacles and reluctance to give up the idea of native citizenship.

THE RIGHT TO ASYLUM AND THE REFUGEE CRISIS

Efforts to atone for the past explain why, until the early 1990s, Germany's asylum law was the most liberal in Europe. Article 16a granted every person persecuted in his or her home country the right to request asylum. Initially, the number was relatively small because the Iron Curtain, a metaphor for the separation of Eastern and Western Europe, prevented many from applying; other avenues were available for economic migrants. When labor migration was restricted in the 1970s, the number of asylum seekers jumped in the following decades.

Table 5.1. Asylum Applications, 1955–2016 (selected years)*

1955	1,926
1965	4,337
1975	9,627
1985	73,832
1992	438,191
1995	166,951
2005	42,908
2015	476,649
2016	745,545

*First-time and follow-up applications.

Source: Bundesamt für Migration und Flüchtlinge, *Das Bundesamt in Zahlen 2016, Asyl*, https://www.bamf.de/SharedDocs/Anlagen/DE/Publikationen/ Broschueren/bundesamt-in-zahlen-2016-asyl.pdf?__blob=publicationFile.

In the mid-1980s, more than two-thirds came from developing countries in the Southern Hemisphere, but in the 1990s, with the implosion of communism and the outbreak of civil war in Yugoslavia, more than two-thirds came from Southern and Eastern Europe, and over 60 percent of all people looking for new opportunities in the EU moved to Germany. In the absence of an immigration law that would regulate the flow of non-EU migrants seeking work and better opportunities, claiming asylum became a loophole for residency in Germany. In 1992 alone, 438,191 people requested asylum in Germany, in particular from war-torn Yugoslavia (122,666), but also Romania (103,787), and Bulgaria (31,540). German authorities granted only a small proportion the right to stay, but the bureaucratic procedures were lengthy, and returning people to their home countries proved difficult; many stayed on. Table 5.1 summarizes asylum applications; the recording of asylum applications often does not coincide with the date of arrival. Thus, although most refugees came to Germany in 2015, many of the new arrivals were only registered in 2016. Although the flow of refugees continued in 2016, the numbers were highest in the second half of 2015.

Revision of the Asylum Law in 1993

Against the first sharp increase in asylum applicants after 1990, xenophobia and violent attacks on foreigners made tightening the law of entry a pressing policy priority. Policy making in this area is particularly convoluted and contentious. The national government sets the legal framework, but the states and local communities are responsible for housing and daily provisions. The debate took a dramatic turn, pitting supporters of the existing liberal asylum regulations against members of the ruling center-right government of CDU/ CSU and FDP who wanted to change policies. Center-left parties favored comprehensive reform of immigration legislation but were outnumbered by those defending the "no immigrant country" position.

In fall 1992, then-chancellor Helmut Kohl proposed far-reaching amendments to Article 16 of the Basic Law. Despite earlier fierce opposition, the main opposition party, the SPD, agreed to the so-called asylum compromise, and the two-thirds majority in the Bundestag necessary to amend the Basic Law was secured. The law went into effect on July 1, 1993. The general provisions of Article 16 were kept in place, but a revised Article 16a severely restricted the individual right to seek asylum. The most important change was the stipulation that any person coming to Germany through a "safe" third country would be returned to that country. Countries were deemed safe when "on the basis of their laws, enforcement practices and general political conditions, it can be safely concluded that neither political persecution nor inhuman or degrading punishment or treatment exists." EU member countries and countries such as Switzerland and Norway were in this category.

Opposition to the new law came from many domestic and international sources, including the UN High Commissioner for Refugees, and such German nongovernmental organizations as Pro Asyl. Several legal complaints challenged the law on humanitarian grounds in the Federal Constitutional Court, which ruled that tightening the asylum regulation was constitutional but demanded better protection of applicants' human rights. As expected, the number of asylum seekers dropped as neighboring countries were deemed safe, and the war in the former Yugoslavia ended in 1995.

European Immigration and Asylum Policies

The EU has not passed immigration legislation or implemented coherent asylum policies that apply in all member states. Rather, a hybrid system of national rules and European regulations coexist. National governments act as gatekeepers to safeguard their country's interests, but they can also actively promote Europe-wide regulations. Four developments pushed asylum and migration onto the agenda of European policy makers: the introduction of the Schengen area, the conclusion of the Single European Act, European citizenship, and the surge in asylum seekers. Until the 1990s, migration and asylum policy were the sole responsibility of individual countries; cooperation was limited to cross-border crimes and terrorism. In 1985, the Benelux countries, France, and Germany agreed to facilitate the free movement of people without internal border controls in the Schengen Agreement; implementation followed in 1990. The borderless area expanded gradually and now encompasses most EU member states and such associated countries as Norway and Switzerland; special opt-out clauses apply to Denmark, Ireland, and the United Kingdom.

Coinciding with the Schengen negotiations, in 1987, the Single European Act aimed to complete the internal market by eliminating most non-tariff barriers, strengthening freedom of movement for services, capital, goods, and people within the EU by 1992 ("four freedoms"). The 1993 Maastricht Treaty introduced European citizenship, granting every citizen of an EU member state the right to move and reside freely in the EU and to stand for, and vote in, European and municipal elections. The combination of these initiatives challenged traditional perceptions of nation-states, called for new border management measures, and clearly set EU nationals apart from nonnationals.

Until the eastward enlargement of the EU in 2004 and 2007, net migration among member states was minor and not a problem. Germany was among those that successfully negotiated transitional agreements limiting work permits for Central and Eastern Europeans. Net migration has gone up, and debates, mostly related to alleged welfare abuse, still flare up on occasion, but the anticipated wave of immigrants from Central and Eastern Europe did not materialize in Germany.

Open borders raised other concerns, including the management of non-EU nationals—in particular, asylum applicants—since they could apply for refugee status in more than one member state. Diverse treaties and regulations make up the Common European Asylum System (CEAS), which established and has confirmed the "country of first entry" principle: the first member state a person enters is responsible for the asylum claim. This principle is the core of the Dublin Convention (now Dublin Regulation), signed on June 15, 1990, and enforced since September 1, 1997; it has been revised and updated several times. Chancellor Helmut Kohl used the provisions of the Dublin Convention to convince opponents at home that a revision of the German asylum law was not only in compliance with the emerging asylum regime of the EU but also a necessary step to limit the number of asylum seekers in Germany (Menz 2009, 185–88). The Amsterdam Treaty, signed in 1997 and enforced since 1999, gave EU institutions greater say over European migration and asylum policies.

Efforts to control and restrict access to the EU are complemented by targeted migration initiatives. An EU program of limited work permits, termed *Blue Card* (referencing the US Green Card, which indicates permanent residence, and the color of the EU flag), came into effect in 2009 to attract highly skilled foreign workers. Geared toward recruitment and temporary work permits, both the German Green Card and the EU Blue Card programs have had limited influence on the overall number of migrants. European countries are still seeking practical solutions to channel immigration and promote integration.

The Refugee Crisis

The situation has changed dramatically in recent years. Geographic proximity and political stability have made Europe the chief destination for many refugees fleeing violence in war-torn areas of the Middle East and Africa. Other forms of persecution and violence and economic misery further add to the stream of asylum applicants. Since 2014, the media have reported heartbreaking accounts of unscrupulous traffickers, boats capsizing in the Mediterranean, drowned refugees, and the overcrowded and often dismal conditions of the detention centers in many southern European countries.

The Dublin system was soon criticized as ineffective and unfair. Southern and Eastern European countries bore the brunt as first entry points for most asylum seekers. Most EU member states disregarded the mandated registration procedures and engaged in "waving" asylum seekers through to another country. Some of the peripheral countries were criticized for not providing adequate accommodations and protection for asylum seekers. The shortcomings of the system became blatant when the number of asylum applications to EU member states rose sharply in 2015 (table 5.2) and 2016.

The EU response to these developments demonstrated its distinct policy limitations; many member states were reluctant to take in refugees. The situation came to a head, prompting the EU to step up border control in the Mediterranean, support countries housing refugees in the Middle East, and encourage non-EU countries to take back refugees departing from their shores; this included a 2016 package deal with Turkey as one of the main countries with large refugee camps.

Table 5.2.   Top Ten EU Recipient Countries for Asylum Seekers, 2015

Germany	476,620
Hungary	177,135
Sweden	162,550
Austria	88,180
Italy	84,085
France	75,750
Netherlands	44,970
Belgium	44,760
United Kingdom	39,000
Finland	32,345

Source: Eurostat (May 11, 2016), reprinted from Bundesamt für Migration und Flüchtlinge, *Das Bundesamt in Zahlen. Asyl, Migration und Integration,* Nuremberg, 2016.

In 2015, citing human rights concerns, the German government allowed refugees to enter the country in large numbers. It applied the sovereignty clause of the Dublin Regulation, which allows member states to examine asylum applications even when they do not necessarily fall under that country's legal responsibility. It is one of two discretionary stipulations in the Dublin system; the other is the humanitarian clause (Wendel 2016). Response was mixed. Many EU member states sharply criticized Angela Merkel's government for what they considered disregard for EU rules and procedures—in particular, the lack of consultation with other member states. According to many within and outside Germany, her actions encouraged migration to Europe. German historian Jürgen Kocka (2016) argued that her government's unilateral decision making exacerbated discord in the EU. On the other hand, many citizens and human rights organizations heralded her actions as pragmatic and humanitarian.

Along with Italy and France, the German government advocated quotas to distribute the refugees more evenly across the EU, but several countries, including the economically less developed postcommunist states in Central and Eastern Europe, blocked the proposal. Several thousand refugees still await transfer to other European countries in camps located in countries of first entry, particularly Greece and Italy, but redistribution is slow. National interests and politics continue to constrain migration and asylum policies.

In Germany in 2015 and 2016, the number of asylum applications reached new heights (see table 5.3). Urgent situations require courage and can bring about change. Faced with the sharp increase in refugees, Chancellor Merkel has emerged as a strong advocate for pragmatic humanitarian approaches. In summer and fall 2015 her position was supported by a wide range of political parties, and the media echoed her positive "let's-get-it-done" approach, not least by reminding citizens that the country weathered a migration surge under difficult conditions after World War II. Commentators not only emphasized the human dimension of the refugee crisis but also the benefits to German society in terms of skilled labor. Citizens from all strata participated in "Welcome to Germany" initiatives across the country; to this day many work in neighborhoods, communities, and schools on behalf of refugees. These liberal trends counteract the nationalistic rhetoric of right-wing groups. Soon, however, the challenges of housing, educating, and training hundreds of thousands of newcomers overwhelmed many communities. Voices turned more critical.

On New Year's Eve 2015 in Cologne, groups of (mostly North African) men sexually assaulted and robbed passing women, raising concerns about safety. Terrorist attacks in Berlin, Brussels, London, Manchester, Paris, and Stockholm, to name only the most prominent, have heightened the need for

Table 5.3. Asylum Applications in Germany, 2015 (in percent)

Country of Origin	%
Syria, Arab Republic	35.9
Albania	12.2
Kosovo	7.6
Afghanistan	7.1
Iraq	6.7
Serbia	3.8
Others	26.7

Source: Bundesamt für Migration und Flüchtlinge, *Das Bundesamt in Zahlen 2015. Asyl Migration und Integration*, Nuremberg, 2016.

comprehensive counterterrorism measures to combat radicalization of young men of Muslim background. Fears about terrorist infiltration into European societies have provided openings for anti-immigrant rhetoric, even though many of the perpetrators are not recent immigrants. The failure to fully integrate immigrants, particularly Muslims, is a recurring topic throughout Western Europe.

Was opening the borders so quickly to so many refugees the right decision? Should Germany introduce quotas, or would they violate international and humanitarian laws granting protection to refugees? How many can German society (and the economy) house and integrate? Integrating the refugees and designing rules for immigration will remain on the agenda for years to come.

In response, Germany's role shifted quickly from open-door policy in summer and fall 2015 to more restrictive measures, although Merkel's government refused to set an upper limit on the number of asylum seekers allowed to enter the country. Administrative procedures for the asylum law were tightened in October 2015 and March 2016. The so-called Asylum Packages I and II fine-tuned application procedures and restricted the eligibility criteria for asylum. New provisions no longer grant all applicants from the western Balkans, Morocco, Tunisia, and Algeria refugee status. Family reunification has been suspended for a two-year period unless applicants are persecuted; family members in refugee camps in Turkey and Syria receive preferential treatment.

Those whose asylum claims are denied are sent back to their country of origin or the first "safe" EU country. Rules about returning migrants to so-called safe countries outside of Europe are now enforced more strictly. In 2016, amid a storm of controversy, some asylum seekers were returned to Afghanistan; in mid-2017, this practice was reversed in response to violence and terrorist attacks in Kabul and other cities.

Persons granted asylum or refugee status receive a temporary residence permit and the same access to the social insurance system as Germans. They are entitled to basic health care, social welfare, child benefits, child-raising benefits, integration allowances, language courses, and other forms of integration assistance. Those whose asylum claim is rejected must leave the country voluntarily or risk being deported. Asylum seekers are distributed to the Länder according to a numerical key, which considers tax revenues, population numbers, and capacity levels. Leaving aside crisis situations where the federal government jumps in with additional funds, the Länder largely cover housing and benefit costs. Germany also introduced legislation addressing the integration of refugees.

INTEGRATING FOREIGNERS

The Discourse

From a legal perspective, the situation of many long-standing migrants has improved significantly, but public perceptions and political rhetoric still struggle with the reality of a culturally diverse society. When desperate migrants from Syria began to arrive in droves, the discourse soon centered on whether and how to integrate them into society. Broadly defined, integration "refers to the processes that increase the opportunities of immigrants and their descendants to obtain the valued 'stuff' of a society, as well as social acceptance, through participation in major institutions such as the educational and political system and the labor and housing markets" (Alba and Foner 2015, 5). In other words, integration entails access to rights and responsibilities equal to those of nationals; it is most often measured in terms of socioeconomic attainment but also refers to feelings of belonging and acceptance (Lenard 2010, 309).

While *integration* has become the term of choice, expectations range from assimilation to multiculturalism. Assimilation mandates that immigrants conform to the host's political and cultural norms, while multiculturalism recognizes and tolerates cultural differences and religious diversity and cherishes newcomers' contributions to society. In retrospect, multiculturalism's heyday in the 1970s and 1980s has been replaced by a layered discourse about the costs and benefits of immigration and more somber assessments of integration. Unlike assimilation, integration is a two-way street. It encourages intercultural dialogue and interaction between nationals and nonnationals, but how it should be advanced and the degree to which the immigrant communities' cultural and religious norms should give way remain disputed and heavily influenced by national trajectories. Per Mouritsen asserts that in Europe, "the dual discrediting of multiculturalism and overt ethno-nationalism" has resulted in a move toward the French model, which emphasizes "nationhood in terms of broad civil-liberal values" (2013, 89).

The 2000 citizenship act was passed during a fierce debate that pitted ethno-cultural against liberal principles. It centered on the idea of *Leitkultur*, a leading or dominant culture to which migrants would have to adjust. They would have to embrace the German language as well as a canon of literature and cultural representation. The argument about learning the language of the host country is common across immigrant societies, but insistence on learning a particular culture stirred controversy. How would German culture be defined; what works belonged to its literary canon? Newcomers had their own literature and other arts. Critics also pointed to the elitism in this notion of culture since most working-class Germans may be unfamiliar with Johann Wolfgang von Goethe, Ludwig van Beethoven, and Albrecht Dürer. They questioned whether particular cultural practices should be required from citizens. In the republican view, acceptance of pluralist political ideas and the social values of a democratic society should be sufficient for integration. Discussions about the meaning of what constitutes *Leitkultur* have emerged routinely.

When German politician and businessman Thilo Sarrazin (2010) argued that Germany attracts the "wrong" kind of immigrants who form a new and growing underclass, he was referring mostly to Muslim residents. He voiced concerns shared by many but also evoked notions of a class war between the educated middle class and a "genetically" determined social underclass, mostly of immigrant origin. His crude appeal to nativism resonated in a climate of economic uncertainty and quickly became a national bestseller.

Speaking for the more cosmopolitan spectrum, philosopher Jürgen Habermas (2010) sharply criticized Sarrazin's publication and the illiberal, nationalist debate about *Leitkultur* that it promoted. He welcomed the modernization of the citizenship law as a long-overdue adjustment to modern globalized societies and defended universalist immigrant rights. Cultural differences should not diminish the right to acquire citizenship; *Leitkultur* was defined too narrowly and negated the cultural and religious diversity that characterizes pluralist, immigrant societies. His arguments resonated with those who favor citizenship reform.

The adoption of the citizenship law demonstrated once again that progress is largely elite-driven and that antiforeigner sentiment can easily be mobilized for political purposes (Howard 2012). This predicament is not limited to Germany: In all advanced democracies, the economic and political consequences of immigration are challenged from a broad spectrum of opinions. As in other countries, German center-right parties tend to promote more restrictions on immigration and citizenship policies as compared to center-left parties, which favor a more open-door policy and support immigrant populations. Parties on the left, such as Alliance 90/The Greens, have generally taken a favorable view of multiculturalism; center-right parties, such as the CDU, oppose it. Chancellor Angela Merkel (CDU) has proclaimed the utter failure of multiculturalism in Germany, a sentiment widely shared by European politicians. In recent decades, anti-immigrant parties, which often espouse strong Euroskepticism as well, have emerged throughout Western Europe. In response, mainstream parties have adjusted their rhetoric if not their policies. These dynamics are common across Europe. Although extreme right-wing German parties have had limited success in the voting booth, their discourse is loud and clear.

Integration in Practice

Discourse and policies have shifted considerably. The predominant question is no longer to what extent immigration should be allowed but rather how residents with migrant backgrounds can be integrated into society and the economy. When new citizenship laws were passed, German language skills and acceptance of the constitutional order were prerequisites. The residence act of 2005, introduced by the coalition government of SPD and Alliance 90/The Greens, added integration courses that familiarize participants with Germany's history, culture, and legal system. These language and orientation classes are mandatory for those seeking permanent residence, but longtime residents can enroll to improve their German language skills. Since 2008, citizenship applicants have had to pass a naturalization test, administered according to the rules of the individual states.

Responding to the steep increase in refugees, the German government introduced further measures to better integrate them and to establish their obligations as German residents. The Integration Law, which went into effect on July 31, 2016, introduced federal guidelines (Bundesgesetzblatt 2016). It was an important administrative move since some Länder were burdened more than others by devising and implementing integration measures, and policies varied widely. Changes included obliging refugees to attend German language classes and the so-called integration classes, which introduce them to basic social facts and customs, political processes, and laws. Funding for the courses was stepped up to meet the increased demand.

Workforce integration is a key goal of the revised rules. Previous practice did not allow asylum seekers to work before their application was approved, a process that takes several months. The new policy supports the food and maintenance services in refugee housing and encourages refugees to join vocational training programs and to find regular work. The obligatory screening by the Federal Agency for Labor to give precedence to German citizens has been suspended for a three-year period to improve refugees' chances of finding work. Those who attend vocational training courses are granted the right to stay (*Bleiberecht*) for the duration of their training. In short, the integration law emphasizes easing access to jobs; policy makers count on the integrative force of work.

The new regulations are significant since more than 80 percent of all refugees are under thirty-five years of age and expected to have good chances for employment once they acquire language and job skills. More contested is the provision that Länder governments can assign refugees to a particular place of residence within their state. This stipulation was introduced to avoid segregation and overcrowding in urban areas, which might contribute to social problems.

Despite long-standing allegations, studies found no significant difference between the rates of crimes committed by German nationals and immigrants (Geißler 2011). Statistics are not always conclusive since different categories of "foreigners" are often lumped together; moreover, the statistics only show arrests but not convictions (Jacobsen and Völlinger 2016). According to data collected by the Federal Criminal Police Office (Bundeskriminalamt 2017), refugees commit very few major crimes, such as homicide and rape. Syrians, Afghans, and Iraqis are underrepresented, while migrants from the Maghreb, the Balkans, and some African countries are overrepresented in relation to their proportion of the migrant population. Since comparisons with Germans based on gender, income, and social status are missing, conclusions about the impact of migration on criminal behavior are difficult to draw.

Due to Germany's federal system, police recruitment and training as well as crime prevention measures vary from state to state. To prevent crime, including terrorist attacks, efforts are under way to improve the flow of communication among states, between the federal government and the states, and between German agencies and EU offices.

Open questions remain. Will integration succeed? How long will it take for newcomers to build a new life? How difficult will they find new customs, a new language, and a secular environment? Is integration easier for an entire family, or will the young, mostly male refugees adapt more quickly? All mainstream parties emphasize the need for integration. Parties on the left favor more and better integration policies and raise human rights concerns when refugees are returned to their countries of origin. Right-wing populist positions stress cultural incompatibility based on religion since most refugees are Muslim.

Muslims in Germany

The Issues

Germany's "diversity transition," a concern in all Western countries, presents both opportunities and challenges. The weight of race versus religion is particularly pronounced when comparing the United States with Western Europe. In the United States, race is a major dividing line; in Western Europe, it is religion, specifically Islam (Alba and Foner 2015, 17). After France, Germany has the largest Muslim population in Europe, and in both countries, its composition is diverse. Approximately two-thirds of the more than 4.3 million Muslims living in Germany are of Turkish origin; smaller groups have arrived from Syria, Afghanistan, Albania, Bosnia, Iran, and Pakistan. Nationality is one dimension of difference; the degree of religiosity and religious affiliation another.

Key concerns in the integration debate have been the alleged formation of "parallel societies" (*Parallelgesellschaften*), gender equality, religion, education levels, and access to the labor market. In 2010, Federal President Christian Wulff (CDU) reaffirmed that, in addition to Christianity and Judaism, "Islam belongs in Germany" but the role of religion in politics and society is contested recurrently. The German Constitution guarantees religious freedom, yet Islam is not recognized as one of the official major religious denominations; the community is diverse and fragmented and no one body represents Muslims vis-à-vis the state. Cultural habits as well as religious practices vary greatly among Muslim communities.

Muslims are often more religious than their Protestant or Catholic counterparts; observance of religious holidays and social values based on religious beliefs are widespread in Muslim communities. At the same time, most longtime resident Muslims consider Germany their home, respect other religions, support democracy, and adjust their values accordingly. For example, attitudes toward same-sex marriage have become more tolerant; about 60 percent view such partnerships favorably. However, the Muslim majority's accommodations to their new home have aroused greater hostility among Germans, and more than half of the persons surveyed viewed Islam as a potential threat (Bertelsmann Foundation 2015). In the corridors of power and the living rooms of ordinary Germans, two questions linger: To what extent will new Muslim arrivals adapt their values? How long will it take?

The introduction of integration courses combined with the backlash against overt multiculturalism have quieted but not extinguished the debate about Muslims in Germany. Antiforeigner sentiment has become more openly anti-Muslim, another characteristic shared across Western Europe.

Although Muslims have long resided here, their growing numbers, the lingering problems of integration, Islamist terror attacks in several Western European countries, and the rise of ISIS in the Middle East have added to anxieties. While cultural and religious differences are still prominent, the integration debate now prioritizes security.

The headscarf debate shows German society struggling with some of the same issues as other European societies with substantial Muslim populations; the debate reflects broader questions of belonging and defining national identity (Korteweg and Yurdakul 2014). Wearing a headscarf can be viewed as an expression of religious freedom, yet many regard it as a symbol of religious Islam and reject it based on secular values or see it as an expression of religious oppression of women.

The headscarf debate in Germany resembles that in neighboring France and Switzerland but not Britain and Austria. In Britain, Sikhs have the right to wear turbans for religious reasons, setting a precedent, and the Muslim headscarf is not controversial. In 1908, the Austro-Hungarian Empire annexed Bosnia, with its mostly Muslim population, and to this day Islam is one of Austria's "official" religions. In contrast, conflicts between secularism and religious beliefs in Germany and France have concentrated on wearing the headscarf and access to education. The French parliament banned the headscarf in public schools, while the German debate focuses on teachers rather than students. Practices vary from state to state. By 2015, eight Länder had introduced headscarf bans for teachers, arguing that wearing them displays a preference for one religion in what should be religiously neutral classrooms; others stress that the headscarf alone is not a problem if teachers do not try to influence students. The Constitutional Court was asked to arbitrate repeatedly, and in 2015, its judges ruled that religious freedom required acceptance of the headscarf. Schools could only ban them in the event of a disturbance of "public order," which had to be supported with evidence on a case-by-case basis.

For security reasons, however, legislation does not allow full-face cover (a burka or niqab). As of 2017, women are no longer allowed to wear a full veil while driving; their identity must be visible. Some private companies in the EU have established dress codes they deemed necessary for their business, including a ban on full veils or headscarves. The ECJ declared this practice legal in a March 2017 ruling.

The majority German discourse dominates the debate about integration, immigration, and Muslim culture; more speak *about* than *with* Muslims. Anti-Muslim sentiment is most vocal in the protest movement Pegida (see chapter 4) and violent attacks on asylum applicants have increased. Right-wing terrorists' verbal attacks and racist propaganda on the Internet and physical attacks on buildings and homes for refugees repeatedly made headlines in 2015 and 2016.

The Turkish Community

The Turkish community is by far the most populous ethnic minority group in Germany. About a third of its members have German citizenship, and many have lived in Germany for decades. Updated citizenship regulations can foster but do not guarantee integration, including societal acceptance. To this day, many German Turks feel torn between two worlds—Turkey and Germany—and often see themselves as marginalized culturally and socially.

The movie *Almanya—Willkommen in Deutschland* (*Almanya—Welcome to Germany*), introduced at the 2011 Berlin film festival, highlighted this conundrum. Based on the experience of the two filmmakers, sisters Yasemin and Nesrin Samdereli, it depicts the life of the 1,000,001st guest worker to arrive in Germany from eastern Turkey in 1970. He comes with high hopes and deep prejudices, believing Germany is constantly cold and Germans are dirty people who eat nothing but potatoes and pork. Two generations later, his grandson in elementary school is trying to come to terms with his identity because all the local sports teams, German and Turkish, reject him. He exclaims, "What are we now? Turks or Germans?" The family has a legal right to acquire German citizenship, but the grandfather surprises them by buying a house in Anatolia, Turkey, and taking them on a journey back. The movie is a comedy, a black comedy at times, and the humorous nature of the unfolding narrative makes spectators laugh and cry at the same time. It echoes the portrayal of a "typical-atypical" German-Turkish family in the documentary feature *Berlin—Ecke Bundesplatz. Der Yilmaz Clan* (2008–9), which followed several individuals living in a quarter of Berlin over the course of twenty-four years.

Increasingly, however, Turkish representatives have taken ownership. Several prominent politicians of Turkish origin, such as Cem Özdemir, head of Alliance 90/The Greens, Aygül Özkan, Social Ministry in Lower Saxony, and Aydan Özoğuz, Commissioner for Immigration, Refugees, and Integration, represent a new generation of Germans born to Turkish parents. The number of MPs from migrant backgrounds has risen slowly: 5.6 percent in the Bundestag elected in 2013. Turkish Germans contribute to a lively discourse in films, books, and media, suggesting that "culture is a substitute for political representation and social equality" (Göktürk, Gramling, Kaes, and Langenohl 2011, 33; our translation). They hold up a mirror to German society as well as Turkish-German identity. Fatih Akin's films have attracted international audiences.

Major impediments to successful integration and gainful employment are lack of language skills and the highly stratified educational system, which separates pupils according to their achievement early on. Although the tracks have become more permeable, navigating the system remains difficult. Turkish-German pupils often lag far behind their German peers. They are represented disproportionally in the lowest track and drop out at a higher rate; fewer go to university. In the past, language instruction targeted ethnic German immigrants; no classes were organized for the migrant workers who came to Germany from the 1960s onward. Now, a wide variety of language classes are offered to different immigrant clienteles; in particular, early childhood education programs are targeted.

IMMIGRATION AND INTEGRATION REVISITED

Due to history, location, and economy Germany was and will remain a major magnet for migrants—both economic migrants and refugees. An aging population and the need for labor provide positive background conditions for a new influx of labor but fears of too much immigration and the loss of control over immigration are ever present. Strong currents of anti-immigrant sentiment can be revived easily, but they are countered by a lively and nuanced debate about the rights and responsibility of immigrants and the successes and failures of integration. At the political level, sharp ideological differences have given way to more nuanced distinctions. The broad consensus holds that Germany needs immigrants, although opinions within and among parties on how to achieve reasonable integration measures diverge.

Even if immigration flows can be channeled, discourse and time matter: when built on broad partisan support, immigration can be framed as a chance and opportunity. In this rare, but not impossible case, chances are enhanced that newcomers find a place in a foreign land and make it their own. Germany's postwar history demonstrated that millions of refugees can be integrated successfully when the political will exists. Most so-called guest workers from Italy, Greece, Spain, and Portugal, arriving in the towns and cities in the 1950s and 1960s, may still be foreigners in name but they are accepted; the lines between nationality and a European identity have become blurred but not erased.

Integration measured in socioeconomic terms (level of income, employment, and education) tends to show considerable variety in outcomes when broken down in distinct categories. Race and religion complicate matters. Social status continues to limit the chances of all children, both with and without a migrant background. Improvements are real, but the gap between

German students and students with a migration background remains. Many working-age migrants do not have a school-leaving certificate, adding to the persistent employment gap between them and German nationals. Inequality and diversity often go hand in hand. The risk of living in poverty is four times higher for non-German nationals than for Germans and twice as high for Germans with a migration background and Germans without. Poverty in old age is pronounced due to lower education and qualification levels and higher rates of unemployment.

In an increasingly interconnected world, identity alone seems to be an erroneous line to take in measuring the success of integration, particularly in an environment where multiple identities are promoted as part of the European project. Just as was the case with the eurozone crisis, the refugee crisis of 2015–16 exhibited the search for a common solution across the EU but it turned complicated because demands for solidarity mixed and often clashed with strong feelings of sovereignty and fear of rising xenophobia, depending on the actors involved. German right-wing parties attract voters but to a lesser degree when compared to neighboring France or the United Kingdom, alleviating the pressure to give in to anti-immigrant demands. Yet, the ugly head of xenophobia is never completely absent either. Although German citizens and the German government received praise for their handling of the 2015 refugee crisis abroad, it was always tempered by apprehension as well as criticism in some quarters both at home and in other EU capitals.

Immigration and integration challenge governments and citizens of recipient countries across the EU, Germany included, and the road to stability and acceptance for many foreign-born nationals is protracted. The need to address the sources of conflict and to design a Europe-wide policy on immigration seems more urgent than ever.

Chapter 6

Political Economy

KEY TERMS

codetermination
coordinated market economy
debt brake
dualization of labor market
economic crisis, 2008–10
economic miracle
economic reforms
energy policy
export surplus
Hartz IV

industrial relations
inequality
minimum wage
model Germany
neocorporatism
post–World War II economic recovery
poverty
reform blockage
unification crisis

Trade and financial expansion, market liberalization, and the addition of new economic players have challenged postindustrial democracies in the last decades, resulting in major adjustments of institutional settings and policies, including features of state regulations (Leibfried et al. 2015). In Germany after 1989, the task of merging the eastern with western economies concurrent with European integration added to globalization pressures. Deliberate and unintended updating and fine-tuning of processes affected industrial relations, corporate strategies, and state actors.

Economic globalization has created winners and losers everywhere, but German businesses weathered the challenges quite well despite some negative trends. The manufacturing sector survived restructuring better than those in many other postindustrial democracies, especially in such areas as machinery, automobiles, chemical products, optical products, and renewable energy technology. Growth in the financial and service sectors was slower, particularly compared to the United States and the United Kingdom. Businesses expanded their exports to new markets and strengthened ties to old ones. They could rely on a highly skilled labor force, solid vocational training, technological innovation, and established patterns of industrial relations. At the same time, despite overall economic growth, inequality increased.

This chapter provides an overview of the major features of Germany's economic system and their evolution in response to the dual challenges of unification and globalization. The final section on energy policy illustrates the interdependence of national, European, and global developments. Chapter 7 will discuss the economic reach of the EU into national politics, particularly in the eurozone crisis.

BACKGROUND

Germany always ranks among the five largest economies in the world—the United States, China, Japan, and India—but it moves up and down with time and measurement criteria; for example, current prices or purchasing power parity (PPP). Its economic status shapes its foreign policy power in general (chapter 8) and its role in the EU in particular (chapter 7). Following unification, its population increased and, after a dip in the last decade, stood at 82.2 million in 2015. Table 6.1 provides data comparing Germany's economic development,

Table 6.1. Germany in Comparison: Selected Political and Economic Indicators, 2014–15

	Germany	France	Spain	Sweden	United Kingdom	United States
Population (in millions)	82.2	64.7	46.1	9.9	65.2	322.8
GDP per capita (PPP; current US$)	47,268.4	39,678.0	34,526.5	46,420.4	41,324.6	55,836.8
Economist Democracy Index	#13 (8.64/10)	#27 (7.92/10)	#17 (8.30/10)	#3 (9.45/10)	#16 (8.31/10)	#20 (8.05/10)
Human Development Index	#6/168	#6/168	#26/168	#14/168	#14/168	#8/168
Transparency International Index	#10/168	#23/168	#36/168	#3/168	#10/168	#16/168

Source: http://www.destatis.de; http://www.census.gov/popclock; http://www.worldometers.info/population/countries-in-europe-by-population; http://www.yabiladi.com/img/content/EIU-Democracy-Index-2015.pdf; http://hdr.undp.org/en/2015-report; https://www.transparency.org/country.

standard of living, and democratic achievement to selected advanced Western democracies. We chose the United States, France, and the United Kingdom due to their role in the international economy and Europe. Sweden, with its small population, represents the well-developed welfare systems typical of Nordic countries. Spain illustrates a southern European country whose market economy developed only after its transition to democracy in 1975. All of them routinely rank high in democratic and economic achievement, and the data show the connection of the economic, social, and political sectors.

The consensus holds that a certain level of economic development is conducive to maintaining democracy. Their interrelationship is at the core of studies examining why some democracies succeed and others fail. Daron Acemoglu and James A. Robinson (2012) emphasize the importance of inclusive political institutions to the development of good economic institutions that guarantee the rule of law, protection of private property, enforcement of contracts, and control of inflation, among other strengths. The Human Development Index measures life expectancy, educational access, and per capita income; it places Germany in the top category, sixth among 188 countries. The detrimental impact of widespread corruption—that is, the illegal transfer of funds to public officials, often as bribes—on the legitimacy of, and trust in, political and economic institutions is widely documented. Corrupt business practices affect the scope of business investment and diminish tax revenues by encouraging shadow economies, among other problems. In such systems, inequality is high. In contrast, economically developed countries have lower rates of corruption, Germany among them.

Globalization and Europeanization often work in tandem, reinforcing or complementing each other. In the 1990s, competitive global pressures accelerated the EU's reach into new policy areas. EU membership acts as a filter through which industries and governments pursue new opportunities for market expansion, outsourcing, and direct foreign investment, at both the European and global levels. Germany's export record attests to the high demand for its goods worldwide. Since 2002, facilitated by the euro's exchange rate on the world market, wage restraint, and increased production, the balance between exports and imports has shifted, many say precariously, in favor of exports. Export surplus is particularly pronounced in trade with the Americas and European countries and has strained relations. Exports have secured jobs at home and promoted technological innovation, but at a cost: consumption and investment within Germany have lagged; competitive pressures lowered actual wage increases and indebted countries to German banks. Globalization also increases competitive pressures; the 2015 Volkswagen diesel emissions scandal showed that manufacturers' ambitions can be counterproductive when they rely on false claims.

Table 6.2. German Foreign Trade, 2015

	Exports			Imports	
Rank	Country	(in 1,000 Euros)	Rank	Country	(in 1,000 Euros)
1	United States	113,990,351	1	China	91,696,618
2	France	102,949,481	2	Netherlands	87,936,963
3	United Kingdom	89,284,282	3	France	66,920,953
4	Netherlands	79,478,999	4	United States	59,641,651
5	China	71,385,193	5	Italy	49,055,143
6	Austria	58,113,881	6	Poland	44,622,292
7	Italy	58,069,405	7	Switzerland	42,467,306
8	Poland	52,180,598	8	Czech Republic	39,294,608
9	Switzerland	49,278,933	9	United Kingdom	38,321,711
10	Belgium	41,155,552	10	Austria	37,289,277
11	Spain	38,783,802	11	Belgium	36,844,638
12	Czech Republic	36,525,461	12	Russia	29,761,263
13	Sweden	23,086,831	13	Spain	26,463,331
14	Turkey	22,411,519	14	Hungary	23,789,763
15	Hungary	21,827,777	15	Japan	20,220,410

Source: https://www.destatis.de/DE/ZahlenFakten/GesamtwirtschaftUmwelt/Aussenhandel/Handelspartner/
Tabellen/RangfolgeHandelspartner.

EU member states remain Germany's most important trade partners, even though exports to them have declined from 67.4 percent in 1992 to 58.6 percent in 2016. France, followed by the United Kingdom, are the most important export destinations for German products. Close business ties with the United Kingdom were one reason German politicians and businesses lamented the Brexit vote. Outside the EU, the United States and now China are by far the most important trading partners (see table 6.2); trade relations are European and global.

GERMANY'S MARKET ECONOMY

The German Model

After its recovery from World War II, the German economic system was widely respected for high productivity and peaceful labor relations and was upheld as an alternative to the neoliberal variant of US capitalism. Since then, the model has been both admired and criticized. In the aftermath of unification, it was declared arthritic, if not dead: labor costs were too high, structural unemployment persisted, and many industries were deemed uncompetitive. However, even before and then during the 2008 financial and economic crisis, its resilience, strength, and capacity to innovate and adapt received new acclaim (Allen 2010). Throughout, "Made in Germany" has stood for high-quality consumer and industrial products. Adjustments made after unification changed some features of economic and fiscal regulation, but the core of the economic model remained intact.

Scholars routinely emphasize the unique blend of historical, cultural, and institutional features that comprise this economic model, variously described as *Rhinelandish* capitalism, *Modell Deutschland*, or coordinated market economy (CME). Manfred Schmidt (2001) referred to West German economics as the "policy of the middle way" between state-interventionist and laissez-faire market economies. Such a middle position was also evident in the classification of welfare states where Germany is cited as a prime example of a conservative welfare system as opposed to liberal and social-democratic welfare regimes (Esping-Andersen 1990). US and British welfare policy patterns, although distinct in scope and programs, illustrate the liberal model, with lower taxes and spending compared to other welfare systems, and many benefits are means-tested. Conservative and social-democratic welfare states share comprehensive safety nets that cover unemployment, social assistance, sick leave, health, education, and family allowances. However, in the social-democratic model, molded by the Nordic countries, universal benefits are mostly based on tax revenues; the conservative model is largely financed through mandatory insurance programs in the form of obligatory taxes, and many benefits are aligned with wages. Labor and family policies in the social-democratic model encourage the participation of both genders; in the conservative system, family and tax policies that support the male breadwinner model prevail. Recent reforms of family and employment policies moved Germany closer to the northern European model (see chapter 4), while the reworking of unemployment benefits inserted elements of the liberal welfare model (Fleckenstein, Saunders, and Seeleib-Kaiser 2011).

Classifications vary but they build on macroeconomic policies, which emphasize price stability, fiscal rectitude, low unemployment, export orientation, and economic growth. Microeconomics combines market liberalism with state regulation. Industrial relations—that is, the relationships among workers, management, and labor unions—were cooperative and close. In terms of the core variables, differences in corporate governance, firm structure, industrial relations, vocational training systems, and interfirm relations define the varieties of capitalism described in the literature (Hall & Soskice 2001). The United States and the United Kingdom are prime examples of liberal market economies (LME), and Germany and Japan exemplify coordinated market economies (CME). Such models are not designed; rather, their distinctive institutional arrangements evolve through adjustments to ongoing global and domestic challenges, including the building of the welfare state and social policies. Their

Table 6.3. Comparison of Coordinated and Liberal Market Economies

Features	Coordinated market economy (CME): Germany, Austria, Japan	Liberal market economy (LME): United States, United Kingdom
Corporate governance and financial system	Dense business network providing insider information	Attentive to current earnings and share prices in equity markets
	Employers' associations and unions—key players	Tolerant of mergers including "hostile takeovers"
	Business reputation crucial	High capital mobility
Internal firm structures	Top managers share decision-making power with boards, including employee representatives and shareholders	Concentration of decision making in top management positions
	Long-term employment contracts	Flexible labor force
		Flexibility in new market strategies
Industrial relations	Reliance on highly skilled labor force	Deregulated labor markets
	Employee-employer cooperation, such as codetermination	Low-cost hiring and firing
	Wage moderation	No codetermination
Education and training systems	Focus on firm-specific skills through apprenticeship and vocational training	Focus on general skills complements a fluid labor market
	Public training systems	Some in-house training
Intercompany relations	Strong industry associations	Strong competition
	Relational contracting and cooperation	Standard setting via the market
	Technology transfer through diffusion and contract law	Technology transfer via the market

Source: Based on Peter A. Hall and David Soskice, *Varieties of Capitalism: The Institutional Foundations of Comparative Advantage* (Oxford, UK: Oxford University Press, 2001).

performances wax and wane, and categorizations gloss over important national distinctions. Also, they are not set in stone. In response to global economic dynamics, institutions change (Thelen 2014). Table 6.3 summarizes the two models in their ideal form; we elaborate on Germany's system below.

Features of the Coordinated Market Economy

Corporate Governance, Financial System, and Firm Structure

Many German multinational companies are household names almost every-where: Allianz Worldwide, Bayer Group, BMW Group, DaimlerChrysler, Siemens, Telecom. To assure that shareholders and stakeholders are represented, separate supervisory and management boards govern such large companies; no one sits on both. Reputation and trust are vital as well as close relations with private banks, which hold a considerable share of equity.

The bedrock of German productivity is the medium-sized company, typically privately owned and often located in small and mid-sized towns with long-standing manufacturing traditions. Many are niche-market leaders, producing innovative, high-value export goods in such areas as renewable energy technology and microelectronics. They benefit from Germany's apprenticeship system, which provides skilled workers, and a collaborative spirit between employers and employees.

Industrial Relations

Germany's system relies on strong trade union and employer associations; their dialogue has been called a social partnership. Although union membership has declined significantly and organizational structure diversified in the last two decades, the legal and legislative framework for industrial relations remains the "steady trestle" that guarantees their influence (Silvia 2013). The system of codetermination (*Mitbestimmung*) grants labor unions, in the form of elected workers' councils, seats on the boards of larger companies, so workers' concerns are voiced and influence management decisions. Codetermination has fostered a consensual decision-making process and secured relative social peace; Germany has one of the lowest strike rates in Europe, although it has increased in recent years.

Education and Training System

Germany's vocational system is widely recognized as the backbone of its manufacturing success. It keeps the youth unemployment rate low (October 2016: 5.1 percent) in addition to providing skilled workers and professional opportunities beyond college education. It follows tracks: prevocational training, full-time vocational training, and dual-system training, which is the most prevalent and combines part-time vocational school with apprenticeship training, or theory with practice. The business community and the state share in covering the costs. The origins of the apprenticeship system reach as far back as the medieval guilds, and the dual system was introduced toward the end of the nineteenth century. The curriculum today is vastly different, but the core principles remain.

Parapublic Institutions

Parapublic institutions are features that distinguished West Germany as a semisovereign state in Peter Katzenstein's portrayal (see chapter 2). They enjoy high degrees of autonomy, but their work is supervised by the state, and they advise government. They bridge the gap between the public and private sectors and carry out important policy functions. Diverse institutions, such as the Council of Economic Advisors and private social insurance funds, coordinate policy with, and provide expertise to, political institutions, building a durable system of economic governance. One institution, the *Treuhand* agency, for example, served as a "shock absorber" after unification. The *Bundesbank* lost its autonomy when the European Central Bank was established in 1999 but represents the successful exportation of the German policy model to the European level (Busch 2005).

FROM ECONOMIC MIRACLE TO UNIFICATION

Recovery of the West German Economy

Prior to World War I, Germany was one of the world's largest trading nations, but afterward, war reparations and the Great Depression hit hard. The 1928–29 economic crisis, with skyrocketing unemployment, was a major reason the National Socialist party rose to power. In the 1930s, state subsidies and work programs sparked an economic revival; Hitler's economic policies relied on extensive state intervention, forced labor, and the exploitation of occupied territories.

The economic system that evolved after World War II adapted major components of late nineteenth-century institutional arrangements and practices to new conditions. The term social market economy came to characterize the German model of capitalism. Under this system, close relations between industrial employers and employees and a strong social safety net were not antithetical but complemented a free market. In the aftermath of defeat and disgrace, economic success helped to lift the country's international standing and sense of identity.

After the devastating war and immediate postwar period, Western Europeans finally started to enjoy some measure of economic stability and improved living standards in the 1950s. British historian Eric Hobsbawm (1994) refers to these years as the Golden Age; the French speak of the "thirty glorious years"; in Germany, this period is called the economic miracle (*Wirtschaftswunder*). Sooner than expected, West Germany reclaimed its place among free-market economies despite its separation from, and loss of, land in the east in 1945. By 1960, industrial production was 2.5 times that in 1950, exceeding the gains achieved by the Nazis' draconian and extortionate methods in 1930s Germany. The GDP rose by two-thirds; the number of employed surged from 13.8 million to 19.8 million; and the unemployment rate fell from 10.3 percent to 1.2 percent. Low unemployment, high demand for labor, and few temporary contracts resulted in high job security and increased wages until the 1970s. The standard of living rose substantially, and consumer goods became readily available. Cars, TVs, household conveniences such as washing machines, fashion goods, and vacation travel concretized the economic upturn for many. In the late 1950s, the government introduced new social programs and expanded others, such as pensions and social security. In many ways, West Germany championed the postwar consensus in Western Europe that linked a mixed economy to a social welfare state at odds with the US model (Nolan 2012). The economic miracle upon which the social model was built owed its origins to diverse factors, both international and domestic.

US Support

Toward the end of World War II, the Allied powers aimed to preclude revival of Germany's industrial prowess, but with the deterioration of relations with the Soviet Union, the onset of the Cold War, and commercial interests, the United States shifted gears and supported Western European economies, including Germany's, through the European Recovery Program (1948–51), better known as the *Marshall Plan*. The impact on the GDPs of the sixteen recipient countries was relatively minor and greatest in the United Kingdom, but having US backing provided a psychological boost. Significantly, funding depended on cooperation among the recipient countries and, in addition to encouraging structural and attitudinal changes in managing economies, facilitated later European integration. The success of the 1948 currency reform, which replaced the almost worthless Reichsmark, and a postwar economy based on barter and the black market with stable prices and goods, depended on the approval and support of the United States. When the Soviet Union cut off supplies to West Berlin to undermine Western action, the United States responded resolutely with the Berlin airlift. Keeping West Berliners supplied with goods and commodities ranging from coal to candy expressed US support for Germany against communism.

European Integration

US influence was only one side of the coin; the other was European. Mary Nolan, for example, contends that "Europeanization seems a more useful narrative thread to capture the transformations of the German economy from 1945 to the present, even if it is in constant conversation, and sometimes competition, with Americanization" (2014, 59). As a member of the European Coal and Steel Community (1952), the European Economic Community

(1958), and the European Atomic Energy Community (Euratom 1958), Germany benefited from increased trade with fellow members France, Italy, and the Benelux countries. These partnerships bolstered industrial modernization and international acceptance.

Social Market Economy

Against the backdrop of communism and the competition between socialist and conservative ideas for postwar economies in Western Europe, the idea of a mixed market economy had widespread appeal. As economic director and, later, Minister of Economic Affairs (1949–63), Ludwig Erhard eliminated price and production controls as part of currency reform against opposition from many quarters. These policies were influenced by the ordo-liberal economic school of thought, which champions the "free play" of market forces but relates them closely to fiscal stability and state regulations. The consensus among business and political leaders held that a free market economy would boost recovery but should be organized to strengthen the industrial base, ensure political stability, and control the money supply. Without directly regulating the economy, the state tried to create favorable market conditions complemented by a system of social provisions and transfer payments.

The economy thrived for most of the 1950s and became the backbone of a new German identity, substituting pride in modernization and economic progress for the fervid nationalism of the first part of the twentieth century. Herfried Münkler (2009, 455–90) submits that emotive appeal, not the balancing of pros and cons, is the crucial prerequisite for successful creation of national myths. Germany's founding myth became the economic miracle, while integration into Western alliance structures, particularly NATO and the EU, only refocused national interests. At its core were the people's work ethic and Erhard's vision; external factors played only a supporting role. The myth initially benefited the conservative parties CDU/CSU, but in the 1970s, SPD leaders coined the term *Modell Deutschland* to stake their claim. Pride in the stability of the German mark expressed pride in the system's economic performance; they merged as identity markers.

Economic Cycles and Reforms in the 1970s and 1980s

The West German economy was not immune to crises. Construction of the Berlin Wall in 1961 cut off the supply of labor from East Germany; a guest worker program that started modestly in 1955 was extended rapidly in the 1960s and enabled continued economic growth and expansion; workers from Italy, Greece, Turkey, and other Mediterranean countries migrated to the industrial centers of the West.

In terms of economic policy, the Grand Coalition government between CDU/CSU and SPD (1966–69) veered toward more state intervention based largely on Keynesian principles. Minister of Economics Karl Schiller (SPD) argued strongly for legislation that would give the federal government and his ministry greater authority. He was convinced that governments had both the obligation and capacity to shape economic trends and to smooth and even eliminate economic cycles. Four sets of data—currency stability, economic growth, employment levels, and trade balance—were thenceforth used to measure Germany's economic success.

SPD-FDP coalitions from 1969 to 1982 expanded the social security system, thereby increasing social budget expenditures. The expansion of educational opportunities for lower and middle-class students also received priority and included the construction of new universities. Mechanisms to strengthen cooperation between employers and employees were implemented, and unions exerted greater influence on policy decisions.

When Chancellor Brandt was forced to resign in 1974 due to a spy scandal, Helmut Schmidt (SPD) faced new challenges in the international realm, particularly the dramatic upsurge in oil prices in 1973–74, which led to a decline in global demand for oil. Given Germany's dependence on the import of oil, the sense of vulnerability and crisis was imminent. For a limited time, a "car-free Sunday" was introduced to save gasoline. By 1976, the economy had recovered, and Schmidt's success led him and his party to claim that they built *Modell Deutschland*. The term captures the peculiar combination of market economy and state regulation that enabled the country to navigate the recession with aplomb.

Chancellor Helmut Kohl (CDU) implemented some of the neoliberal policies heralded by British Prime Minister Margaret Thatcher and US President Ronald Reagan in the 1980s, but with less fervor. Expenditures, taxes, and government restrictions and regulations were reduced, and the flexibility of the labor market improved. His government also executed a series of privatization measures, selling shares of various state-owned institutions, such as Volkswagen, Lufthansa, and Salzgitter, a major steel producer. The state's role in the economy declined, but recovery remained sluggish; growth and inflation figures improved only marginally; few jobs were created, and high unemployment persisted, reaching four million by the end of the decade. Only in the late 1980s did the economy begin to grow again, but unemployment declined only slightly.

Economic Opportunities and Costs of Unification

In the GDR, leaders legitimized their rule with recourse to antifascist roots and ideals, but this rationale resonated with the public for only so long. The lack of democratic freedoms coupled with the shortcomings of a strictly planned economy characterized by fixed production targets and state oversight of all sectors could not compete with the open and free markets in the West. For citizens behind the "Iron Curtain," Western freedoms were inseparable from "perceptions of material abundance" (Kopstein 1997, 4). All communist systems struggled with these challenges, especially when the ideology wore thin, and political acquiescence was built on the promise of economic delivery. However, the standard of living was increasingly hard to improve, and by the late 1970s, governments across Central and Eastern Europe relied on subsidies from the Soviet Union and loans from Western institutions.

The East German economy may have been the "brightest star in the region," but it shone "in an otherwise dim socialist economic universe" (Kopstein 1997, 3). SED functionaries were in an especially precarious position since citizens compared their economic status less with fellow communist states than with West Germany's. To promote economic and technological development, the government made East Germany dependent on West German hard currency, received in exchange for the release of political prisoners, as visa payments, and, in 1983 and 1984, as part of commercial bank loans. The decay of economic performance helped to topple the communist regime, and after the opening of the Berlin Wall in November 1989, the draw of West German currency, consumer goods, and overall prosperity propelled unification, which was quick and unexpected. In the long run, it created new economic opportunities, but the immediate impact was a deep economic crisis that lasted into the mid-2000s.

In fall 1989 and spring 1990, the implosion of the communist government unleashed immense pressure for fast political, economic, and financial solutions. The first democratic election in the GDR (March 18, 1990) resulted in a coalition government that advocated swift unification with West Germany. On May 18, 1990, the two German states signed the Treaty Establishing a Monetary, Economic and Social Union between the German Democratic Republic and the Federal Republic of Germany, enacted on July 1, 1990, with the Deutschmark replacing the East German mark as the official currency. With this treaty, East Germany transferred its financial policy sovereignty to West Germany, and the west moved to subsidize the eastern budget and social security system. The fiscal and currency union created a viable framework for the political union that followed on October 3, 1990. Deliberately building on the founding narrative of the Federal Republic—currency reform, then economic miracle—Chancellor Helmut Kohl promised that unification would deliver, not only the German mark, but also "flowering landscapes" (Kopstein 1997, 200; Münkler 2009, 474–75). In the 1990s, desolate factories and deserted lands denied the flowery promises, and the project of German unity was strained.

The large-scale restructuring of a planned economy into a functioning market-based economy proved far more challenging than anticipated. In the uncertain terrain of trial and error, East Germany had distinct advantages over other postcommunist countries undertaking a similar project. West German economic institutions and practices could be transferred along with western expertise and workforce, and massive financial transfers buffered such social hardships as rising unemployment. However, advantages were freighted with challenges. Some policies introduced in the transition period were hastily designed and politically motivated. In particular, the unrealistically high exchange rate of East to West German currency (1:1 for wages and salaries and 1:2 for financial assets) together with wage pressure made eastern goods virtually obsolete; former export destinations in Central and Eastern Europe and the soon-to-be former Soviet Union could no longer afford them.

Tweaking the West German economic system to postcommunist circumstances had other limits. Specifically, most East German companies could not compete on the global market, and productivity was less than half that of the west. Infrastructure in the east needed fundamental modernization; environmental degradation due to socialist industrialization and the industrialist expansion of agricultural production was intolerable in many regions. Restructuring the economy would require large-scale privatization since all large and most small firms had been state-owned. The Trustee Agency (*Treuhand*), which played a unique role in the privatization of state-owned assets, required investors to submit a business plan outlining modernization concepts but lacked the authority to follow up or enforce them. Many eastern German companies were turned over to investors who later closed them; by late 1994, only 350 of 1,378 enterprises survived (Kopstein 1997, 201). Industrial production plummeted, and large regions deindustrialized, causing high unemployment. Early retirement was the only option for many people over the age of fifty-five, and those who remained employed often had to change jobs and undergo training and retraining. Aside from personal hardship, these measures put a financial strain on social coffers and eastern German citizens. Optimistic expectations for a swift economic transformation were replaced on both sides of the former Iron Curtain by talk of "unification crisis." High unemployment remained a problem for the new Länder well into the 2000s, peaking at 18.7 percent in 2005, but it has since declined steadily (see table 6.4).

Fast forward to 2015: a transfer of funds estimated at over two trillion euro has reshaped the eastern German economic landscape. The physical infrastructure has been modernized to an enviable level; the standard of living has markedly improved, and productivity has more than doubled since 1991. Still, unemployment remains higher, and productivity lower in the east than

142   Chapter 6

Table 6.4. Unemployment in West and East Germany, 1995–2015
(in percent)

Year	Germany	West Germany	East Germany
1995	9.4	8.1	13.9
2000	9.6	7.6	17.1
2005	11.5	9.9	18.7
2010	8.6	7.4	13.4
2015	6.4	5.7	9.2

Source: Bundesagentur für Arbeit: *Arbeitslosigkeit im Zeitverlauf 01/2016.*

the west (see tables 6.4 and 6.5). Income and wealth disparities between the
regions persist. The solidarity surcharge (*Solidaritätszuschlag*), an additional
fee on the income tax, capital gains tax, and corporate tax was introduced in
1991 and remains in place today. It was justified to help with the costs of unification, the Gulf War, and assistance to the countries in Central and Eastern
Europe. Importantly, the federal government and the Länder agreed to yearly
transfer payments to defray the costs of the political, economic, and social
transformation of the eastern Länder (Solidarity Pact I and II). Payments under this system will expire in 2019, but financial support of approximately ten
billion euro per year will continue to help deprived regions and communities
in the east and west.

Perhaps most important, the economic landscape in the east is a patchwork
of booming cities and rather desolate towns. The first draw new investments
and create jobs; the latter have declining populations since job opportunities
for qualified young people are scarce. Variation among regions and between
urban and rural areas is pronounced, and statements about east versus west re-

Table 6.5. West-East German Comparison of Selected Economic Data

	West Germany*		East Germany*	
	1991	2015	1991	2015
Population (in millions)	61.9	65.5	14.6	12.5
Labor force (in millions)	27.2	31.8	6.44	5.27
Unemployed (in millions)	1.60	2.02	1.01	0.77
GDP (in billions euros)	1,404.6	2,570.9	107.4	330.8
GDP per capita (in euros)	22,687	39,270	7,342	26,453
Compensation (in billions euros)	731.8	1,305.6	84.8	170.3
Compensation per employee (in euros)	26,895	40,994	13,164	32,340

*Without Berlin.

Source: Adapted from "Jahresbericht der Bundesregierung zum Stand der Deutschen Einheit 2016," edited
by Bundesministerium für Wirtschaft und Energie (Berlin: Bundesministerium für Wirtschaft und Energie,
2016), 98.

quire qualifiers since economic diversification increasingly runs along north/ south trajectories. The economic impact of these changes is not restricted to the eastern Länder, although they bore the brunt. The German welfare system was under pressure to reform before unification; the "price of German unity" (Ritter 2011) strained it further, and global market expansion added costs. In response, Germany's capitalist model required adjustments.

REFORMING THE MODEL

German unification occurred when Western capitalist systems were also under duress. Initially, reforming the German social and economic systems to meet the challenges of rising unemployment and budget deficits was put on the back burner; the problems associated with unification were too critical, and energy and resources were channeled into rebuilding the economy in the new Länder. However, the pressure mounted. Critics cited high labor costs, persistent structural unemployment, soaring healthcare expenditures, and dated social institutions, such as universities and schools, as reasons for lack of competitiveness in the emerging global market. "The unease that East Germans brought to united Germany came to be increasingly matched by the malaise emerging in the wider society" (Maier 1997, 329). By the end of the 1990s, debates about reform blockage (*Reformstau*) dominated the domestic discourse. In the early 2000s, reforms targeting labor market practices and the social welfare system began in earnest.

Labor Market Reform and Agenda 2010

Responding to the rising costs of welfare state policies, structural changes in the labor market, and globalization pressures, most European countries introduced major changes to their social systems throughout the 1990s. Herbert Kitschelt (2000, 218) wondered whether "the two midwives of policy innovation could be crisis and leadership." He was proven correct. As crisis indicators, particularly high unemployment, mounted, much-needed reforms were finally delivered in 2003 by a leftist government of SPD and Alliance 90/The Greens. Agenda 2010 was a comprehensive package that overhauled labor market policies and the pension system and cut taxes and healthcare benefits. The so-called Hartz reforms—after Peter Hartz, then-director of Volkswagen and head of the government-established commission—introduced thirteen "innovation modules" that were divided into distinct packages. Hartz I–III measures were implemented between January 1, 2003 and 2004, and Hartz IV went into effect on January 1, 2005.

The policy changes associated with Hartz IV were highly controversial. They restructured unemployment benefits, introduced welfare-to-work and retraining programs, and remodeled the government agencies that administer unemployment claims and benefits. The duration of unemployment benefits was shortened and mandatory retraining introduced. The reforms drew mass protests and criticism from the unions and the left wing of the SPD, which formed a new party, the Labor and Social Justice Party (WASG). It later merged with the PDS under the name The Left. Particularly unpopular among workers, these policies hastened the end of the Red-Green coalition government; elections were called one year early.

The Financial Crisis of 2008–9

The global financial crisis set off by the subprime mortgage and financial crisis in the United States acted as a catalyst for the eurocrisis (see chapter 7) and also affected Germany. Immediately following the collapse of Lehman Brothers and other US financial institutions, German banks and finance organizations connected to US partners faced turmoil. In 2008, a first bank "rescue package" was implemented; large banks, such as Hypo Real Estate and Commerzbank, were the first to receive government aid followed by several smaller banks on the state level (*Landesbanken*). The government hastened to assure citizens that "savings are safe," yet public trust quickly eroded. The deep crisis in many European countries negatively affected German exports, which declined sharply in 2009, lowering the overall growth rate to -5 percent. Facing an even more severe crisis in 2010, the German government introduced a large stimulus package targeting investments in public infrastructure, traffic, public building renovations, and tax relief for small businesses; it was the largest stimulus program in postwar Germany.

The Debt Brake

Keeping public debt in check was a concern from the moment the euro was designed and implemented. The convergence criteria that set the basis for acceptance into the eurozone and the criteria governing the euro both stipulated a debt-to-GDP ratio that could not be exceeded, but many eurozone member countries, Germany among them, could not adhere. The German finance minister attributed the country's inability to comply to the high costs of unification and evaded official sanctions from Brussels.

Rising public debt is a concern in all postindustrial democracies. Governments struggle to find ways to limit spending and the public deficit. Some, including the United States, introduced debt ceilings. Sweden uses expenditure ceilings, and the United Kingdom, spending reviews. Switzerland implemented a so-called debt brake in 2003. In Germany, public debt rose substantially in the 1990s, dipped in the mid-2000s, but rose again when the financial crisis unfolded. In 2009, the Bundestag and Bundesrat agreed to amend the constitution by introducing a debt brake (Art. 109, 3). In contrast to a debt ceiling, which tries to limit new credits, a debt brake requires balanced budgets and limits expenditures without recourse to new public borrowing. It also encourages the federal government to apply fiscal policy to moderate economic cycles. Budgetary surpluses in economic boom periods should temper expenditures during economic downturns. Barring exceptional circumstances, such as a severe economic crisis or natural disaster, the federal government cannot run a structural deficit of more than 0.35 percent of the GDP.

The new regulations went into effect in 2011, but a transition period allowed time for adjustments. Mandatory enforcement of the debt provisions for the central government started in 2016, although in 2015, for the first time since 1969, a balanced budget had been achieved. Länder governments will have to balance their budgets when the debt brake begins for them in 2020.

These measures are not without controversy. For example, exceptions and loopholes, such as outsourcing public debt to special agencies and institutions, raise doubt about the transparency of implementation. Some economists, concerned about the effects of borrowing limits on investment and economic growth, disagree with the government about the benefits of a strict debt brake.

REVISITING THE GERMAN MODEL

A Changing Labor Market

Labor market reforms, wage restraint, and strong export demand are the cornerstones of Germany's economic recovery. They enabled companies to preserve and expand traditional markets and to weather the consequences of the economic crisis of 2008–9 better than those in many other European countries. The measures associated with Agenda 2010 sought to bolster Germany's attractiveness as a business location and, in a climate of high unemployment, to provide job security for those who had jobs, instead of risking more layoffs due to high labor costs. Unions and employers shifted away from industry-wide collective bargaining agreements, which used to be the norm, toward plant-level agreements to stem wage increases. These measures contributed to the rapid export increase and a swift drop in unemployment from an alarming 11.7 percent in 2005 to 6.1 percent in 2016.

However, reforms came at a price. Real wages have increased as of late but only after a period of decline, which has had important consequences for consumption and investment. Employment patterns today differ distinctly from those in the early 1990s. Not all workers are protected equally. Anke Hassel (2014) argues that liberalization and coordination patterns, hallmarks of the German CME, complement, rather than oppose, one another. They protect core workers but also accommodate flexible, lower-paying jobs. Kathleen Thelen (2014) makes a similar argument: even the more egalitarian system of CMEs, when under pressure to liberalize, respond with institutional change. In Germany, the core institutions have survived, but the principle of social solidarity has been undermined. The dual labor market protects the privileges of those who have jobs but discriminates against those who are unemployed or in precarious jobs.

Conditions for acquiring long-term or unlimited work contracts have changed, as time-limited and part-time jobs replace full-time careers. The range of low-paid, so-called mini-jobs, has increased, in particular allowing many women to enter the workforce at lower pay scales but eroding job security, benefit entitlements, and levels of social security support. In addition, a growing number of young employees, many with academic degrees, work on term-limited, part-time contracts, often without benefits. "Generation internship" is a trend in a country proud of its work ethic and highly trained, well-organized workforce. Many citizens entering the labor market find less favorable terms than in the past, and the inequalities increase over their lifespans (Bönke, Giesecke, and Lüthen 2015). Precarious forms of employment may also endanger the long-term goals of high productivity and competitiveness in an increasingly knowledge-based economy. The rapid expansion in low-paid and short-term employment and the decline in sector-wide collective wage agreements negotiated by unions and employers continued even after Germany emerged from the eurocrisis.

Social Inequality and Poverty

The shift toward neoliberal policies since the 1980s has increased social inequality. While the middle- and upper-income groups see higher incomes and assets, people in low-income groups, often stuck in precarious employment, have stagnated. German discourse introduced the term two-thirds society (*Zweidrittelgesellschaft*) in the 1980s to describe the growing gap between the middle-income two-thirds and the low-income and poor one-third. The Gini coefficient is a widely used statistical measure to gauge a society's inequality; it does not measure relative wealth but the distribution of income between rich and poor. A zero indicates complete equality; one, perfect inequality. Often, the coefficient is multiplied by 100 and expressed in percentages, and in 2015, it stood at 31 percent for the EU member states. At 30.1 percent, Germany is in the midrange of all advanced industrialized countries but decidedly lower than the United States and higher than the Nordic countries.

Income distribution is linked to the relatively high percentage of people who live at the poverty level or in danger of slipping to it. The EU defines the "risk of poverty and social exclusion" as income below 60 percent of a country's median income, and reporting on poverty in Germany, the German Joint Welfare Association adopted this definition. In 2014, the median income was 917 euro per month for a one-person household, and 1,926 euro for a family of four. The report warned that although poverty declined slightly from 2013 to 2014, it was still at 15.4 percent, affecting about 12.5 million people. Hardest hit are the unemployed, single parents, children, and, increasingly, the elderly. Former part-time employees and many women who interrupted their professional career to care for children are among those whose pensions often no longer guarantee a decent standard of living in old age. Leaving aside the western city-state of Bremen, the poverty rate was higher in the east than in the west, but regions differ greatly (Deutscher Paritätischer Wohlfahrtsverband 2016).

Minimum Wage

The overwhelming majority of EU countries have a minimum wage policy, albeit at different rates. Germany set one only recently, although labor union and left-wing SPD members had long demanded it. In contrast to a time when unions and employers annually negotiated and agreed on wage regulation, the minimum wage is a statutory arrangement, and the government took the lead. In summer 2014, the law passed with 535 out of 630 votes; only five MPs voted against it, and the Left Party abstained. About 17 percent of workers in the west and 27 percent in the east were projected to benefit. The law has been in force since January 2015; the minimum wage (as of 2017) was 8.84 euro per hour, up from 8.50 euro when it was introduced in 2015. The law did not affect higher wages negotiated by unions and employers but covers low-wage workers in temporary or insecure employment, who are not included in collective bargaining agreements. These groups often had to supplement their income with social welfare to make ends meet. The introduction of a minimum wage adjusted but did not reverse earlier labor market reforms (Mabbatt 2016). Until 2018, several exceptions to the minimum wage apply; critics fear that these exceptions as well as the low figure will undermine guarantees of a decent standard of living through work.

What brought about this policy reversal? Several factors came into play, particularly a shift in favor of the policy among the governing SPD and criticism from economists both inside and outside of Germany for not investing enough in its human capital. Unions were divided. Service, food, and public sector unions favored adoption of a minimum wage. Others, such as the traditionally influential metal workers' union and the chemical workers' union feared the negative consequences on their collective bargaining power (Behrens and Pekarek 2016). Employers' associations and free-market proponents had long opposed minimum wage regulations, but paradoxically, market liberalization and intense global competition may have reduced their ability to act strategically to fend off government regulations. In the end, minimum wage advocates prevailed, arguing that the economic system had failed to deliver a decent wage for many workers and placed an undue burden on the social system that had to supplement inadequate incomes with (public) social assistance.

Social Partnership and Neocorporatism Redefined

The West German system of industrial relations privileged close employer-employee cooperation and supported it with labor laws, labor courts, and parapublic institutions, particularly the Federal Employment Agency (Silvia 2013, 41). The current status of these relations is contested. In a Europeanized and globalized market, national solutions to economic problems carry less weight, and the shift from industrial to service-centered economies has changed the function of labor unions and the significance of the social partnership. A few numbers illustrate the decline: in 1950, 42.5 percent of the West German workforce was employed in the industrial sector (agriculture 24.6 percent; services 32.5 percent); in 1990, the percentage was 36.6 (agriculture 3.5 percent, services 59.9 percent); by 2015, for the unified Germany, it had shrunk to 24.4 percent (agriculture 1.5 percent, services 74.1 percent).

In addition, the drastic restructuring of the eastern German economy, coupled with high unemployment, undermined the role of work councils. Companies sought to lower labor costs, and fewer and fewer workers were covered under wage settlements reached by the industry-wide collective bargaining that had been the norm. The number of employees covered under such regularly (mostly annually) negotiated bargaining agreements is still higher in the west (2015: 51 percent) than in the east (2015: 37 percent), and although overall, values and orientations still emphasize cooperation between employers and employees (Behrens 2015), firm-level agreements have become more common.

The neocorporatist system in Germany evolved in the 1960s and 1970s. Corporate or economic interests have more influence than other societal groups, and the state plays the important role of mediator. It captures the arrangement in many advanced capitalist societies favoring state regulation, collective bargaining, and strong unions (Streeck 2009). Close cooperation among the major economic actors and the state aims to increase international competitiveness and to manage economic challenges efficiently; it worked well in smaller Western European countries, such as Austria, and countries with a strong, unified labor movement, such as Germany.

In Germany, the state's role has centered less on direct intervention and more on setting framework conditions through laws, courts, and parapublic institutions. Tripartite bargaining among state, unions, and employers has been reserved for times of economic crisis, and here, patterns have changed. In 1996 and between 1998 and 2003, a so-called Alliance for Work involving the government, employers, and unions failed to reach agreements on labor market reforms. In contrast, at the onset of the financial crisis in 2008, in three summit meetings with the chancellor, the government, employers, and unions successfully negotiated programs to stimulate the economy (Anders, Biebeler, and Lesch 2015, 30–31). The new minimum wage circumvented the established tripartite relationship, with the state taking the lead.

ENERGY POLICY IN GERMANY

Energy legislation has a long trajectory due to the highly resource-dependent German economy (see table 6.6) and reflects national, European, and global developments. The ambitious 2010 and 2011 energy transition (*Energiewende*) proposes to achieve efficiency and security by cutting demand and greenhouse gas emissions and curbing overreliance on imported resources. Can such a highly industrialized nation achieve the proposed goals for energy efficiency and sustainability? Will Germany be a trendsetter or an outlier in the concert of European states? Do national initiatives about renewable energy coexist with or supersede EU frameworks? The policy shift raises questions with relevance beyond Germany's borders.

Germany's Energy Evolution

Historically, the coal mines of the Ruhr Valley and, until the end of World War II, Silesia (now part of Poland) were major energy providers, accelerating the growth and development of steel production and such large-scale industries as automobile manufacturing, shipbuilding, machinery, and rail infrastructure. In West Germany, coal was considered so indispensable that

Table 6.6. Comparison of Energy Dependence and Consumption in the EU

	2012	*2014*	
	CO_2 Emission per Resident (tons)	*Energy Dependence (%)*	*Renewable Energies/ Final Gross Energy Consumption (%)*
Germany	10.0	61.6	13.8
France	5.7	46.1	14.3
Italy	6.5	75.9	17.1
Poland	8.4	28.6	11.4
Spain	5.9	72.9	16.2
United Kingdom	7.6	46.5	7.0

Source: https://www.destatis.de/Europa/DE/Staat/Vergleich/DEUVergleich.html.

the government largely subsidized its production, and along with steel, it supported the successful economic model. However, in the 1960s, with oil readily available on the world market and nuclear energy a promising new energy source, coal lost its significance as the backbone of modernization. Resources were limited, and production became more and more costly.

The shift from coal to oil was rudely interrupted in the 1970s, when the rise of the Organization of the Petroleum Exporting Countries (OPEC) demonstrated just how vulnerable a resource-poor country like Germany was. At the same time, public awareness of the environmental costs of economic growth increased, and political parties responded, not least because of the Green Party's success in attracting voters and attention. Diversification was again on the agenda. Nuclear energy expanded but never reached the significance it had in other countries, such as the United States and France. Next to coal and lignite, gas and oil imported from the Soviet Union became major energy sources, and new pipelines were built in the 1980s.

Unification did not solve the energy question. East Germany was equally resource-poor, relying on lignite, which is economically less efficient than hard coal, and production was in dire need of modernization; many lignite-producing sites closed after 1990. East German nuclear plants were deemed unsafe and phased out. The push toward renewable energy was one of the many unintended consequences of unification. Christoph H. Stefes (2010) argues that energy providers and others who opposed carbon-free sources were busy setting up a new utility network in the eastern part of the country, thereby inadvertently allowing passage of a new utilities law that introduced the feed-in tariff model. Feed-in tariffs come in different forms, but they share the goal of accelerating renewable energy use through long-term contracts. Germany pioneered one that guarantees long-term price stability and the ability to sell renewable energy to the grid; many other countries have emulated the plan. In 2014, new legislation substantially altered the feed-in tariff provisions and set targets for the share of renewable energy in electricity consumption—40–45 percent by 2020; 55–60 percent by 2035.

By the late 1980s, Germany was a leader in wind energy technology, surpassed only by pioneering Denmark and, later, the Netherlands. Research in other renewable energy technologies advanced, and small and medium-sized companies began to specialize in their development and production. Even though parliament voted to curb subsidies for wind energy in 2016, it remains Germany's major renewable energy source. Today, windmills define the landscape, and large wind energy production sites are located offshore in the North Sea. Storage and transport still need improvement, and several companies, universities, and technical colleges are involved in research and development. Wind energy is the fastest-growing renewable energy source, and cross-border cooperation with the Netherlands, for example, accelerates technological progress. Germany's investments in renewable energy now rank third in the world, after China and the United States.

Nuclear Power and the Energy Transition

Germany was one of the first European countries to build and use nuclear power plants. As early as 1970, the first plant began operating in the north, and several others followed. However, support dwindled as questions about waste management, high research and development costs, and risk remained unresolved. Vocal popular protest never ceased, especially because most of the plants were located close to densely populated areas.

The search for alternatives to nuclear power intensified in reaction to the April 1986 accident at the Chernobyl Nuclear Power Plant in what is now Ukraine but was then part of the Soviet Union. It released radioactive clouds that drifted over most of northern and central Europe. Left-of-center parties had long favored other energy sources, and leadership change in 1998 provided the opportunity to follow rhetoric with action. A hallmark of the SPD and Alliance 90/The Greens government (1998–2005) was 2001 legislation to phase out nuclear power (*Atomausstieg*) and to accelerate the development of renewable energy. This decision, though strongly opposed by the energy sector, the FDP, and parts of the CDU, held until 2010.

In 2010, the government of Angela Merkel (CDU) outlined goals for a complete energy policy overhaul. International climate-change negotiations within the framework of the UN were well under way, and the EU strongly supported internationally binding benchmarks. Merkel's policy aimed to augment energy supply options and to achieve energy security within the next forty years (Federal Ministry of Economics and Technology 2015). CO_2

emissions were to be reduced by 80 percent, primary energy consumption by 50 percent, and renewable resources increased to at least 80 percent of the energy mix by 2050. In a reversal of previous policy, the lifespan of nuclear power plants was extended but then quickly annulled. In summer 2011, new legislation mandated the immediate closure of older nuclear power plants and phasing out nuclear energy altogether by 2022. The catalyst was the Fukushima nuclear disaster in March 2011, but the ground was prepared by the high costs of nuclear waste management, concern about energy security, and growing inter-European energy cooperation. With an already apprehensive public and upcoming regional elections, Germany followed other countries phasing out (Belgium and non-EU member Switzerland) or abjuring nuclear energy entirely (Austria, Denmark, Greece, Italy, Portugal, and the Baltic states). Replacement energy sources are in development, and despite the cost, the public supports the turnaround.

Recycling and the Environment

To halt or reverse climate change by reducing emissions and replacing fossil fuels with renewable energy sources is a main objective of energy policies. Legislation promotes energy efficiency and energy-saving strategies through tax breaks and subsidies, among other mechanisms. Reducing energy use is complemented by policies to salvage materials, and this strategy applies not only to factories and production sites but everyday life. Germany is a European leader in recycling community waste; according to some figures, 87 percent is recycled. Extensive local recycling programs were a major feature of German public policy even before unification; both West and East Germany encouraged citizens to recycle paper, glass, and metal, although for different reasons. In the east, early recycling programs were motivated by resource poverty; in the west, the major impetus was overflowing landfills. Today, children are taught to save energy and to recycle trash. Every household has separate bins for glass, paper, biowaste, and other trash, which are collected by communal waste services, and citizens can discharge large quantities of specialized items at central public locations free of charge. A second system shares the burden of collecting, sorting, and recycling packaging materials; businesses are obliged to accept and to recycle packaging according to a complex system of green and yellow dots on products. Refundable deposits on bottles are common. Recycling rules vary from place to place and can be cumbersome. Searching "recycling in Germany" on the Internet, you will find lighthearted good advice on how to steer clear of trouble with the neighbors to participate in the national passion!

Future Challenges

Despite favorable developments and considerable political and public support, the German energy transition has encountered problems, including opposition from parts of the energy sector. Large energy providers, who are highly organized, seek support from the federal government, but the government considers the companies responsible for the transition to an adequate energy mix. Goals set in 2014 can be changed or dropped if they prove too costly or meet resistance from key corporate players and the share of fossil energy sources such as coal remains high.

Consumer costs are another concern. Energy prices have increased three-fold since the transition began, and they are among the highest in Europe. While so far consumers have been willing to pay, critics argue that energy companies should provide affordable supplies; energy companies contend that they must pay for developing technological innovations. Some critics also fear that rising prices harm industrial competitiveness.

Other items on the agenda include the need to modernize the power grid, unresolved technological problems associated with transportation and longer storage of renewable resources, the continued reliance on coal, and the slow progress in reducing greenhouse gas emissions.

Energy Policy and the EU

Energy and environmental policies cannot be solved solely at the national level, but national leaders and policies can set examples. Germany works through international organizations, particularly the EU, to reach its goals. Over the past two decades, the EU has become an important actor in energy policy, increasing its engagement in energy security and budgetary outlays for climate-related policy initiatives promoting renewable energies. It is a trendsetter in international negotiations on climate change and takes an active role in UN-related climate initiatives.

Energy Security

Energy security and the push for renewable energy drive European energy policy. Better coordination of energy policies would make EU member states less dependent on imports from conflict-ridden regions or authoritarian regimes. High on the agenda is reducing imports from Russia, but cost considerations have deepened long-standing disputes over the relative priority of environmental and climate-related policies and energy security. The Russian-Ukrainian crisis revitalized European concerns about disruptions in the natural gas supply as experienced in 2006 and 2009, and the EU changed its supply chain, further diversifying imports and better connecting member states. After 2004, Russian natural gas imports to the EU declined, but they rebounded in 2014, albeit to a lower level—37.5 percent as opposed to 43.6 percent in 2004. The share of Russian solid fuels stood at 29.0 percent in 2014 (2004: 18 percent), and Russia remains the main supplier of Europe's oil and natural gas (Eurostat 2016b).

Environmental Policy and Renewables

The reach of EU economic policies has increased, and the energy sector illustrates the spillover effects from one policy area to another envisioned by the architects of European integration. Looking back at its history, energy played an important role from the very beginning. Coal was a crucial resource in the postwar years, and cooperation within the internal market for coal and steel, both crucial for war production, diminished fears of a German rise to power among the European allies, notably France. After the European Coal and Steel Community (1952), the Treaty Establishing the European Atomic Energy Community, or Euratom (1958), created an international organization to address nuclear power in Europe. The Treaty of Lisbon (2009) advanced the goal of a common European energy policy while guaranteeing individual member countries limited sovereignty in determining the sources and structure of their energy supply.

Although not mentioned in the founding treaties of 1958, growing concern about pollution and global warming made environmental policy integral to the EU agenda. Its Renewable Energy Directive (2009) established binding benchmarks to increase renewable energy sources to 20 percent and, in the transport sector, 10 percent of the energy mix. The directive is part of the 20-20-20 climate and energy package, which also mandates a 20 percent reduction in greenhouse gas emissions and a 20 percent improvement in energy efficiency over 1990 levels. In February 2015, it launched a European "energy union" to drive the "transition to a low carbon, secure and competitive economy" (Eurostat 2016a). Its guidelines and directives are in line with the 2015 Paris Climate Change goals; member states agreed to comply with the overall goal to limit greenhouse gas emissions.

The energy mix and dependence ratio vary widely among EU member states, as do their policy preferences (Strunz, Gawel, and Lehmann 2014). The share of renewable energy has been expanded significantly in some countries, where wind (Denmark, Netherlands, United Kingdom), solar (Spain), and water (Austria) power account for a significant portion of the energy market. In several countries, local communities have generated innovative sustainability projects. Although a common EU energy market is not in place, voluntary bilateral and multilateral cross-border cooperation is increasingly common and constitutes a form of Europeanization that occurs without centralized decision making.

Germany and several other member countries are on schedule to meet the EU targets. For example, in 2015, renewable energy production (wind, biomass, solar, hydropower) generated 29 percent of German electricity, followed by lignite (24.0 percent), hard coal (18.3 percent), natural gas (9.4 percent), nuclear energy (14.2 percent), and oil (0.9 percent). Efforts in the areas of heating and transportation must follow. Electric cars, for example, account for a very small percentage of transportation options (Bundesministerium für Wirtschaft und Energie 2016).

THE GERMAN ECONOMIC MODEL IN MOTION

Germany's economic performance has seen ups and downs prompted by domestic and international developments and crises, and because it is the EU's leading economic power, these changes are followed closely all over the world. In the early 1980s, West Germany looked miraculous compared to its neighbors—that is, until the "performance crisis" of the 1990s, when two intimate observers of German politics and economics suggested that "there is little hope for the German political system to overcome its present immobility, making continued social and economic decline the most likely scenario for the future" (Kitschelt and Streeck 2004, 2).

Twenty years later, headlines tout Germany's strong economy, stable politics, and rising international status when many other European countries are struggling. Germany mastered the financial crisis quite well and its economic strength is back both at home and abroad (Dustmann et al. 2014). However, economic stability is not without challenges. The labor market has witnessed both positive and negative changes. The competitiveness of German goods has grown, but any country that depends on exports will be affected by the increasingly hostile debates about economic globalization, including criticism of trade imbalances from partners and calls for lower taxes and more investment (Jacoby 2017). Technological development poses another constant challenge. For example, German car manufacturing—one of the leading export commodities—must transition from fuel-based technology to electricity. In 2016, automaker Volkswagen announced a large-scale restructuring program, laying off 30,000 workers and shifting to more advanced electro-car production technology. Other companies may follow; with fierce international competition, pressure on the relatively open German economy to advance cutting-edge technologies is increasing. The European market remains most important, but export destinations have become diversified, and trade with the Americas and China is increasing.

Germany has also seen major shifts in energy policy based on its resource dependence, concern about climate change and environmental degradation, and unease about nuclear power. The EU not only provides a vibrant market for exports; it has also become the frame for new energy technology development, research, and benchmarking practices. Germany is a bold trendsetter, conceptualizing a complete overhaul of its energy supply, but success largely depends on further European cooperation. Only if the EU as a whole works to achieve greater energy security and deeper integration will Germany realize its ambitions.

Radical change is not a hallmark of German economic policy. Rather, the country fine-tunes its institutions and alters the mechanisms of its economy without abandoning the core features of its CME. Once again, these changes illustrate that once chosen, pathways persist. Cultural preferences and institutional structures have deep roots, and adjustment processes evolve slowly. Building on traditional strengths, such as a highly skilled labor force, solid vocational training, and cooperative industrial relations, has served the country well, but the triple challenges of unification, the eurozone crisis, and globalization challenged traditional approaches. Germany must be able to adjust them to new concepts.

Chapter 7

Germany and the European Union

KEY TERMS

Brexit
democratic deficit
European integration
EU enlargement
EU history
EU institutions
EU treaties

Euroskepticism
eurozone crisis
future of Europe
intergovernmentalism
neofunctionalism
supranationalism

Challenges to European integration have defined Angela Merkel's chancellorship. Shortly after her election in 2005, her government took the lead in negotiating the Treaty of Lisbon, which amended existing treaties and salvaged elements of the stillborn treaty that would have established a European Constitution. In 2010, the eurozone crisis usurped attention, and German leadership's hesitant, austerity-centered approach was widely criticized abroad. With the refugee crisis of summer and fall 2015, Merkel took a more decisive yet still controversial role in pushing for coordinated EU policies. Other potentially destabilizing developments loomed: the rise of Euroskeptic parties and movements across the continent, democratic decay in some Central and Eastern member states, Russian grandstanding in Ukraine, and the autocratic turn in Turkey before and after the failed military coup of 2016. The 2016 referendum in the United Kingdom and the subsequent decision by the British government to leave the EU added to the list of woes. Anti-EU and antiestablishment sentiments have reinforced each other, and the future of the EU is under review. Germany is not immune to Euroskepticism, but so far its impact has been more restrained than dramatic.

Germany's preoccupation with European affairs is not surprising. Being "European" is part of German identity; the country exercises most aspects of its foreign and security policy as a member of multinational organizations, primarily the EU. The relationship is reciprocal; EU progress and global standing rely on Germany's active participation and often leadership. The British news magazine *The Economist*, not prone to hyperbole, called Angela Merkel and, by implication, Germany, an "indispensable European" (*Economist* 2015b). Emerging strains in relations between the United States and the EU during the first months of the Trump presidency reinforced Germany's crucial role in the Western alliance.

A brief overview of the history of European integration after World War II provides the framework for a discussion of selected policies. We will introduce the reader to the EU's institutional organization and then elaborate on Germany's position, preferences, and policies. Economic integration is at the core of the European project, and we will discuss the significance of the eurozone crisis and Germany's handling of it. We will analyze the intersection of German and European interests with reference to the EU's expansion into Central and Eastern Europe. Germany acted as a driver for including these countries, and EU enlargement is usually viewed as a positive factor in their political and economic transformation. The prolonged and, for the time being, aborted negotiations with Turkey about full membership in the EU also demonstrate some of the unpredictability of expansion. In the next section we explore the UK decision to leave the EU—a first in the history of the organization—and Germany's stake in it. In the concluding segment, we reflect on the various predictions and prescriptions of prominent German scholars about Europe and its future.

BACKGROUND

Article 23 of the Basic Law commits Germany to active promotion of European integration. This provision was only added after unification, but commitment to European integration is deeply rooted in Germany's post–World War II history and has characterized its external relations since the 1950s. This stance has been beneficial both economically and politically: far from limiting Germany's authority, which was the intent of fellow alliance members, it allowed Germany to reclaim a place among the major European powers. Its pivotal role in the European project facilitated its unification and the swift incorporation of East Germany into the European Community in 1990. Later, the inclusion of many countries in the former communist bloc broke down the larger East-West divide. Membership in multinational European institutions enables German leaders to express and press policy preferences while acting in concert with other countries.

Germany's economic role is also pivotal. With 510 million inhabitants, the EU is the world's largest economic market, and Germany is its anchor; EU countries account for nearly 60 percent of German trade. The introduction of the euro and the addition of new members only increased Germany's international economic standing. Based on its GDP, it makes the largest contribution to the EU budget and the recently established rescue funds to assist economies in crisis.

Political scientists often discuss the hierarchy of agency and structure to explain policy continuity and change. *Agency* refers to the role of individuals and groups in shaping decisions and behavior, while *structure* emphasizes conditions and institutions. Following World War II, agency and structure worked hand in hand to realize European integration. The peaceful, prosperous vision of the "fathers of Europe" would be built on permanent institutions in order to bind member states together. These "fathers" include, but are not limited to, Konrad Adenauer (Germany), Alcide De Gasperi (Italy), Jean Monnet and Robert Schuman (France), and Paul-Henri Spaak (Belgium). Major treaties mark the evolution of these structures and the expansion of policy areas (see table 7.1), but their intersection with national and regional institutions makes decision making complex and lengthy, relying on bargaining and compromise, building coalitions, and securing package deals. As the most populous and economically powerful country in the EU, Germany's consent to major decisions is a necessary, but not sufficient, condition for agenda setting and policy formulation.

INTRODUCTION TO EUROPEAN INTEGRATION

European integration refers to economic, political, legal, and cultural processes that link European countries in a dense network of transnational relations not restricted to, but primarily promoted by, the EU. Several European organizations exist to promote closer cooperation in distinct policy areas, but EU membership entails voluntary transfer of sovereignty, which is "pooled" at the EU level to achieve goals that could not be achieved if states acted individually. However, states do not abandon their sovereignty completely, and many policy areas remain solely in their hands. Even when the EU enjoys legal status in international organizations—for example, the WTO and the UN—the member states are still represented separately. EU citizens enjoy

Table 7.1. Major EU Treaties

Year	Treaty	Goals/Major Provisions
1952	Treaty of Paris	Creating the European Coal and Steel Community (ECSC): free access to the production and free movement of coal and steel among member states
1958	Treaties of Rome	European Economic Community (EEC): creating a common market by eliminating tariffs among member states and introducing a common external tariff and a Common Agricultural Policy (CAP) European Atomic and Energy Community (Euratom): developing the nuclear energy industry
1987	European Single Act (SEA)	Creating a single market focused on the free movement of goods, persons, capital, and services Reforming decision-making procedures affecting the Council of Ministers, European Parliament, and the Commission Expanding community policies (e.g., introducing a cohesion policy to support less-developed regions of the Community)
1993	Treaty on the European Union (Maastricht)	Merging existing institutions into the European Union Extending policy competences and introducing a pillar structure (terminated in 2009): economic, social, and environmental policies; foreign and security policy; justice and home affairs Introducing the concept of European citizenship Strengthening the European Parliament Establishing a timetable for implementation of the Economic and Monetary Union (EMU)
1999	Treaty of Amsterdam	Changing decision-making procedures—in particular, extending the powers of the European Parliament Incorporating the Schengen Agreement into treaty structures, extending asylum, immigration, and visa policies Creating the Office of High Representative for EU Foreign Policy
2003	Treaty of Nice	Changing voting procedures and the institutional structure in anticipation of EU enlargement (e.g., extending qualified majority voting [QMV] and vote distribution in the Council of Ministers)
2009	Treaty of Lisbon	Amending the Treaty of Rome and Treaty on the European Union; replacing the unratified EU Constitutional Treaty (2007) Awarding legal status to the Fundamental Rights Charter Replacing unanimity with QMV in the Council of Ministers as a standard procedure in most policy areas Officially granting the European Council the status of an EU institution; creating the position of president Extending the co-decision procedure between the European Parliament and Council of Ministers Creating the High Representative for Foreign Affairs and Security Policy and an External Action Service (Foreign Service) Office Distributing EU competences into areas of exclusive, shared, or supporting competence

Source: Compiled by the authors.

free movement and the right to reside and work in any member state. National identity is embedded in being "European," even though the scope and depth of European identity varies across countries and time.

Drivers of Integration

Regional integration schemes experienced major growth spurts after World War II and again at the end of the Cold War; on the European continent, globalization and regionalization are conjoined. After World War II, the first pan-European institution was the Council of Europe (1949), an intergovernmental organization that now includes forty-seven member states. It is not a part of the EU but sometimes confused with it since they share the European flag—twelve golden stars against an azure background. The Council of Europe is mainly concerned with human rights, democracy, and the rule of law. Unlike the EU, it cannot make binding laws, but its Human Rights Convention, following the 1948 UN Declaration of Human Rights, binds member countries, whose citizens can appeal to the European Court of Human Rights in Strasbourg, France. Human rights norms developed by the Council of Europe, including its firm stance on abolishing the death penalty, were later adopted by the EU and included in its canon of rights.

European integration was never a smooth process, but several factors propelled progress despite occasional setbacks. Sharing normative goals of peace and political and economic stability, leaders from Belgium, France, Germany, Italy, Luxembourg, and the Netherlands joined forces in the late 1940s and 1950s, propelled to integrate their markets by the tacit support of the United States and the looming communist threat in the east. Democracy promotion, first in southern Europe (1970s and 1980s), then in Central and Eastern Europe (1990s and 2000s), and then, less forcefully, in other parts of the world, became a new mission. Furthermore, representing Europe in an increasingly interconnected global society means encompassing the voices of both large and small member states.

The roots of what is now the EU reach back to the formation of the European Coal and Steel Community (ECSC 1952). Hopes of building on its momentum to establish a European Defense Community, headquartered in Paris, were shattered in 1954 when the French parliament opposed it. Rather than allowing cooperation to stall, leaders returned their focus to economic integration as articulated in the founding Rome Treaties (1958). In the 1950s and 1960s, the establishment of a free trade zone and a common external tariff to establish a customs union developed as a trade-off between German and French interests, a pattern since repeated. Initially, it strengthened France's capacities through massive agricultural subsidies and Germany's industry by eliminating tariffs and creating a common external tariff to open trade channels.

No account of Germany's role in the EU can ignore the special role accorded its bilateral relations with France. They are often described as a marriage of convenience but indissoluble since divorce would harm both sides. Cooperation and power sharing dilute suspicions of national dominance and support coalition building and legitimacy. The personal relationship between their leaders is often used to gauge the health of the partnership. Legendary friendships or at least amicable relations mark milestones: the 1963 Élysée Treaty (Charles de Gaulle and Konrad Adenauer); the 1979 European Monetary System (Valéry Giscard d'Éstaing and Helmut Schmidt); the 1993 Maastricht Treaty (François Mitterrand and Helmut Kohl); and the 2009 Lisbon Treaty (Angela Merkel and Nicolas Sarkozy). Initial strains and differing ideological predispositions can lose their edge as in the relationship between Angela Merkel and François Hollande. Scholars routinely point to divergent interests, political structures, and political cultures, only to conclude that they have been navigated successfully. Established, multilayered networks in civil society and such businesses as the Airbus industry buffer national relations from the vagaries of personal chemistry; they rest on the institutionalization of close bureaucratic connections, professional networks, and joint consultation.

The conflict-solving potential of this special alliance has been tested. While Germany's population and economic power increased with and after unification, France has been plagued by economic woes. In the postwar decades, grassroots cultural exchanges, in particular town twinning and youth exchanges, anchored the high politics of reconciliation between the former enemies, but they have lost importance as new generations become more cosmopolitan, and the peace idiom no longer resonates: a war between France and Germany seems impossible today. The success of the EU is tied to close Franco-German relations, which have been taken for granted based on power rationales. Such cooperation remains vital and requires targeted nurturing to succeed. German media and politicians widely praised the 2017 election of Emmanuel Macron to the French presidency and the success of his new party *La République en Marche* in the parliamentary election shortly thereafter. Both have rekindled expectations for increased European integration, although the difficulties of reconciling German and French economic and financial interests are real. Macron ran his campaign on a decidedly pro-European platform to counter the Euroskeptic message of his main contender, Marine Le Pen.

Explaining the EU

What Is the EU?

Simply put, the EU is an organization of twenty-eight member states as of 2017. Member states voluntarily share sovereignty with *supranational institutions.* The EU is less than a state but more than an international organization; it shares elements of a federal system and a confederation. Most scholars view it as a distinct polity and a prototype for regional integration schemes around the world. Its institutional structure has evolved considerably since European integration began in the 1950s, and with each step, its unique characteristics have become more pronounced. The EU is comprised of executive, legislative, and judicial branches, but the distribution of power among them and their relationship to member states distinguishes them from the state structures found in political systems across the globe. Compared to other international organizations, its policy reach is deeper and national and supranational interdependence more entrenched.

Some policy areas, in particular, trade, are decided mostly at the European level, while others, such as culture and education, remain firmly grounded in national politics. However, an "open method of coordination" increasingly supplements legislation, providing guidelines, benchmarks, and best practices that member states are encouraged to follow. Peer pressure, not legal sanctions, encourages emulation and convergence—for example, in gender equality, LGBT policies, and environmental policy.

Decision-making rules allow for differences in the adoption and implementation of EU decisions; a "multi-speed" Europe is already under way. For example, Ireland and the United Kingdom did not sign the Schengen agreement with its open-border policies, but non-EU members Iceland, Norway, Liechtenstein, and Switzerland did. Currently, nineteen of the twenty-eight member states belong to the eurozone; their finance ministers form the Eurogroup in the Council of the European Union, but most members are also expected to introduce the euro in time. EU expansion to include more and more diverse members may increase the range of policy decisions on which countries diverge, including, for example, a common foreign and security policy.

Theories of Integration

Two competing and complementary integration dynamics are responsible for the EU's ambiguous status and institutional architecture. The first is *neofunctional* pressure to move to an "ever-closer union," as one "father" of European integration, Jean Monnet, and later political scientist Ernst Haas (1958) describes it; the second is intergovernmental bargaining between member states. Neofunctionalism refers to the spillover from the economic arena to other types of cooperation; it relies on supranational organizations, such as the ECSC, to ensure national compliance with goals and norms laid out by EU leaders. For example, economic integration ultimately necessitated cooperation on environmental policies, and the free movement of people across national borders has increased police cooperation and affected visa and asylum policies. Incremental change advanced integration, and neofunctionalists argued that the more integration, the more loyalties would shift to the supranational European level and national-level institutions would adjust their policy actions accordingly.

Intergovernmentalism, on the other hand, emphasizes state preferences, the bargaining processes driving cooperation, and only partial integration (Moravscik 1998). This view finds integration strongest in the economic arena since it can effectively reduce transaction costs for trade between states, but weaker in areas such as foreign and asylum policies. In fact, it does not account for the many policy activities related to social and employment coordination, foreign and security policy, and justice and home affairs in the post-Maastricht era. According to Uwe Puetter (2014), integration is a paradox. EU member states recognize the need for EU action to address common problems but are unwilling to cede further powers to the supranational level. Rather than rely on legislative/regulatory action, they pursue novel forms of decentralized consensus building, a development he calls new or deliberative intergovernmentalism.

Social constructivist theorists add yet another lens to explain institution building. They argue that European integration is mainly shaped by norms and ideas, including preserving peace or respecting human rights. According to constructivists, European integration is not only based on economic benefits; rather, ideas guide human action, and actors can be socialized into "being European" and feeling loyal to the EU. In this process, communication plays a major role, and constructivists highlight the creation of a European public sphere—for example, through media and transnational dialogue. To reach deeper integration, the extension of powers to the EU is contingent on the development of a common European identity that has yet to be realized (Risse 2010).

A byproduct of increased integration is its politicization. A new cleavage characterizes European party systems; most still support the European project but some dispute integration, and openly Euroskeptic parties have gained popularity. EU integration is no longer viewed as a mostly elite-driven process. Liesbet Hooghe and Gary Marks (2009) posit a post-functionalistic theory of integration; no longer driven by incremental political change, its scope and depth are contested politically.

In the history of European integration, both intergovernmental and supranational/neofunctional models have proved useful; neither can claim universal explanatory power. With the Maastricht Treaty (1993), more power was given to institutions, such as the EP, and regions throughout Europe. *Multilevel governance* has become the code word to describe authority dispersed across local, regional, national, and supranational institutions, and the EU is the prime example (Hooghe and Marks 2001). European states operate within a complex matrix, with pressure exerted from EU institutions above and regional institutions below. Thus, pinpointing the degree to which legislation originates with the EU has become difficult.

Institutional Design and Decision Making

European Parliament

Every five years since 1979, citizens in EU member countries vote in elections to the EP. It is the only directly elected political body among EU institutions, and, with 751 members (2014–19), it is the largest democratically elected parliament in the world. Meetings alternate between Strasbourg and Brussels. The members are organized around party families, not nationality. For example, members of the CDU/CSU who are elected to the EP vote as part of the center-right European People's Party group; members of the SPD belong to the Progressive Alliance of Socialists and Democrats. In response to pressure exerted by the members of the European Parliament (MEPs) and the public, the EP's role has gradually been upgraded from advisor to co-legislator with the Council of the European Union, commonly called the Council of Ministers or Council. EP rights also include budgetary approval and consent to enlargement. MEPs can propose legislation to the Commission; they cannot initiate it. The EU does not levy taxes, and about 40 percent of budgeted expenses are earmarked for agricultural subsidies and structural funds; the Commission drafts and must balance the budget.

The number of MEPs depends on the size of the country but is not exactly proportional to population to keep the parliament's size in check and to assure a representational balance between the few large and many smaller member states. Germany has the most MEPs (ninety-nine) based on population size but the highest ratio of population-to-individual representative. German MEPs are relatively independent of their national parties, and most consider work in the EP their political vocation. Their high rate of reelection has granted them political capital and seniority in committee and leadership positions (Daniel 2015). Still, most politicians prefer a career in national politics to election to the EP; few move from the state or national level to the EP (Borchert and Stolz 2011, 217).

Council of the European Union

The Council is the other important law-making body in the EU. It is organized around policy areas, and the national ministers responsible for a particular portfolio make final decisions. They meet in Brussels, the unofficial capital of the EU. The Committee of Permanent Representatives (COREPER), whose members reside in Brussels, provides administrative support to the Council. Through intensive bargaining, the Council often arrives at compromises before a formal vote is held. Voting has changed over the decades from required unanimity to more complex mechanisms that allow progress in integration without consent by all member states; they aim to prevent large or small member states gaining unfair advantages. Unanimous agreement is still required in some areas, but in others, consensus among at least 55 percent (sixteen out of twenty-eight) of member states, who together comprise 65 percent of the EU population, is necessary for a vote to pass. Germany holds the same number of votes as the other large countries: France, Italy, and the United Kingdom. This so-called double majority voting is a consensus-building mechanism; a government in a losing minority usually does not want the electorate at home to think it failed in Brussels, so joining an emerging majority can be an effective face-saving strategy.

European Commission

The executive branch, the European Commission, is headquartered in Brussels. It is comprised of twenty-eight commissioners nominated by each of the member states; one of them acts as president. Chosen by the European Council, he or she is formally elected by the EP. The president plays a major role in coordinating activities and representing EU affairs in public. The members of the Commission are committed to serving European, not national, interests, making it a good example of a supranational organization. They have the right to initiate legislation, to draft legislative proposals, to monitor implementation of EU policies, and to represent the EU in international organizations, such as the WTO or the UN. Overall, decision making is based on the principle of collective responsibility; that is, the commissioners have equal rights and voting power and, once a decision is made, must support the Commission's action. Decision making is consensus based, but votes can be taken upon request.

European Council

The intergovernmental quality of the EU is most visible in the European Council, which sets the political agenda and discusses matters of fundamental importance, such as the Ukrainian crisis or international terrorism. It was formed in the 1970s and became an official EU institution with the Lisbon Treaty. Aside from heads of state and government, it convenes the president of the EU Commission, the High Representative of the Union for Foreign Affairs and Security Policy (HR), and national ministers—normally, the foreign ministers. Its president, usually a former head of government and currently former Polish Prime Minister Donald Tusk, chairs its quarterly meetings. It represents the highest level of cooperation among EU national governments.

Court of Justice of the European Union

The CJEU, which rules on matters pertaining to EU treaties and legislation, is another prominent example of a supranational institution. It is located in Luxembourg and consists of two courts: the Court of Justice and the General Court. Its jurisdiction overrides national law in areas where the EU has responsibility. Judges come from the EU member states, but they rule in the name of European, not national, interests. To protect their impartiality, no dissenting voices are published. The Court's caseload has increased over the years, requiring the addition of new chambers and the revision of procedural rules. It remains a powerful actor and facilitator of European jurisdiction and integration.

European Central Bank

Another important institution is the European Central Bank (ECB), located in Frankfurt am Main, Germany. The ECB is the central bank for the euro and administers eurozone monetary policy; for example, it has the exclusive right to authorize the issuance of euro banknotes. The capital stock of the ECB consists of shares provided by central national banks, such as the Bundesbank, or German Federal Bank, of EU-member countries. Modeled on the Bundesbank, with its anti-inflationary monetary policy, the ECB's main objective is to maintain price stability. In 2014, it shifted to a more flexible approach to lending money and buying bonds in response to the euro crisis.

Leadership positions in EU institutions are generally assigned through horse-trading among the member states. With time, their prestige has grown, and former prime ministers serve as presidents of the European Council and the European Commission. These positions are filled only after complex political bargaining among heads of state and government. German nationals seldom hold the primary leadership positions but increasingly serve in second-level positions, such as vice commissioner or committee chair.

Revisiting the Democratic Deficit

Due to its hybrid nature as a supranational *and* an intergovernmental political body, the EU's democratic credentials are sometimes called into question.

Strong in support of democracy and the rule of law, the European polity is haunted by a "democratic deficit." EU citizens' only direct influence on EU decisions is through elections and petitions to the EP, except for Ireland, which has a constitutional prerogative to submit major EU treaty adaptations to a public referendum. Although EU referenda have become common in many member states, they are not allowed in Germany.

Powerful decision makers, such as the presidents of the European Commission and the EU Council as well as the EU Commissioners, are appointed via intergovernmental negotiations behind closed doors. The Commission is the only institution with the right to initiate legislation, but it also monitors policy implementation, so legislative and executive powers are intertwined. To many, Brussels bureaucrats seem to be driving, with the elected MEPs stuffed in the back seat. As a result, citizens take little notice of their work, and voter turnout to the EP has steadily declined since the first direct elections in 1979, despite the fact that the EP has gained more influence on policy making over the years (in 1979, EU average voter turnout was 61.99 percent; in Germany, 65.7 percent; in 2014, the numbers were 42.61 percent and 48 percent, respectively).

Against the democratic deficit argument, some contend that those making the major decisions at the EU level received their mandate in national elections. They ask whether the EU should be compared to nation-states or other international organizations. Are its decision-making bodies and mechanisms any less transparent than those of nation-states?

The alleged democratic deficit has many facets, and scholars disagree on how serious the problems are for the EU as a polity. When the EU was established, it had no blueprint for its institutional design. Institution building followed a pragmatic path, and many of the functions it now fulfills were not even envisioned at its founding. In 2004, shortly before the "big bang" of eastern enlargement, EU and national leaders agreed to draft an EU constitution to support the legitimacy and efficiency of its institutions. Short the necessary votes, the Constitutional Treaty was not ratified, and a compromise, the Lisbon Treaty, took its place.

EUROPEAN ECONOMIC INTEGRATION AND THE EURO

Significance of the Euro

The history of European integration has been written in different ways, contrasting goals with reality or achievements with setbacks. Some focus on major decisions that expanded policy areas, enlarged the union, and influenced institutional and policy-making mechanisms, while others portray an elite-driven project with varying popular and elite support. The one constant is economic integration. Ambitions have shifted from creating a customs union to completing a common market and, for a subset of countries, greater economic union with a common currency. This movement has been both supportive and divisive. In the *Eurobarometer*, a biannual public opinion survey conducted by the European Commission since 1973, many Europeans consistently consider the economic situation and unemployment among the most pressing concerns facing the EU; its fate is closely tied to the economic performance of its member states.

Several factors, including the preferences of the major political actors, must align for a major EU policy initiative to come to fruition. Changes in the global environment must shake policy entrepreneurs into action, and political and economic rationales must fuse or, at the very least, not clash. The introduction of the euro is a particularly good example of the necessary confluence: increased economic interdependence across borders, the end of the Cold War, and German unification. A common currency was long seen as a way to increase Europe's global competitiveness and to reduce its dependence on the US dollar, the ill effects of which became evident when US currency was overvalued in the 1960s, and the US government abandoned the fixed exchange rate mechanism in 1971. EC member states had long called for reduced transaction costs in the flow of goods and, in particular, exchange fluctuations. Various measures to control them proved unsustainable; in March 1979, the European Monetary System (EMS) replaced this ad hoc system, and the European Currency Unit (ECU) was introduced. The Maastricht Treaty carried these measures to their conclusion with the European Monetary Union (EMU). A common currency would obviate currency fluctuations and bank transaction costs and make price comparisons across member states more transparent.

Political and economic rationales overlapped in 1990 with the unofficial end of the Cold War. The unanticipated collapse of communism in the Central and Eastern European countries and their desire to join the EC as quickly as possible made the need for economic integration more urgent. In addition, the prospect of unification would make Germany by far the most populous country in the EC, further strengthening its economic power. France, Italy, and the United Kingdom greeted this prospect with mixed feelings, if not outright concern. Memories of a powerful, destabilizing Germany in the center of Europe lingered, and the period of National Socialism as well as World War II were still fresh in many minds. Would a united Germany use its economic power to become a military power and threaten peace and stability in Europe?

To bind Germany even closer to Europe was one way to defuse these concerns. German unification required the approval of the four allied powers, and their blessing could be used as leverage. French President François Mitterrand linked his government's consent to European integration—specifically, advancement toward a common currency. At the end of the 1980s, the completion of the Single European Act had priority; a common currency was the logical next step but seemed far off. Chancellor Helmut Kohl, a convinced Europeanist, did not oppose monetary union but was in no hurry to push it. In the end, he consented even though the Deutsche Mark was stable, and the federal bank and most of the population opposed it (Sarotte 2009, 82–85). He championed monetary union as a symbol of a strong European identity and closely linked national unification to European integration. Consequently, the Maastricht Treaty laid out a roadmap introducing the euro on paper by 1999 and in practice by 2002.

Aware of Germany's crucial role, the CDU/CSU-FDP coalition government insisted on what seemed like strict conditions for joining the euro and the functioning of the currency union. Certain "convergence criteria" had to be fulfilled, such as stable exchange rates and low inflation, budget deficits, and public debt, and countries had to report on these macroeconomic data before they could join the euro. Rather than derail the larger project, countries could opt out of using the joint currency, and the United Kingdom, Denmark, and, later, Sweden did. Once the currency was in place, the Stability and Growth Pact would guarantee the fiscal discipline of eurozone member countries. The ECB was headquartered in Frankfurt, the seat of the famed German Federal Bank, which was best known for ensuring price stability and low inflation. The timing of the euro's introduction, the conditions for joining the eurozone, and the mechanisms that govern it were closely aligned with German preferences.

The first few years of the new currency were promising: it quickly turned into the second-largest reserve currency behind the US dollar, a position it still holds. Exports took off, and citizens and corporate strategists adjusted quickly to the new landscape. The potential negative side effects, predicted by critics and downplayed by advocates, did not appear until some years later.

The Eurozone in Crisis

Catalysts and Root Causes

The EU has seen its fair share of crises and battles to recover from them, but the eurozone crisis occupies a special place because the response went beyond the customary institutional and policy adaptations. At least four crucial differences stand out. First, the crisis affected and, to some extent, involved the member states' citizens and political actors more than any before, sparking publicity both in Europe and abroad. Second, it exposed deep rifts between groups of countries, pitting north against south, or what is sometimes referred to as the core against the periphery. Although this taxonomy is too simple, real policy divisions expressed durable national stereotypes that European integration had failed to address. Third, the actions and discourse surrounding the crisis shifted from an exclusive focus on financial markets and the euro's survival to larger questions about the future of Europe. Would more or less integration solve them? Should reforms seek to fine-tune the status quo or to promote greater differentiation? Fourth, the crisis catapulted German policies and Germany's place in Europe and the global economy to the forefront.

The eurozone crisis or euro crisis played out differently in different countries. It developed in the aftermath of the US subprime crisis, which reverberated throughout Europe and the world. The exposure to bad and overextended debt in the United States triggered the banking crisis; with reduced liquidity, access to money became tighter, investment slowed, tax receipts declined, and a recession ensued. In addition, many large European banks had issued nonperforming loans to southern European countries. The international crisis only deepened with worrisome public debt projections in some eurozone countries. The banking system in Ireland collapsed due to risky transactions following market liberalization and increased sovereign debt. In Spain, the collapse of the housing market caused economic difficulties and sharply increased sovereign debt. Slow growth in eurozone countries overall added to economic anxiety, and concerns about a ripple effect led the EU to take emergency measures to avert a default. Governments were confronted with a sovereign debt crisis since they had difficulty repaying debt, and sluggish economic growth made creditors doubt their future ability to do so.

Greece had a prominent place in the evolving drama. It became the scapegoat for everything that went wrong with the euro and in the ensuing crisis, although what happened there was not representative of developments in other crisis-stricken countries. By becoming a eurozone member in 2001, Greece gained easier access to loans and borrowed more than it could shoulder. Its economy had experienced difficulties for some time, including a budget deficit out of line with the strict Maastricht criteria. Its economy relied on a small industrial sector but had a bloated public administration encouraged by the patronage systems on which both the Panhellenic Socialist Movement (PASOK) and New Democracy had relied; imports vastly outweighed exports; and productivity remained low, despite access to the common market. By 2010, its public debt hit 120 percent and kept increasing. The imminent loss of confidence in the Greek economy due to sharply rising sovereign debt triggered the larger eurozone crisis and threw the Greek economy into its most severe crisis since democracy was established in 1974.

If the global financial crisis and developments in indebted countries cata-lyzed the eurozone crisis, attention soon focused on faults in the design and implementation of the euro. From the beginning, critics on both left and right questioned the viability of the common currency since it was implemented without integrating Europe's economic, fiscal, and social systems, which di-verge greatly. Hall (2012), for example, argued that the asymmetry between the northern and southern European countries was due to long-standing differences in economic policies. The north pursued growth- and export-oriented strategies, while the south depended on demand-led strategies fo-cused on domestic markets, which were often accompanied by substantial increases in public and private debt. In other words, the anticipated economic convergence of eurozone members was spotty and limited to certain mac-roeconomic indicators, such as inflation. As members, however, individual governments could no longer weather an economic crisis through monetary policy—for example, by devaluing their currencies.

In addition, when the euro was first implemented, political rationales could trump economic considerations; for example, the criteria for using the euro (such as limited sovereign debt) were applied inconsistently. Germany and France were among the countries that did not meet Stability and Growth Pact criteria shortly after the introduction of the euro. From the outset, many criti-cized these criteria as unrealistic and too inflexible. Paradoxically, the strictly rule-bound approach of the ECB became a pitfall for the common currency under crisis; it required reforms and a new approach to monetary policy.

Responses: Bailouts and Institutional Reforms

The EU responded to the crisis by implementing rescue packages to assist crisis-stricken countries with loans backed by eurozone member states, the International Monetary Fund (IMF), and the ECB (the "Troika"). As the larg-est economy in Europe, Germany shoulders the largest burden in backing the bailouts, at least in absolute numbers, but it is not disproportional (Schieder 2014). These bailouts spurred institutional changes with important conse-quences for the scope of EU policies. The EU first established the European Financial Stability Facility (EFSF) in May 2010; the EFSF could back the loans of the eurozone countries in trouble, recapitalize banks, and buy sov-ereign debts. After some discussion about whether EU treaties, especially the Maastricht Treaty, allow such bailouts, EU leaders decided to replace the EFSF with the European Stability Mechanism (ESM), which is based on an amendment to Article 136 of the Maastricht Treaty. It went into force in Oc-tober 2012 and provides permanent rescue measures. By October 2013, the EU had improved coordination of its banking policies, introducing oversight mechanisms to establish common bank capitalization rules. As a result, the ECB can monitor large banks in countries using the euro. These measures alleviated immediate challenges and avoided dissolution of the eurozone or the exit of individual states, and the EU introduced institutional changes to guard against future shocks. In 2014, under Mario Draghi's presidency, the ECB lowered interest rates and increased readily available money supplies to accelerate growth; yet the crisis lingers.

Reform Perils and Problems

Three bailout packages were given to Greece between 2010 and 2016, each linked to austerity policies that demanded cutbacks in welfare, state subsidies, and other government expenditures to balance the budget. The conditionality, strictly monitored by the EU, the IMF, and the ECB, has since frequently fueled public protests and caused friction between the Greek government and EU institutions. Many blamed the EU, particularly Germany, for the harsh conditions of aid and "rescue" packages, even when domestic factors contributed to the economic woes. A debt-release program would ease the problems, but several actors, including the German government, opposed such measures, fearing they would send the "wrong" message to the Greek government by undermining its structural reform efforts.

Recovery in Greece has been sluggish; unemployment and debt remain high; some economists argue that the reforms deepened the recession. Greece alone was granted 322 billion euro in loans, but critics point out that the biggest chunk was used to recapitalize Greek banks, repay debts, and serve interest payments without providing relief to the Greek population. Only a small portion was invested in restructuring the economy and creating jobs. Large-scale cuts of wages and pension and social benefits as well as layoffs in the public sector added to the suffering. By 2015, nearly 20 percent of Greeks could not meet their daily food expenses. Homelessness in cities skyrocketed, and the overall health situation deteriorated.

Greek citizens were not alone in having to deal with the fallout of the financial and euro crises: In many of the affected countries social suffering was widespread, unemployment rose sharply, and young people (fifteen- to twenty-four-year-olds) paid a particularly heavy toll. According to Eurostat, the statistical office of the EU, in 2013, unemployment in eurozone countries reached a record high of 12 percent, but this number concealed wide disparities. In Austria and Germany, for example, unemployment stood at 4.9 and 5.2 percent, respectively, but it was 27.5 percent and 26.1 percent in Spain and Greece, respectively. By June 2015, unemployment had fallen to 11.1 percent overall but remained at stubbornly high levels in Greece (25.5

percent) and Spain (22.5 percent); youth unemployment rates were a staggering 53.7 percent in Greece and 49.2 percent in Spain. At the other end of the spectrum were Germany (4.7 percent) and the Czech Republic (4.9 percent). Germany was the only euro-area country in which youth unemployment was under 10 percent (7.1 percent).

Political developments left their mark as well. In Greece, for example, a fractured multiparty system replaced the long-dominant PASOK and New Democracy. New parties emerged, and minor parties saw their electoral fortunes soar. Political mistrust and alienation flourished; Greek citizens who were once strong supporters of the EU became its ardent critics.

Germany and the Eurozone Crisis

Not surprisingly, Germany was pivotal during the eurozone crisis, and its role remains controversial. Its businesses and those of other export-oriented core countries benefited greatly from the introduction of the euro; it sheltered their goods from higher currency exchange rates with non-EU members and stimulated exports. European export-oriented economies, banks, and financial institutions argue strongly for keeping the euro in place. Chancellor Angela Merkel once warned that if the euro failed, so would Europe.

Facing a potential breakup of the eurozone as the crisis deepened, in late 2010, the government moved swiftly to negotiate bailout packages and aid conditions. Three preferences stand out. First, eurocrisis measures and responses became the prerogative of the executive. Chancellor Merkel and Finance Minister Wolfgang Schäuble were the main actors in the negotiations with EU members and played a major role in designing and negotiating the rescue packages. Parliament approved the bailout packages, but it did not alter the rules set by the "Troika." Second, Germany favored anti-inflation policies. According to the government and German representatives on the ECB board, the ECB's monetary policy should follow tight money supply guidelines. They rejected proposals to use monetary policy to ease the indebtedness of euro member countries. Third, the German government insisted on strict austerity policies to balance budgets in the countries receiving aid and bailout packages. Many international observers fiercely criticized this approach, but the government did not veer from its course.

Germany's position on strict austerity caused considerable resentment in southern Europe, and many international observers described it in pejoratives ranging from perverse to sadistic. Germany was not alone in supporting the austerity policy but was its major proponent. Its leaders found strong allies in Finland, the Netherlands, and particularly the Central and Eastern European states, which had experienced stringent economic reform after the fall of communism. Mark Blyth (2013, 5–8) is one of many outspoken critics of austerity measures. He concedes that debt matters but emphasizes that, excepting Greece, the eurozone was mainly "a transmuted and well-camouflaged banking crisis." The blame, according to the author, was "shifted . . . from the banks to the state." Austerity has not worked to stimulate the economy and to reduce debt and it cannot work when all countries pursue such a policy. Some must spend if others want to save.

Outside criticism has focused on Germany's initial reluctance to assume leadership and its later insistence on austerity measures for troubled economies. In early discussions about rescue measures, the chancellor asked whether the EU should be held accountable at all since the original Maastricht Treaty did not prescribe bailing out other eurozone countries. Many argued that dawdling at critical junctures exacerbated the emergency as well as uncertainties about Europe's role in the globalized economy. At the height of the crisis, *The Economist* (2013) warned that European economic recovery required Germany to take the lead, yet styled it the "reluctant hegemon."

This behavior should not be attributed to inaction but rather to caution and restraint. Wade Jacoby (2015) draws attention to "the timing of politics and the politics of timing." By his account, the "'intrusion' of the German voter into the domain of financial politics" required informed consent. Voters had to be prepared, which took time; during the delay, the cycle of emergency measures and bailouts restarted, and public skepticism grew. Abraham Newman also reflects on timing and concern for the electorate but traces the lack of open solidarity with debt-ridden countries to the lingering effects of German unification: the large-scale monetary transfers from west to east and the painful structural economic reforms that the whole nation endured to overcome its economic malaise (2015, 208, 120).

The debt discourse was confounded with moral arguments. The German word *Schuld* means both debt and individual guilt, or moral failure, and the term *austerity* is rarely used in German discourse, which instead emphasizes concepts like savings policy or budget balancing. The debt-ridden countries were portrayed as overindulgent, and by implication, Germany as responsible and restrained. Some of the criticism invoked the past; relations between Greece and Germany remain burdened by memories of Nazi occupation, and in some Greek newspapers, Angela Merkel and Wolfgang Schäuble were depicted in SS uniforms. Tabloid-fueled stereotypes and prejudice on both sides strained formerly amicable Greek-German relations. Others attributed Germany's conservative monetary position to the collective memory of the high inflation that brought down the Weimar Republic and gave rise to National Socialism, but most observers ascribed divergent views on how to assist crisis-stricken countries to a clash of

economic philosophies. This reading closely associates the German preference for balanced budgets with the influence of ordo-liberal economic
thought, which favors rule-based economic policies, state regulation, and a
tight monetary policy to control inflation and support long-term solutions
(Hillebrand 2015) and requires the economies of indebted countries to un-
dertake structural reforms. Similarly, the moral-hazard argument proposes
that nations avoid covering for their counterparts' risky behavior lest they
embolden further risk. In contrast, Keynesian economics relies on increased
expenditures and lower taxes to stimulate demand and lower expenditures
and higher taxes to curb an overheated economy. By this argument, depress-
ing demand as part of an austerity policy only slows economic recovery.
Germany did not buy it; no influential political group seriously challenged
the government's approach, and German voters largely approved.

Another critique focused on trade imbalances between Germany and its EU
partners. According to this view, Germany's export surplus has made recovery difficult for countries attempting to increase their exports and revive their
economies, such as Greece and even France. The Organisation for Economic
Co-operation and Development (OECD) and other expert panels have called
on Germany to correct these imbalances through domestic reforms, including
investing in social infrastructure and childcare, lifting wage suppression, and
reducing taxes for lower-income families. All of these measures would accelerate domestic demand and potentially correct trade imbalances, but from
the German government's perspective, the surplus reflects competitiveness in
the global market.

The crisis also confronted EU leaders with a host of political questions:
How much sovereignty do member countries want to transfer to the EU level,
and how important are national priorities? Pressured to achieve solutions, do
national governments have sufficient time to investigate and negotiate, or are
they condemned to rubber-stamp decisions made in Brussels? Should governments succumb to pressure to integrate social and economic policies, or should
they secure and protect their national economic models and domestic welfare
states? The eurozone crisis tested the strength of arguments for and against integration between those who wanted more Europe and those who wanted less.
Originally conceived as a symbol and tool to unite Europe, the euro has exacerbated economic and political divisions, strengthening Euroskeptic voices on
the left and right of the political spectrum, and aided in the renationalization.

The Rise of Euroskepticism

Until the 1990s, the elite largely drove European integration, with the public
looking on. The Maastricht Treaty politicized the project by extending pow-

Table 7.2. Trust in Institutions: Supranational vs. National
How much do you trust certain institutions? (German responses in parentheses)

	Tend to Trust (%)			Tend Not to Trust (%)		
	EB 2008	*EB 2012*	*EB 2016*	*EB 2008*	*EB 2012*	*EB 2016*
European Union Institutions	50	31	36	36	60	54
	(43)	(30)	(37)	(44)	(61)	(43)
National Government	32	28	31	62	67	64
	(36)	(39)	(51)	(59)	(56)	(53)

Source: Standard Eurobarometer 69 (November 2008); 77 (July 2012); and 86 (December 2016).

ers and introducing the EMU. Expansion into Central and Eastern Europe, the failure to ratify the EU's Constitutional Treaty, the eurozone crisis, and the European refugee crisis raised louder criticism. The once permissive consensus between elites and the public is fraying, although measuring sentiment about the EU is tricky.

Euroskepticism has become a catch-all term for a variety of positions. *Soft Euroskepticism* defends aspects of state sovereignty against transfer of power to supranational EU institutions and/or critiques specific policy initiatives, while the *hard* version questions the entire integration project, but the lines are fluid. Are those who advocate more economic but less political integration Euroskeptics? Does the move toward populist parties on the left and right represent a rise in Euroskepticism or a protest against the mainstream parties for not providing choices related to European integration policies and/or perceived policy failures? Are gains by Euroskeptic parties in the May 2014 elections to the European Parliament evidence of growing Euroskepticism across the EU or country-specific problems? They still hold fewer seats and are divided among themselves. Moreover, their success varied greatly across EU member states, in most of which voter turnout was low. Political distrust of the established parties and Euroskepticism often go together and are difficult to separate. In most member countries, EU institutions still claim higher levels of trust than national governments and parliaments; Germany is an exception (see table 7.2). European leaders are often blamed for failures when problems lie at home, and Klaus Armingeon and Besir Ceka (2014), for example, emphasize the connection between low trust in national governments with low trust in the EU.

Outlier Germany

In German politics, despite some grumbling, the European consensus holds. During the euro crisis, when governments were voted out of office across

Europe, Merkel and the CDU/CSU prevailed, although coalition partners alternated from SPD to FDP and back. Even when the SPD was in opposition (2009–13), an "informal grand coalition" between the two parties may have been based on two premises: that German economic performance was strong, and that the integrity of the eurozone should be saved (Zimmermann 2014, 322–23). European integration has had minimal impact on national party competition; up until 2017 all parties represented in the Bundestag agreed that membership in the EU is not only desirable but advantageous to Germany. Still, within this broad consensus, there has always been room for disagreement; for example, over Turkey as a future EU member.

The Left Party and the AfD are the most outspoken, while the CSU's position depends on topic. The Left Party is typical of soft Euroskepticism in supporting European integration and opposing particular policy measures. Hard Euroskepticism, which entails leaving the EU, has been limited to right-wing fringe parties with no national political influence (Niedermayer 2016). Controversies about the EU have played hardly any role in national election campaigns, even in 2013, when the EU was in the throes of the eurozone crisis. This lack of attention to EU matters in national elections did not change in the 2017 campaign to the Bundestag.

Constitutional challenges to new EU treaties and bailouts also signal growing polarization. Representatives on both the political left (Left Party) and right (CSU) have turned to the Federal Constitutional Court to challenge stipulations of the Maastricht and Lisbon treaties as well as the permanent euro bailout fund, the European Stability Mechanism, and the Fiscal Compact. In each case, the court reaffirmed Germany's strong ties to Europe but strengthened parliament's control over European legislation. Subsequent legal provisions granted more space to deliberate European treaties and other measures proposed by the EU; for example, the German parliament must approve each rescue package.

GERMANY AND EU ENLARGEMENT

Crossing the East-West Divide

The EU has grown from six countries (Belgium, France, Germany, Italy, Luxembourg, the Netherlands) to nine (United Kingdom, Ireland, Denmark) to twelve (Greece, Portugal, Spain) and, at the end of the Cold War, fifteen (Austria, Finland, Sweden). In 2004, eight former communist countries joined (the Czech Republic, Estonia, Hungary, Latvia, Lithuania, Poland, Slovakia, Slovenia) along with Cyprus and Malta. In 2007, Bulgaria and Romania followed, and Croatia was admitted in 2013. The draw continues, as

Albania, the former Yugoslav Republic of Macedonia, Montenegro, Serbia, and Turkey are recognized as "official candidates." The citizens of Norway rejected formal membership via public referenda in 1972 and 1994, and in 2015 Iceland withdrew its pending application; in 2016 Switzerland withdrew its suspended membership application, but their polity and policies are closely intertwined with the EU.

Enlargement remains on the agenda, despite deeply entrenched public and even elite fatigue following the ambitious extension of membership to Central and Eastern Europe. Communism collapsed unexpectedly, and EU leaders had no master plan to address it. A "first-aid" program (PHARE) was designed mainly to assist Poland and Hungary during their initial, massive economic restructuring and political change. In response to pressure for membership, the Copenhagen Criteria (1993) outlined new conditions for EU accession, setting high benchmarks compared to the previous rounds of enlargement. They state:

> Membership requires that the candidate country has achieved stability of institutions guaranteeing democracy, the rule of law, human rights and respect for and protection of minorities, the existence of a functioning market economy as well as the capacity to cope with competitive pressure and market forces within the Union. Membership presupposes the candidate's ability to take on the obligations of membership including adherence to the aims of political, economic and monetary union. (European Council 1993)

By the mid-1990s, most of the countries in Central and Eastern Europe had officially applied to join, with countries in the Balkan region following.

Accession to the EU follows a detailed protocol with thirty-five chapters that cover all of the EU legal acts that must first be adopted and concluded. Candidate countries must make major adjustments to their legal, social, and economic systems to become full EU members. Existing member-state attitudes toward enlargement were deeply influenced by their own location, economic interests, and political calculations of costs and benefits. Those in favor emphasized the positive effects of stabilizing difficult political and economic transitions in the former communist countries, which would enhance Europe's global standing. The more reluctant stressed the gap in economic development between Western and Eastern Europe, the cost of redistributing EU funds to less-developed regions, and the need for institutional reform of the EU. Some feared that Germany would gain disproportionately, both economically and politically. Both advocates and opponents were concerned about a potentially large influx of labor migrants, the consequence of freedom of movement within the EU.

German governments strongly advocated enlargement into Central and Eastern Europe, based on a policy driven by norms and concrete political and economic interests (Jeřábek 2011). After unification, they grabbed at the opportunity to be surrounded by friendly neighbors and built a new *Ostpolitik*, or eastern policy. Reconciliation with Poland, Czechoslovakia, and the former Soviet Union already figured prominently during the chancellorship of Willy Brandt (SPD) in the early 1970s; the fall of the Berlin Wall opened a new range of opportunities to cement this policy of rapprochement and reconciliation (Feldman 2012).

Skillfully wielding "rhetorical action" and appealing to the self-proclaimed EU values of democracy, liberty, and rule of law, political elites in the emerging democracies of Central and Eastern Europe "shamed" their western counterparts into standing by their promise that any democracy in Europe could become an EU member (Schimmelfennig 2001). Such appeals were difficult to dismiss and fell on particularly fertile ground in Germany, where political actors emphasized political advantages, such as contributions to democratic stability, but also moral obligations deriving from the Nazi past. Poland and the Czech Republic (before 1992, part of Czechoslovakia) bore the scars of Nazi occupation, concentration camps, war, and destruction. As Germany's closest neighbors to the East, they received high priority in foreign relations, which, after 1990, drew on earlier successful reconciliation patterns with France, including youth and student exchanges, cultural projects, and joint economic ventures. For their part, the new leaders in Central and Eastern Europe quickly realized that the road to Brussels led through Berlin. As a result, relations improved in a remarkably short time. The recent nationalist backlash in Hungary and Poland has raised deep concern in Germany and other European countries. EU membership was supposed to bolster democracy and pluralism, yet, once countries are full members, the EU has limited leverage to induce changes in domestic politics.

German governments also expected to gain economically from including Central and Eastern European countries in the common market. Given their low labor costs and high skill levels, these countries promised to reward foreign investment and joint ventures with future profits, and their draw was of particular interest to the highly export-oriented German economy. As early as 1990, Germany was the most important trade partner for most Central and East European countries; dense German business ties and direct investment accelerated quickly, in particular in the so-called Visegrád Group—the Czech Republic, Hungary, Poland, and Slovakia—named for the Hungarian town where they held a summit on February 15, 1991 (Gross 2013).

Even a generally positive disposition toward extending EU membership did not erase concerns about the potential costs; pragmatism and realism always counterbalanced normative sentiments, and Chancellor Gerhard Schröder (1998–2005) irritated Central and Eastern Europe's leaders when he refused to set an EU accession date during the negotiations in the late 1990s. He was concerned that certain EU policies supporting poorer regions with agricultural subsidies and structural funds would increase Germany's net contributions to the EU budget. Labor unions feared competition from Eastern European workers; the German government joined most other EU countries in insisting on the maximum transition period for labor mobility—seven years. After the restrictions were lifted, the expected wave of migrants from the new member countries did not materialize; while more east central Europeans work in Western Europe today, economic development in their home countries often motivates them to stay.

The Special Case of Turkey

No EU membership application has been as drawn out and controversial as Turkey's. A NATO member since 1952, Turkey became an associate member of the EEC in 1963 and submitted its official EU membership application in 1987. German businesses have especially strong ties with Turkey, and the largest Turkish minority community in the EU calls Germany home. Even as economic and political relations deepened, membership remained on the back burner. When the enlargement to Central and Eastern Europe took shape, Turkey felt slighted and, with the active support of the United States, increased its pressure. In 1995, it signed a Customs Union Agreement with the EU and was finally officially recognized as a candidate for full membership in 1999. Several reforms, including modifications to the penal code, improvements in women's rights, separation of the government and military, and abolition of the death penalty moved it closer to membership. Negotiations started in 2005 but stalled shortly thereafter. The stop-and-go pattern continued until, in 2016, the EU officially put talks on hold.

In Germany and elsewhere, economic, geopolitical, security, and identity considerations have shaped debates. In the past, advocates of membership, in particular the SPD and Alliance 90/The Greens, argued that Turkey could help to improve relations and to alleviate conflicts with the Islamic world in the Middle East and to foster recognition and integration of the Turkish minority living in Germany. On the other hand, conservative and Christian groups and parties have long felt that Turkey does not belong in their idea of Europe, founded on Judeo-Christian traditions and rooted in Christian values. Turkey has a predominantly Muslim population of 79.8 million (2017) and could quickly emerge as the most populous country in Europe, with the attached advantages.

Members' official positions toward Turkey's inclusion have vacillated from openness to skepticism based on general enlargement fatigue and fears about further labor migration in a time of economic and financial stress. Expectations that Turkey and its ruling Justice and Development Party (AKP) would present a model of democracy for Muslim countries have been disappointed. Violations of Kurdish minority rights, conflicts with Greece over Cyprus, the crackdowns on the 2013 protest movement and following the 2016 military coup, and the move toward authoritarianism under former prime minister and now President Recep Tayyip Erdoğan played into the hands of those advocating a "special relationship," short of membership, particularly leaders of Austria, France, and Germany.

No matter how future relations evolve, Turkey and the EU are bound by historical, economic, and societal ties. The crisis in Syria and the rise of ISIS demonstrate Turkey's crucial geopolitical role; cooperation in controlling the flow of refugees from Syria to Turkey has led to EU-Turkey agreements to control migration to the EU. Still, EU membership is unlikely in the near future, especially since the Erdoğan government, which is in the midst of reorienting its foreign and security policy, is no longer seeking it.

BREXIT AND BEYOND

On June 23, 2016, 51.9 percent of the British electorate voted in favor of leaving the EU; 48.1 percent voted to remain. Voter turnout was high at 72.2 percent. Most observers were surprised, if not shocked, despite the long-standing reluctance of the United Kingdom to be part of the European project. It joined the union (then called the EC) only in 1973, and a public referendum immediately challenged the move, although 67 percent of the electorate voted in its favor. Motives for joining were purely economic; policy makers never pursued closer integration or European identity. The British role waxed and waned under different prime ministers. As one of the most powerful member states, it was crucial to economic integration, security policy, and enlargement questions, but even constructive membership could not disguise its reservations. It is not a member of the Schengen Treaty or the eurozone and used opt-out clauses in other policy areas as well.

British relations with the EU divided its political parties, although tides shifted. Initially, the Labour Party criticized the EU's neoliberal economic policies but took a more positive view under Prime Minister Tony Blair. Concurrently, the Euroskeptic wing of the Conservative party gained momentum. The United Kingdom Independence Party (UKIP) emerged in the 1990s; it became the first prominent hard Euroskeptic party, calling for the United Kingdom to withdraw from the EU. Its appeal increased during the eurozone crisis, and, in

2014, it was the strongest British party in the elections to the European Parliament, with 28 percent of the votes (Goodwin and Milazzo 2015).

In 2013, facing increased electoral competition from UKIP and opposition from the ranks of his own party, Conservative Prime Minister David Cameron declared his intention to hold a referendum on EU membership should he be reelected in 2015. He was, and he immediately set out to negotiate more favorable conditions for the United Kingdom with the European Commission, but increasing fears about immigrants and refugees lifted anti-EU sentiments to new heights. Cameron and most of the political establishment campaigned for remaining in the EU but a slim majority of voters disagreed. The generational divide was clear; voters between eighteen and twenty-four years of age voted overwhelming to remain in the EU (73 percent), while 60 percent of citizens sixty years or older voted to leave. Differences were pronounced between urban areas, in particular London, and economically depressed areas such as the Midlands. Scotland and Northern Ireland voted to remain, England and Wales to leave. The vote in Wales left many observers puzzled; it has been a major beneficiary of EU funds.

The result of the Brexit referendum sent shockwaves throughout the United Kingdom and EU member countries. The value of the British pound plummeted amid uncertainty about future economic development. Prime Minister David Cameron and his cabinet swiftly resigned, and Labour leader Jeremy Corbyn was blamed for having botched his party's pro-EU campaign. Cameron's successor, Prime Minister Theresa May, expressed her determination to move swiftly: "Brexit means Brexit." The British government formally invoked Article 50 of the Treaty of Lisbon in March 2017; it has two years to negotiate the legal and practical exit procedures with the EU. How these negotiations will pan out is still an open question. Prime Minister May called for early elections in June 2017 with the hope of gaining seats for the Conservative Party and strengthening her negotiating position vis-à-vis the EU. However, this move backfired. The Conservatives lost their majority and now must rely on the votes of MPs from the Northern Irish Democratic Unionist Party to pass legislation.

In EU countries, Germany included, the Brexit vote hit a raw nerve. The United Kingdom has been one of the most important economic and political players in the EU, and the impact of its exit on the organization's international standing and Common Foreign and Security Policy (CFSP) is unclear. Thus, everyone involved in the exit negotiations has a vested interest in maintaining close ties with the United Kingdom, perhaps none more than German politicians and businesses. Britain is Germany's third-largest trading partner, with an export volume of roughly 90 billion in 2016 euro. More than 2,500 German companies have subsidiaries in the United Kingdom, and about 3,000 British companies have subsidiaries in Germany. With Britain leaving the EU market, these close connections could become complicated. Untangling complex ties in such areas as business and scientific research will take time, and the results may be less or more dramatic than hoped for or feared by different constituencies. Questions at the core of the exit negotiations are British access to trade preferences, free movement of British and EU citizens, and British budget contributions to the EU.

The timing was also unfortunate, coming on the heels of the eurocrisis and amid heightened anti-EU sentiments. Not surprisingly, Euroskeptic leaders across Europe rejoiced, among them the AfD. Marine Le Pen (2016), president of the French National Front, expressed her belief that the EU had "become a prison of peoples" and a "people's spring was now inevitable." The British vote revealed deep divisions not only within the United Kingdom but also in Europe (Hobolt 2016).

Although predicting the political, financial, and economic consequences of the Brexit is premature, leaders must balance British against EU interests while keeping relations amicable and close. Granting the United Kingdom free-trade preferences without open borders might invite other countries to follow the British example, but they are not a given. The British vote reflected the specifics of the campaign, protest against the political establishment, and a long history of Euroskepticism that does not translate to other settings. It also sheds light on a long-standing theoretical controversy: Is EU integration driven mainly by economic motifs and cost-benefit-analysis or by a socially constructed vision of a united Europe tempering strong national identities? Economically, the United Kingdom has benefited from EU membership and the open market, increasing its exports of goods and services, including financial services. The free movement of EU citizens across member states opened opportunities for more than one million UK citizens to live on the continent, but about three million Central and Eastern Europeans moved into the United Kingdom, which was one of only three countries that did not impose restrictions on the new member. This influx stirred anti-EU sentiments among many Britons.

Attitudes toward the EU are never based solely on a cost-benefit analysis but always involve geopolitical identities constructed by historical events, media, and national narratives that are reinforced by school curricula among other sources. These identity-forming agents have long reinforced British separation from the continent. It is an island; it was a colonial empire with continued ties to the Commonwealth. In stark contrast, German identity construction after World War II strongly emphasized the economic and international benefits of belonging to Europe. Despite growing Euroskepticism, the great majority of German citizens still approve EU membership. One day prior to the British referendum, they expressed regret about the prospect of the United Kingdom leaving but confirmed their commitment to the EU and its future: 79 percent of those polled favored EU membership (*Frankfurter Allgemeine Zeitung* 2016).

No matter the outcome of negotiations, the Brexit was a wake-up call for EU leaders. Many members may take the tangible and intangible benefits for granted; others mistrust globalization and consider the EU an integral part of it, while counting on the effects of globalization to lessen the impact of leaving the EU. The blurring of states' sovereignty and the rise in immigration also strengthen identity politics. The EU must find new ways to engage citizens of member states in its future.

EUROPE AT A TURNING POINT?

"European unity started as the dream of a few; it became the hope of the many. Then Europe became one again. Today we are united and stronger: hundreds of millions of people across Europe benefit from living in an enlarged Union that has overcome the old divides" (Rome Declaration 2017). In March 2017, this celebratory statement featured prominently in commemorations of the sixtieth anniversary of the signing of the Rome Treaties in 1957, paired with sober reflections about the future. Acknowledging the challenges ahead, Jean-Claude Juncker, president of the European Commission, outlined five scenarios: (1) preservation of the current integration agenda; (2) emphasis on the single market; (3) differentiated membership according to the degree of willingness to pursue integration; (4) cutbacks to, and extensions of, the EU's reach into policy areas; and (5) expansion of the current integration agenda (https://ec.europa.eu/commission/white-paper-future-europe-reflections-and -scenarios-eu27_en).

Not surprisingly, Juncker omitted one option: break up, which skeptical voices keep predicting, however prematurely. Many EU (and German) citizens remain optimistic about the union's future but pessimistic views have increased in the last decade (see table 7.3). In the post–World War II decades, it built peace and helped to spread prosperity. Now, coping with international terrorism, new border control problems, and the integration of millions of refugees requires new forms of cross-national communication and cooperation. Cultural, religious, and regional diversity notwithstanding, sharing burdens and problem-solving will be required for Europe to thrive. A United States more focused on its own agenda and less on international leadership may also push Europeans to take more responsibility on the continent and worldwide.

Table 7.3. The Future of the EU

Would you say that you are very optimistic, fairly optimistic, fairly pessimistic, or very pessimistic about the future of the EU?

	All EU Members			Germany		
	2008	2012	2016	2008	2012	2016
Total Optimistic (%)*	63	49	50	64	53	50
Total Pessimistic (%)*	28	46	44	26	42	45

*Combined scores of very and fairly optimist/fairly and very pessimistic answers.

Source: *Standard Eurobarometer* 69, 77 (November 2008); 77 (July 2012); and 86 (December 2016).

Nevertheless, the challenges to Europe's future are real, the international environment has shifted, and national interests diverge. Political observers and scholars also differ in pinpointing not only the major sources of the problems and Germany's role in remediating them, but future prescriptions. Claus Offe argues that Europe is politically "entrapped"; policy measures urgently needed to solve its economic problems are also extremely unpopular and virtually impossible to implement by democratic means. What must be done, he argues, cannot be sold to the voting public of the core member states because they are less affected by the crisis, nor can the conditions they try to impose be easily sold to voters in the indebted countries. In his view, divides are deepening between the German-dominated "core" and the southern "periphery," between the winners and losers in the adoption of the common currency, between the advocates and opponents of greater integration, between technocrats and populists. Rifts opening throughout the continent are obstructing the EU's ability to deal with a crisis that has already caused massive suffering on its periphery and is threatening to derail the entire project (2015, 4).

Critics concerned with the democratic deficit, such as political philosopher Jürgen Habermas (2012), contend that recent developments have shifted power to the executive branch, threatening EU legitimacy. Jan-Werner Müller (2016b) emphasizes that "weakly Europeanized national public spheres" are insufficient to address the challenges of the future but can see no formula for creating a discourse across borders. Ulrich Beck (2013) also stresses the need for greater public input, a view echoed by social media and pro-EU citizens groups. From his perspective, the best way to reinvigorate Europe is to bring ordinary Europeans together to act on their own behalf. Wolfgang Streeck (2011) would like to see Europeanization scaled back—for example, discontinuing the transfer of competences to the European level—to safeguard the German welfare state. Others favor more Europeanization to supplement the common currency with unified economic and social policies. The effort should not affect German dominance but rebuild Europe through a bottom-up, democratic process as opposed to a top-down, technocratic model.

By 2015, the refugee crisis overshadowed the euro crisis, raising arguments about how best to respond. Germany's role remains controversial; German politicians see it as problem-solving and mediating, but their greater assertiveness leads foreign analysts to wonder whether national interests are prevailing over the EU's.

The nexus between European and domestic policy may be a two-sided coin. When interests clash, which will dominate? Signs of renationalization have challenged the European project and only deepened during the euro crisis. When Angela Merkel responded to the disappointing outcome of the G-7 meeting in May 2017 and the erosion of automatic trust in long-standing partnerships and called on Europeans to "really take our fate into our own hands," she can count on the support of Germans.

> Foreigners often get Mrs. Merkel all wrong. She is not the queen of Europe, nor has she any desire to be it. She is a domestic leader and politician whose mounting international stature is always a function of her ability to serve the interests and predilections of German voters. It is predominantly because Germans, for deep historical and cultural reasons, feel so "European" that she talks and acts in a "European" way. (*Economist* 2017)

Europe's future will depend on the degree of common political will to meet challenges as one polity, not separately. The idea of Europe has become more complex, and, because of the recent crises, publics across Europe are asking questions. Rebuilding a ship at sea is risky: reforms rely on a patience and persistence often lacking under high pressure. Moreover, the multilayered decision-making process binds negotiations to EU procedures and institutions, and it can be blocked by vetoes. Informal governance is increasing as established decision-making channels are dispersed, confusing the public's grasp of links between events and outcomes. However, crises also spark discussions that can lead to rejuvenation.

Such rejuvenation may well require policy shifts in Berlin, especially regarding economic integration, greater willingness to take on and share responsibilities, and, always, joint leadership with Paris. A frank discussion of the necessary sacrifices and rewards of continued integration must supplement the time-honored rhetoric of peace, stability, and prosperity.

Chapter 8

Germany in Global Politics

KEY TERMS

Bundeswehr
civilian power
constructivism
geo-economic power
hard and soft power
hegemony
liberal institutionalism
military missions abroad

multilateralism
NATO
neorealism
power restraint
Russia
security and alliance structures
transatlantic relations
United Nations

The dramatic upheavals of World Wars I and II, division into two ideologically opposed states, and the Cold War from 1947 to 1990 circumscribed West Germany's external relations. Caught on the front line of East-West confrontation, its priorities were peace and stability, national unification, and integration into Western alliances (*Westbindung*), such as NATO and the European Community (Haftendorn 1983). On the other side of the Iron Curtain, East German policies were intimately tied to Soviet ambitions; they emphasized strict demarcation from the West and unquestioned loyalty to the Warsaw Pact and the Council for Mutual Economic Assistance.

With the end of the Cold War and unification, Germany regained complete sovereignty, turned its location in the heart of Europe from ideological battleground to bridge between East and West, and, for the first time since World War II, engaged its armed forces in peacekeeping, conflict resolution, and counterterrorism missions. These changes are embedded in global developments, in particular, challenges to US hegemony, the rise of China, the revival of Russia as a great power, and instability in the Middle East. They went hand in hand with the emergence of the EU on the international stage.

Fast-forward to 2015: in November, *Time* magazine selected Chancellor Angela Merkel as person of the year, recognizing her leadership in the euro and refugee crises and during the standoff between Ukraine and Russia. Earlier in the year, prominent German politicians from Federal President Joachim Gauck to Foreign Minister Frank-Walter Steinmeier (SPD) and Defense Minister Ursula von der Leyen (CDU) called for a stronger role in confronting international challenges together with its alliance partners in NATO and the EU. According to Gauck, Germany's prosperous and stable democratic system entailed responsibility for greater involvement in international affairs. Many German scholars have promoted a shift in priorities from restrained power to greater involvement (Münkler 2015). Have German elites finally heeded the calls for leadership expressed by both international and national pundits? Early developments during the presidency of Donald Trump have challenged both the EU and Germany to assume greater responsibility on the international stage.

This chapter highlights the evolution of Germany's foreign and security policy. We begin with debates about its trajectory after unification before turning to specific implications. A brief overview of German relations with selected countries highlights both economic interests and the continued legacy of history. International diplomatic engagement as well as European integration are central to Germany's identity; these core principles and applications were discussed in chapter 7, which also addressed Germany's relationship with France and the United Kingdom.

Russia and the United States are introduced separately as prominent although very different touchstones of Germany's foreign policy priorities. In the conclusion, we return to the key question since unification: how have change and continuity meshed in foreign and security policy?

BACKGROUND

Accounts of Germany's foreign and security policy invariably gauge the blend of continuity and change, a calculation that starts with its most important alliance partners: France and the United States. Franco-German relations were the motor for deeper integration in Europe after World War II, and their interdependence continues. Formally, they are still equals in European affairs, but the international clout has tilted in favor of Germany. The end of the Cold War somewhat diminished Europe's role in US foreign policy calculus, but successive US governments have called on the EU (and Germany) to share the burden of international leadership in the face of periodic conflicts in Eastern Europe, upheavals in the Middle East with consequences for state sovereignty from Kosovo to Ukraine, the fight against terrorism, and the promotion of democracy and protection of human rights seemingly everywhere.

These calls have challenged policy makers, especially when they involved military action. Unlike other major European players, Germany's military engagement is limited out of necessity and by choice. First, it does not hold nuclear or chemical weapons, and its army is capped in size and fully integrated into NATO. Second, due to a long-standing policy of military restraint, it adheres to multilateralism, acting within the framework of NATO and EU, and sees military action as a last resort. Third, the German government prioritizes measures associated with peace building, conflict resolution, democracy promotion, and multilateral diplomacy. Coalition building with other governments and cooperating with international organizations is the baseline of Germany's foreign engagement, and active participation in the EU, a sine qua non for its leaders who portray their actions as carrying out and working on behalf of EU interests. The Maastricht Treaty aimed to strengthen the external profile of the EU; amid many trials and errors, the EU's standing in the world has increased. The creation of a new post, High Representative for Common Foreign and Security Policy, in 1999, following the civil war in the former Yugoslavia, was one important step in shaping the EU's foreign policy profile; Javier Solana (1999–2009), a former secretary general of NATO, first held the post. In 2009, the Treaty of Lisbon upgraded the High Representative to the position of Vice President of the EU Commission. Today, the EU's legation includes the High Representative of the Union for Foreign and Security Policy and the European External Action Service (EEAS), the diplomatic service of the EU. The EU's Common Foreign and Security Policy (CFSP) provides a platform to pursue national and European interests abroad. It supplements, rather than replaces, the foreign and security policy stances and initiatives of individual member states. Depending on the issue at stake, experts either laud examples of successful European cooperation or criticize the EU as a political lightweight since sovereignty often still trumps European considerations. German actions illustrate both. For example, in December 1991, German leaders unilaterally recognized the breakaway republics Croatia and Slovenia and in 2011, breached Western consensus by abstaining from support of a no-fly zone over Libya in the UN. On the other hand, they were crucial when the EU successfully implemented economic sanctions against Iran and Russia, negotiated a truce in Ukraine, and promoted democracy around the world.

In accordance with its general support for international organizations, Germany is the third-largest contributor to the regular UN budget after the United

States and Japan and among the top contributors to the UN's peacekeeping budget. Several UN organizations are based in Germany, including the International Naval Court. Germany participates in peace-building operations after the conclusion of military conflicts and is a major donor of development aid. It is less generous in providing personnel; in 2015, approximately 185 soldiers and police personnel were assigned to international UN operations. Since the late 1990s, German governments have occasionally tried to gain a seat as a permanent member of the UN Security Council. The proposal was initially tied to general UN reforms, such as the effort to include countries from Asia, Latin America, and Africa as Security Council members without veto powers. These reforms stalled in 2006 and were thwarted when opposition grew to adding another European country besides France and the United Kingdom, which have been permanent members of the Council since its inception. Germany has been a nonpermanent member of the UN Security Council five times.

Strong backing of international cooperation extends beyond UN missions, NATO, and the EU. For example, in 1998, Germany was one of the first signatories of the Rome Statute, which established the International Criminal Court (ICC) to prosecute crimes against humanity, genocide, and other war crimes. German leaders supported the Kyoto Protocol (1997) to reduce carbon dioxide emissions and renegotiating a later protocol on climate change in Paris in 2015. In line with the country's efforts to implement the transition to sustainable energy, the German government endorsed this internationally nonbinding agreement of 195 UN member countries reached on December 12, 2015, as a significant sign of multilateral cooperation to remediate climate change. The United States has since vowed to abandon the agreement, while EU leaders continue to endorse it strongly. Despite some criticism from environmental activists and NGOs that the Paris Agreement did not go far enough, these multilateral agreements enjoy broad public and political support in Germany.

With the partial exception of the Left Party, governments can rely on broad cross-party consensus in matters of foreign and security policy, bolstered by domestic political institutions—in particular, the need for coalition government. The chancellor, together with the foreign minister, shapes and executes foreign relations, and the views of the coalition partner matter. Since 1990, these partners have varied from the FDP, Alliance 90/The Greens, to the SPD, then to the FDP and back to the SPD; as the holder of the foreign-affairs portfolio, the smaller coalition party has bargaining power and enjoys international visibility. For example, FDP politicians have shaped German foreign policy for many decades. Hans-Dietrich Genscher, foreign minister from 1974 to 1992, is closely associated with efforts to promote better relations with the East. Green foreign minister Joschka Fischer (1998–2005) pushed for a strong human rights approach to foreign relations and a deepening of European integration.

Ostpolitik—that is, relations with Central and Eastern Europe and the Soviet Union—have been one important backbone of Germany's foreign policy before and after unification. During the Cold War, the pursuit of diplomatic relations with countries across the Iron Curtain culminated in nonaggression treaties and the recognition of postwar borders. West Germany's active involvement in détente policies, such as the Conference on Security and Cooperation in Europe (CSCE), helped to pave the way for the peaceful revolution and subsequent unification in 1989–90. After 1990, close political and economic ties with the former communist bloc assisted in the accession of new member states from the region to the EU and in bridging the East-West divide.

THE IMPRINT OF HISTORY ON
FOREIGN AND SECURITY POLICY

Factors Shaping Policies before Unification

Drawing on the lessons of misused power in the first half of the twentieth century, West Germany sought to limit power politics. The Basic Law was written to implement a complete break with its authoritarian, militaristic, and violent past; it commits German leaders to pursue peace and peaceful conflict settlement and places a constitutional ban on wars of aggression and possession of nuclear weapons. NATO membership, in place since 1955, granted West Germany a security umbrella, sanctioned its place in the West, and allowed it to focus on economic reconstruction. Since no peace treaty was signed after 1945 due to Cold War divisions, only with unification did the four former wartime Allies—the United States, France, the United Kingdom, and the Soviet Union—terminate their rights over Germany.

The power constraints imposed by history and international obligations became deeply embedded in the German public and political elites and infused the Two-Plus-Four negotiations between the two German states and the four former Allies from January to September 1990. These negotiations resembled the settlements usually laid out in a peace treaty; they included territorial regulations, membership in international defense organizations, and the size and capabilities of the German army. The final treaty confirmed the borders of the united Germany as the borders of the former West Germany and the GDR, settling any potential land conflicts with Poland and then Czechoslovakia. It also strictly limited Germany's military force to no more than 350,000 soldiers, and possession or production of any nuclear or chemical weapons remained off limits. Unification settlements terminated Allied rights, and by 1994, US military bases were reduced, and troops from the Soviet Union left for good. Only troops under NATO command stayed, with certain limitations on their deployment in the eastern part of the country, or what was formerly the GDR. The conclusion of these negotiations was a prerequisite for German unification in October 1990.

Some East German oppositional groups favored demilitarizing altogether and forming a neutral, nonmilitarily aligned, united Germany. Alternatives ranged from regional security cooperation to a new security architecture that would include the Soviet Union to complete neutralization (Albrecht 1992). They were never realistic. A sense of urgency for international settlement with the Soviet Union after the end of the GDR prevailed, and political leaders chose the "prefabricated house" of NATO (Sarotte 2009). It reformed its strategy, expanded its territorial scope, and stepped up its mission, much to the chagrin of the Russian leadership. Germany's commitment to NATO aimed to demonstrate its reliability as a partner and the continuity of its pre-unification security policy.

Continuity and Change after Unification

Unification triggered extensive soul-searching among international foreign-policy experts over future priorities. Would the nation become more introspective and concerned with its own interests or more "normal" in international relations; that is, would it pursue a stronger role as a midsized power? The answers varied widely, depending on which view of state power and international relations theory was invoked. *Neorealists* assume that states strive to maximize power in international relations to provide security, stability, and economic well-being for their citizens. Cooperation is seen as effective only insofar as it reflects national interests. West Germany's post–World War II foreign and security policy confounded these assumptions in deliberately downplaying the concept of power. In the aftermath of unification, neorealist academics argued that due to size, geographic location, and economic power, Germany would secure its own national interest and aim to assume a leading role in world politics. Scholars such as John J. Mearsheimer (1990) speculated that it could step up its weaponry and acquire nuclear weapons.

Liberal institutionalists pointed to the international interdependence that would continue to shape and constrain united Germany's power. Membership in the NATO alliance, the United Nations, and, above all, the European Union all serve to limit Germany's national power by prioritizing cooperation rather than unilateralism. Peter Katzenstein (1997) described the unified Germany as a "tamed power" largely due to its ties to the EU and preference for soft power, and Helga Haftendorn (1996) compared it to "Gulliver in the center of Europe." Reinforcing Germany's history of constraint, *constructivists* highlight the collective identities of political actors and the public in considering foreign policy. They posit that foreign policy goals and concepts are not fixed or given but are social constructs shaped by norms, ideas, and values. In Germany's case, the historical and political ruptures of World Wars I and II, defeat, and division have indelibly marked its identity so that the culture of remembrance overrides power-driven national interests (Bach 1999).

Over the years, commentators and scholars have struggled to describe Germany's new international position. It has been called reluctant but indispensable, a gentle power, a central power, a middle power, as well as passive and provincial, inconsistent, and diffident yet dominant, to cite just a few attempts. Some contend that Germany's power ambitions are embedded in the rise of Europe as an economic power (Crawford 2007). Other observers characterize Germany's approach to power as new geo-economics; that is, economic motifs drive global influence and power ambitions (Kundnani 2015; Szabo 2015), with little interest in a global political role. On occasion, economic interests rest uneasily with security considerations and the promotion of democracy and human rights.

Today, military power restraint and multilateralism remain core tenets of foreign and security policy, but increasingly, the political elite embraces assertiveness and willingness to take on leadership roles. These changes reflect generational turnover, international encouragement, if not pressure, and adaptations to new security challenges. Starting with Chancellor Gerhard Schröder (1998–2005), a new generation of leaders for whom World War II was no longer the defining experience sits at the helm of governments. Schröder's assertive foreign-policy rhetoric and, to a lesser extent, action led some to argue that Germany was weighing the benefits of self-restraint against enlightened self-interest (Haftendorn 2006). US leaders were first to call on Germany to step up its foreign-policy ambitions, including its willingness to consider military engagement and a stronger role in Europe. Angela Merkel carefully carved out another approach. She espoused diplomacy and resilience in negotiations with European leaders during the various EU crises. If the euro crisis gradually changed European leaders' reluctance, anxiety about too much German power can be resurrected at any time, although usually by domestic constituencies in Poland, for example, or southern European countries. More important, changes in the international environment have thrust European leadership on Germany, among them the rise of Russia under Vladimir Putin, the consequences of Middle Eastern instability for Europe, the refugee crisis, and, not least, the EU's emerging international participation.

Lacking a consensus on the depth and span of German power, most commentators agree on its commitment to *civilian power* and preference for *soft power*. First applied to the European Community, the concept of a civilian power remains an apt characterization of the EU's foreign and security policy (Börzel and Risse 2009), but it has also been applied to Germany and Japan, among other nations. At its core, a civilian power uses its international influence to promote such democratic norms as human rights and the rule of law and considers military action a last resort only after diplomacy and international negotiation have failed. Applied to German foreign and security policy, problem solving in concert with others has been variously described as "never alone" or "reflexive multilateralism" (Harnisch and Maull 2001). Time and again, policy advisors and politicians evoke this concept to argue in favor of diplomacy, negotiation, and conflict resolution without the use of force.

The *soft power* concept shares the intuitive appeal and murky definition of civilian power; politicians and scholars apply different meanings to it. Introduced by Joseph Nye (1991) with reference to the United States, soft power implies leading by good example in contrast to *hard power*, which takes a stick-and-carrot approach to pursue policy priorities. However, the criteria that should be used to measure soft power remain ambiguous. In recent years, global soft power rankings by the British magazine *Monocle* and the US-based consulting firm Portland, among others, consider measurements of culture, government, education, and business as well as expert opinions. The rankings routinely assign Germany a top place with the United States and the United Kingdom.

Other sources rely exclusively on public opinion data to gauge a country's soft power appeal. Citing an April 2010 BBC survey in which 50 percent of respondents affirmed that Germany has a positive influence in world affairs, two German political scientists deliberated tongue-in-cheek about the indicators: "It probably involves a mixture of Goethe and Mesut Özil [a prominent German soccer player of Turkish origins], Mercedes and green tech, dealing with the past and multilateralism." They also cautioned that "attraction alone is not power—the aforementioned conjectures may shape Germany's image, but they do not necessarily lead to support for German policies. It is necessary to turn international respect into influence" (Kleine-Brockhoff and Maull 2011). In other words, soft power is only effective when backed by the will and the tools to exert authority.

In reality, different power concepts mix, and no one description fits all policy positions. For example, Germany adheres more closely to a neorealist view in defending its economic interests abroad and a civilian power approach in pursuing its security policy. In its recent policy toward Russia, many forms of power were at work: hard or compulsory power through economic sanctions; institutional power through coalition building as part of the EU negotiations with Russia; and civil power that framed Russia as the uncivil power that resorts to military action and illegal annexation (Fix 2015).

German leaders may have taken the international stage, but the process has been cautious and incremental, especially in terms of security policy. Step by step, Germany has expanded its engagement in military and peacekeeping operations, shaping a new defense policy unthinkable at the time of unification.

POWER RESTRAINT AND NEW RESPONSIBILITIES

After World War II, West German military operations outside of German or NATO territory were out of the question. The 1990 Gulf War and wars in the former Yugoslavia in the 1990s increased pressure on German leaders, particularly from the United States, to augment financial with military support for Western action, but when the governing coalition of CDU and FDP under Chancellor Helmut Kohl (CDU) made tentative steps to accede, domestic opposition was strong. German military units participated in naval mine-sweeping missions during the Gulf War in 1990–91, and antiaircraft missile units operated in Turkey during Operation Desert Storm. German military personnel also participated in stabilization missions in Somalia and humanitarian missions in Cambodia. However, Alliance 90/The Greens, the SPD, churches, and unions rejected any policy change toward military involvement abroad. They thought that such actions violated the constitution, which they interpreted as allowing military action only in defense of the home territory. The Federal Constitutional Court was called upon to act as final arbiter and, following a heated debate, ruled in 1994 that German forces could participate in military actions other than self-defense (that is, "out-of-area operations"), but only under two conditions: under the umbrella of international organizations, such as NATO, the EU, the UN, or the Organization of Security and Cooperation in Europe (OSCE); and with the German Parliament's approval (*Parlamentsvorbehalt*). The legitimacy of international military action is significantly, if not formally, enhanced when the UN endorses it.

The Kosovo War in 1999 marked a departure from abjuring the use of military force outside of NATO territory. Despite legal concerns about the lack of a UN mandate, Germany took a more active role in foreign deployment and peacekeeping missions as part of NATO and EU missions. The coalition government of SPD and Alliance 90/The Greens, parties with strong pacifist credentials, shifted the discourse: evoking the Holocaust, Foreign Minister Joschka Fischer argued that Germany had a moral obligation to intervene to prevent genocide and atrocities against the Albanian majority population in the Serbian province of Kosovo. German leaders also advocated engagement in the war-torn region of the former Yugoslavia and strongly supported the

1999 Stability Pact for Southeastern Europe, with important implications for peacekeeping, economic support, and promotion of democracy.

After the September 11, 2001, attacks in the United States by the Islamic terrorist group Al-Qaeda, Germany participated in the UN-supported war against the Taliban in Afghanistan. A clear majority of the Bundestag voted for troops to join the International Security Assistance Force (ISAF) mission, and Parliament renewed the mandate each year until 2014, when the United States officially ended its military mission in Afghanistan. Although a positive vote was never in doubt, Chancellor Gerhard Schröder (SPD) used a vote of confidence to get his coalition government in line; public support was always more muted.

The underlying foreign-policy consensus favoring multilateral settings allows participation in operations, both civil and military, within the framework of alliances, such as NATO and, increasingly, the EU's European Common Foreign and Security Policy network. Unlike France and the United Kingdom and certainly unlike the United States, Germany remains a limited military power. After unification, with the merger of the two formerly opposed conscription-based armies, the West German *Bundeswehr* and the East German National People's Army, troop strength was reduced significantly, and the move to a professional army began only in 2011. Conscription was suspended; mandatory social service for conscientious objectors was replaced by voluntary social service.

In 2016, the German army comprised approximately 178,000 soldiers, far below the level granted in the Two-Plus-Four Treaty of 1990. This number is low compared to the United States, with close to 1.5 million active military personnel, but commensurate with other major European powers. In any case, numbers alone are insufficient to gauge military preparedness; equipment and perceived fighting strength matter greatly.

By 2015, more than 300,000 soldiers had served abroad but often for relatively short times; overall, foreign engagement peaked at around 10,000 soldiers in 2002. In August 2014, for example, about 4,000 German soldiers served in different NATO, UN, or EU operations abroad, including missions in Afghanistan and Uzbekistan, KFOR in Kosovo, and the EU-led Operation Atalanta fighting piracy off the coast of Somalia. In 2015 and 2016, the numbers were 2,800 and 2,900, respectively. Balancing international needs against its capacities, Germany prefers to provide support in its areas of strength: conflict mediation, capacity building, administration, specialized technological equipment, and training such personnel as police forces in postconflict areas.

Overall, German military expenditures rank among the highest in the world but below NATO's recommended 2 percent of the GDP, despite recent increases in absolute numbers (see figure 8.1). In response to US president Donald Trump's sharp criticism of Germany and other European NATO allies, CDU leaders reiterated their intent to move toward the 2 percent within a decade, as agreed upon in 2014, but this move is unpopular and challenged by the left. Angela Merkel and Defense Minister Ursula von der Leyen emphasized that a modern security concept extends beyond defense expenditures and should include development and foreign aid. Although not mentioned in the public debates, an increase to 2 percent of the GDP would make Germany the largest spender in Europe outside of Russia. Germany's arms exports reflect its technology-heavy economy and global business interests more than its military inclinations.

A skeptical public that strongly endorses restraint is checking any greater assertiveness in military affairs. In 2015, only 25 percent of Germans agreed that Germany should play a more active military role in helping to maintain peace and stability in the world. Just over two-thirds (69 percent) believed that, given its history, Germany should limit its military role in world affairs. Notably, there was no partisan difference: 78 percent of CDU and CSU members and 77 percent of SPD adherents oppose a greater military role. Public attitudes about greater sharing of the global security burden also reflected reticence. About half preferred that countries deal with their own problems. Such reluctance may not be surprising given the political and security environment; in the same study, the US public gave similar answers (Pew Research Center 2015).

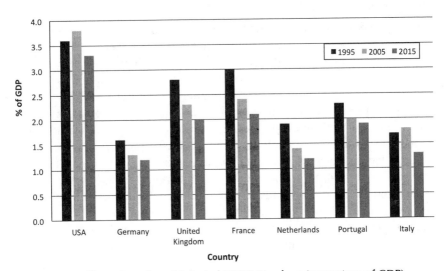

Figure 8.1. Military Spending of Selected NATO Members (percentage of GDP)
Source: https://www.sipri.org/databases/milex.

            Chapter 8

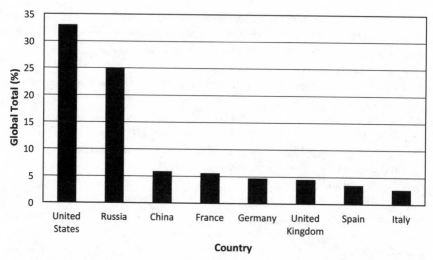

Figure 8.2. Top Arms Exporters by Country, 2011–15

Source: Adapted from https://www.sipri.org/research/armament-and-disarmament/arms-transfers-and-mili
tary-spending/international-arms-transfers.

GERMANY AND THE WORLD

Recasting German Interests on a Global Scale

Israel and the Middle East

The major geographic area of Germany's international engagement is Europe,
but it has widened. Due to the Holocaust, Israel has a special place in German foreign and security policy. In the 1950s, West German leaders reached
out to Israel, setting themselves apart from East Germany, which to its very
end maintained strained, if not hostile, relations. The SED leadership allowed
Palestinian terrorist groups to train on its soil and refused to accept any responsibility for the Holocaust. The West German policy of reconciliation and
support for Israel has strengthened close cultural, political, and economic
ties, but tensions have arisen. With the EU, German governments endorse a
two-state settlement to accommodate Palestinian claims, and they condemn
Israeli settlements in East Jerusalem and the West Bank. German politicians
often mediate in EU negotiations with Israel, but the stalled peace process and
the hardline rhetoric of the current Israeli government and some Palestinian
groups complicate relations.

Iran

Relations between Iran and the Western powers have long been tense, particularly during Mahmoud Ahmadinejad's presidency (2005–13). His aggressive rhetoric toward the West and Israel, support for the militant Palestinian-Sunni group Hamas, and accusations by the International Atomic Energy Association that Iran's nuclear program failed to comply with international obligations led to an ice age after 2005. In 2007, the EU joined in US and UN sanctions and expanded them in 2010 and 2012. Germany's emerging international role and economic and political interests in solving the conflict with Iran led to inclusion in the nuclear negotiations with Iran that commenced in 2006 alongside the five members of the UN Security Council and the High Representative of the EU. In 2013, when Iran's presidency changed to a more pragmatist leader, nuclear policy negotiations took off and concluded in summer 2015. Sanctions lift gradually as Iran complies with international rules regarding nuclear proliferation. The EU welcomed this outcome as a breakthrough that will allow its once profitable economic relations with Iran to resume.

China

Germany's relations with China illustrate the dominance of economic interests. Since Gerhard Schröder, German chancellors have visited China almost yearly with CEOs and business managers from some of Germany's leading industries in tow, particularly producers of automobiles, railway systems, telecommunications, and renewable energy, and Chinese political and economic leaders visit Germany frequently. Trade relations have deepened and benefited both sides, yet concerns about Chinese practices, including limited market access and appropriation of technology by investing in Germany and other European countries, also raise concerns. Human-rights issues overshadow these economic relations only tangentially. Cultural exchange is another important avenue. Increasingly, Chinese students enroll at German universities, and German language institutes, such as the Goethe Institute, have offices in major cities such as Shanghai and Beijing.

Africa

On the African continent, economic trade relations have concentrated on the north, but security concerns following the rise of Islamist terrorism severely damaged the status of Egypt, Tunisia, and Morocco as favorite German tourist destinations, and regime instabilities, particularly in Libya and Egypt, have diminished economic interest in the region. In other parts of Africa, Germany supports the UN Millennium Development Goals and its follow-up programs to reduce poverty and improve gender equality, the environment, and education; about half of Germany's total development aid goes to African countries. Support and cooperation are organized through government agencies, such as the German Society for International Cooperation (GIZ), efforts by the Lutheran and Catholic Churches, political foundations (*Stiftungen*), and a dense network of NGOs.

Unlike France and Britain, Germany's colonial past is only a faint memory, and former colonial ties, except for Namibia, play almost no role in contemporary relations. Germany was late in securing colonies and had to give them up after World War I. However, in Namibia, a former German colony, the empire waged an extermination campaign against the Herero and Nama peoples, who mounted resistance from 1904 to 1907 in the Herero Wars. German governments were slow to acknowledge the crimes; only in 2016 did they refer to the massacre of tens of thousands of people as genocide and start to discuss possible reparation payments. Atonement is also linked to new forms of remembrance: in 2016–17, the German Historical Museum in Berlin staged a widely acclaimed exhibit on German colonialism.

Germany and Russia

Germany's relations with the Soviet Union and, after 1991, Russia remain complex. Security concerns dominated during most of the Cold War, but trade gained prominence. After unification and the collapse of the Soviet Union, economic relations took center stage, but not for long: now security and economic interests have merged (Pond 2015).

During the Cold War, the Soviet Union acted as gatekeeper to any improvement in relations between East and West Germany. A precondition for German unification was Soviet assent, and the German narrative underlines the constructive role President Mikhail Gorbachev played in the swift, peaceful merger. Afterward, German businesses welcomed the transition to a mixed market economy in Russia, and trade increased, making Germany the country's most important trading partner (Stent 1999). Chancellors Helmut Kohl, Gerhard Schröder, and Angela Merkel tried to bind Russia to Europe. Russia's transition from communism to a market economy and a new political system was particularly challenging. The chaotic years under President Boris Yeltsin and perceived humiliation by the West, in particular the expansion of

NATO into Central and Eastern Europe, paved the way for a shift in foreign policy orientations under Vladimir Putin. For a short time after his ascent to the presidency in 2000, close relations with Germany continued, but the steady move toward authoritarianism, nationalist rhetoric, and great-power ambitions gradually have taken their toll. Still, the divide between the once close and amicable nations came as a surprise to their leaders.

Most important, it has quenched German aspirations to include Russia in Europe's security structure. Putin has repeatedly denied that Russia belongs to Europe, rather invoking its special status as a Eurasian power with its own development path, independent of Western interference. When he stepped up efforts to suppress domestic opposition and to reassert Russia's role in the Near Abroad, the territory of the former Soviet Union, clashes with Germany and the West were inevitable, and they escalated with Russian incursions in Ukraine in 2014.

As part of its 2009 European Neighborhood Policy (ENP), the EU tried to foster closer relations with Armenia, Azerbaijan, Belarus, Georgia, Moldova, and Ukraine, all territories that were once part of the Soviet Union. Ukraine has historical, political, and economic significance to Russia, and while most western Ukrainians see their future allied with the EU, many eastern Ukrainians are tied to Russia through language, culture, and business. The territory soon engaged in a tug of war. In November 2013, the Ukrainian government canceled signing an association agreement with the EU under pressure from Russia, which had plans for its own customs union with Eastern European countries, including Ukraine. This reversal triggered a wave of demonstrations and civil unrest in Kiev's Maidan [Independence] Square. Protesters demanded the president's resignation and an end to widespread government corruption, abuse of power, and human rights violations. Unrest turned violent. In February 2014, the government of President Viktor Yanukovych was overthrown; he fled to Russia, and a new government was formed.

Russia then annexed Crimea, arguing that the transfer of the Black Sea peninsula from Russia to Ukraine in 1954 had violated Soviet law and the rights of ethnic Russians. A hasty public referendum overwhelmingly sanctioned annexation, but Western governments immediately questioned its legitimacy, and relations deteriorated with Russia's military support for separatists in eastern Ukraine. They hit a new low when a Dutch passenger plane was shot down over eastern Ukraine in summer 2014. From March on, the EU and other Western countries applied and widened sanctions against Russian individuals and businesses and separatists in Ukraine. Russia responded with its own sanctions, including a ban on food imports from the EU, the United States, Norway, Canada, and Australia.

The Ukrainian crisis has been an important test case for EU resolve: it demonstrated that the EU could speak "with one voice" and apply hard power. Chancellor Merkel and Foreign Minister Steinmeier, along with French president Hollande, acted as chief negotiators in efforts to resolve the crisis, including a 2015 truce in eastern Ukraine. The crisis also exposed long-standing tensions about Russia in the German political establishment and public opinion. So-called Russian sympathizers or pragmatists questioned the use of sanctions and Russia's exclusion from the G-8. They explain Russia's behavior as a reaction to the continued violation of its interests by Western institutions, in particular NATO, but also the EU. Others, including the German government and many influential media outlets, pointed to Russia's encroachment on Ukrainian sovereignty and ruthless power politics at the expense of its neighbors.

Economic and energy interests remain crucial to German/Russian relations. Germany's entry into the Russian market with large-scale projects, such as Siemens's engagement in modernizing the Russian railway system and Gazprom's activity in the German/European energy market, created great opportunities for both profit and corruption (Szabo 2015). Energy has become critical to economic relations, not only between Germany and Russia, but across Europe. The Nord Stream project, a gas pipeline serving several northern European countries and Germany but circumventing Ukraine and the Baltic states, is highly profitable for energy companies in the East and West. Steve Szabo bluntly points out Putin's ties to former Stasi officers and their role in Nord Stream and Gazprom management; former chancellor Schröder (with no Stasi ties) also featured prominently in the Gazprom deal.

Under the leadership of Angela Merkel, Germany has emerged as the power broker in EU relations with Russia as evidenced by its role in negotiating a peace deal in Ukraine and its backing of economic sanctions on Russia. As the Ukrainian crisis showed, support for rule of law and democracy can outweigh economic interests, at least temporarily. Political and security considerations also play a role. Russian actions intent on spreading misinformation through social media and its own international TV channel and breaking into computers and servers of parties, parliaments, and/or governments in the United States and Europe, Germany included, have become bolder and more widespread. Their goal is to influence electoral outcomes, deepen discord among Western allies, and deepen rifts within Western democracies. These massive challenges notwithstanding, the German government keeps the lines of communication open, especially since Russia is a key player in settling security challenges, such as Iranian nuclear policy and the civil war in Syria. Observers agree that German-Russian relations have cooled considerably but disagree over the degree of shift (Siddi 2016).

Germany and the United States

US involvement in Europe after World War I under President Woodrow Wilson was short-lived; World War II overturned its isolationist tendency in favor of global superpower status. In Germany and elsewhere in Europe, it shaped the forms democracy would take and aided in economic recovery. Under its auspices, NATO provided a much-needed security umbrella against the communist threat. US influence was also felt in media and cultural development, higher education, and consumer goods (Nolan 2012, 3). Maybe nowhere in Europe was the Americanization of culture more pronounced than in West Germany. With France, the United States was the fulcrum of West German foreign relations, and soon the former occupying power became a friend and partner, fostering a close network of political, business, and civil society ties. US support helped to cement unification against the reluctance of some European allies (Zelikow and Rice 1995).

The high priority assigned to German/American relations continues: all postunification governments have promoted them, and economic, cultural, and political ties have remained strong and counterbalanced emerging tensions. The continued presence of NATO troops on (West) German soil emphasized US security interests. During the 1990s, US Presidents George H. W. Bush and Bill Clinton viewed Germany as a key ally and demanded greater engagement and cooperation in shouldering burdens. In 2003, transatlantic relations grew strained when the US government favored military action in Iraq. Germany and France advocated continued negotiations and settlements through international organizations such as the UN and openly doubted US claims that the Iraqi government harbored weapons of mass destruction. Public opinion shifted dramatically; Germans grew skeptical of America's hegemony in world affairs, and mistrust of political actions can cause a crisis of legitimacy. Germany's refusal to participate in the war was a severe setback for the once amicable relations.

Strains relaxed after the election of Barack Obama in 2008 (Rudolf 2010). In fact, approval ratings for his policies, including foreign policy, were higher in Germany than in the United States, although some citizens were subsequently disappointed by unfulfilled promises—for example, to close the military prison in Guantanamo Bay—and uneasy about seemingly omnipresent US security and secret service operations in Germany and Europe. During the Cold War, intelligence cooperation between the two countries was intense, especially since US initiatives had built Germany's intelligence institutions. However, the German public condemned the surveillance practices of the US National Security Agency (NSA) exposed by programmer Edward Snowden in 2013. Revelations that a close ally had tapped the cell phones of Angela Merkel and government ministers and collected data from a number of institutions, including businesses, forced the German government to distance itself from such practices and intensified long-standing calls for greater independence (German Marshall Fund of the United States 2014), even though the public later learned that Germany also spied on the United States, albeit on a much smaller scale. Intelligence cooperation between the two countries remains vital in such areas as cybersecurity and the fight against terrorism.

With the EU's rise as a global actor, relations between individual European countries and the United States became increasingly embedded in joint actions. Recurring disputes suggested different belief and value systems shaped by enduring features of political culture. The Iraq War in particular triggered much soul-searching about the significance of cultural differences and their impact on foreign and security policy. Robert Kagan (2003) borrowed the metaphors Venus and Mars to characterize the value rift between Europe and the United States, respectively. European integration and multilateralism were contrasted with US unilateralism and the view that reluctance to use military force is cowardice. Such cultural codes form over the course of history, fostering understandings and misunderstandings in transatlantic relations (Jarausch 2006b). Others downplayed cultural chasms as "the narcissism of minor differences" (Baldwin 2009). They tempered important distinctions among European countries and emphasized the many similarities the United States and Europe share.

Are tensions in transatlantic relations a normal byproduct of close interactions and shifting foreign policy stances or an expression of growing anti-Americanism? This term is notoriously difficult to define; it can point to US cultural hegemony, the values it represents, or political actions and foreign policy. For some, criticism of US policies should not be confused with anti-Americanism; stereotypes and generalizations must be distinguished from political opposition and critical assessment (Leggewie 2004). Others explain recent waves of anti-Americanism as part of European identity building (Markovits 2007). Whether anti-Americanism is couched as critique or critique labeled as anti-Americanism, motives and targets for shifts in popular opinion vary with time.

The election of Donald Trump as forty-fifth president of the United States stunned the German public and political elites and ignited concerns about the future of transatlantic relations. Two crucial cornerstones of US foreign policy and transatlantic relations, support for NATO and European integration, have been challenged. Will German-American relations enter a new stage, with an assertive US president calling on Europe (and Germany) to take on more of the burden in NATO? Would such a policy ultimately push the EU to greater military engagement and is such an extension of the EU's power desirable? Will the joint US-European stance toward Russia be jeopardized?

Another area of potential conflict is trade. Peter Navarro, director of the White House National Trade Council, accuses Germany of unfairly manipulating the euro to its advantage by keeping its value low. This claim has been widely rejected in Germany and abroad because the ECB is independent in setting its monetary policy, but the fact that the trade surplus has become a source of contention and concern keeps it alive (see chapter 6). What impact will Trump's protectionist rhetoric have on economic policies, including the stalled TTIP negotiations? Will strong political and economic networks provide a sufficient buffer to settle disputes amicably? What spillover effects will the antiglobalist and populist mood that helped to propel Trump into office have on Germany and Europe? Ultimately, will a policy to make "America great again" provide another push for Germany to accept greater leadership in Europe? In a period of uncertainty, the German public follows US policy steps attentively. The German government is stepping up efforts to coordinate joint European efforts in maintaining amicable relations with the United States despite disagreements over trade and security.

A BALANCE SHEET OF CONTINUITY AND CHANGE

Power is at the core of international relations. Its attributes rest primarily on a country's military and economic capabilities but also reflect population size and geopolitical location, reputation in the international community, and willingness to apply its advantages. When the country was divided, West Germany was frequently called an economic giant but a political dwarf; after unification, expectations about Germany's rise as a political power sparked both promise and deep concern.

The economic foundation of Germany's power is undisputed, but what kind of political power it is and wants to be is less clear: is it a middle power or increasingly a great power? A great power exerts global influence, whereas a middle power has regional influence but occasionally ventures into select areas of global politics. What would Germany's goals as a middle power be, and how would a great power operate in a multipolar world?

Gunther Hellmann (2016) summarizes the current debate about a "new" German foreign policy: one view, advanced by the government, sees Germany as a benevolent power that actively shapes global relations (*Gestaltungsmacht*), while the other describes Germany as a new hegemon. Indeed, within the German academic community the term *hegemon* is viewed negatively. German political scientist Sebastian Harnisch puts it bluntly: "The unified Germany is no hegemon, not in Europe and not in the world," even if it has taken on international leadership (2014, 17; our translation). He points to the insufficient material and immaterial resource base as well as institutional constraints and reminds us that leadership and hegemony differ: leadership can be temporary. German leadership has also aroused critique, particularly in southern Europe, as the culture of restraint gives way to self-confidence. Others see hegemony as an analytical, not solely negative description of Germany's new role, describing it as a full-fledged hegemon or a reluctant EU hegemon (Bulmer and Paterson 2013). No matter the terminology and approach, these controversies point to Germany's increased stature in international politics.

Policy priorities and instruments have adapted to an evolving international environment in gradual and reactive processes. Political actors did not seek new responsibilities or leadership in international relations but reluctantly adjusted policies to a world in transition. Recent international developments have catapulted Germany and its political leaders to the forefront, and postunification fears of German aggression gradually yielded to calls for stronger leadership.

The cornerstones of this leadership rest on proven policy modus operandi: emphasis on multilateralism; preference for civilian/soft power tools; Europe as the core of German interests followed by strong transatlantic relations. History's lessons are not forgotten. Parliamentary control of all security institutions and support for international conflict resolution guide and constrain security policy. Even if military actions are gaining acceptance, they are far from routine.

Chapter 9

Looking Backward and Forward

The past decades have challenged and changed Germany, and the captions in the special reports of the British news magazine *The Economist* provide kaleidoscopic impressions: "Divided Still" (1996), "An Uncertain Giant" (December 2002), "Waiting for a Wunder" (February 2006), "Older and Wiser (March 2010), and "The Reluctant Hegemon" (June 2013). They allude to the difficulties of unification, qualms about taking on greater international responsibility in a rapidly changing Europe, the challenges of reforming its economic and social systems, its successful economic recovery, and, again and again, its ambivalence about its growing international role. This book has analyzed these challenges and opportunities, explored institutional characteristics, and addressed policy questions that have absorbed politicians and citizens. In this concluding chapter, we revisit some of the major themes, highlight findings, and ponder some of their consequences.

A NEW GERMANY

The unexpected unification of East and West Germany in 1990 created a new Germany, sometimes called the Berlin Republic, in the heart of Europe. However, *new* is always temporary, and here it meshed with considerable continuity; once patterns settled, the term lost significance. Some innovations proved largely symbolic—for example, moving the capital from the provincial town of Bonn to the bustling metropolis of Berlin. Others were more substantial, such as the accession of the eastern Länder and the emergence of new parties.

In 1990 and immediately afterward, the amalgam of new and old was a subject of speculation and concern. While some expected only marginal

209

adjustments, others feared a resurgent nationalistic Germany. Neither was correct. History and culture still constrain Germany's actions and shape its outlook on the future. Institutionally, the new Germany resembles West Germany more than any other model. Decision making still relies on gradualism and bargaining in interwoven, often interlocking institutions. The cornerstones of the German political system remain in place, but utilities and policies have been updated and transformed. Domestically, the political party landscape has changed; the east has adopted the institutional diversity of the western Länder; and dramatic policy adjustments in the east had repercussions in the west. Former West German mainstream parties continue to dominate politics, but overall, the political landscape has become more diverse and multilayered. The political elite remains predominantly western, but "politicians who came from the East" (Ther 2016) include Angela Merkel and former civic movement activists, such as Joachim Gauck, president from 2012 to 2017. The communist successor party, the PDS, presented a political force that spilled into the west and led to the creation of the Left party. The anti-immigrant Pegida movement is staffed mostly by East German right-wing activists. Some twenty-five years after unification, scholars still debate the legacies of communism in the east but also how much "east" is in the "west."

Germany also had to redefine its role and place in international affairs. Unification did not occur in a vacuum. It coincided with the end of the Cold War, but instead of a peace dividend, new security challenges emerged quickly. Confronted by the disintegration of the former Yugoslavia in the 1990s, terrorist attacks, the Ukrainian crisis, and the refugee challenge, Germany could no longer avoid responsibilities abroad, including military engagement, participation in peace-building operations, and leadership in international crises. Fundamental adjustments in legal provisions, policy guidelines, and even the logistics of security policy were necessary. German foreign and security reticence gradually and often reluctantly gave way to greater activism. Most Germans today acknowledge that their country's international influence has grown, and many are willing to support conflict-ridden countries (Wike 2016). Nonetheless, German power remains predominantly economic and somewhat controversial both in and outside of Europe due to the handling of the euro crisis, its trade surplus, and its economic dominance in the EU. International calls, particularly from the United States, to adjust its economic policies to promote domestic consumption and investment are becoming louder and beginning to resonate among German politicians. Still, shifting priorities and policies have to be sold to the German voter.

THE COMPARATIVE PERSPECTIVE

Throughout the book, we highlighted political and economic features that are similar to, or differ from, those of other Western democracies. Some aspects of Germany's political and economic systems have served as prototypes of consensual democracy, a conservative welfare state, a coordinated market economy, and civilian or soft power shaped by its history and the collective memory of the twentieth century. The interplay of distinctive political networks, a system of coalition government, federalist arrangements, and parapublic institutions, sets Germany apart from other European democracies. Some institutional features, such as the prominent role of labor unions, reach back to the nineteenth century, while others, such as the electoral system or the concept of defensive democracy, are rooted in the recasting of democratic structures after World War II. According to the founding fathers and mothers of the (West) German democratic state, never again would authoritarianism, Nazism, or any other dictatorship rule the country, and certain institutional features have been adopted and modified in other settings. The Federal Constitutional Court and its judicial review, for example, have served as a model in many countries, including the evolving democracies in Central and Eastern Europe. The foundations (*Stiftungen*) of the major political parties and their role in promoting democracy have inspired similar efforts elsewhere. Germany's policies for dealing with a history burdened by war and genocide in the first half of the twentieth century have gained it respect, and some of its approaches, among them reparations for victims of Nazism and policies of reconciliation, have diffused to other settings.

Germany also illustrates trends in advanced European democracies that have deepened in recent decades, among them greater party fragmentation and the rise of minor parties; the advance of advocacy democracy to complement and, at times, defy reliance on representative democracy; struggles over authority between center and periphery; decreasing membership in labor unions and political parties; the growing role of constitutional courts; the strengthening of the executive at the expense of parliament and the downgrading or, at the very least, transformation of traditional notions of sovereignty; and responses to EU encroachment on sovereignty. These trends are more pronounced in some European democracies than in others, but increased cross-border communication and political action framed by EU policies have encouraged greater interdependence and the spread of norms, ideas, and practices. Germany mirrors these developments and, in some cases, premiered them.

REVISITING UNIFICATION, EUROPEANIZATION, GLOBALIZATION

The book explored the complexities, challenges, and fruitful interchanges among unification, Europeanization, and globalization. Their processes are separate, but their logic, paths, and dynamic are intimately interwoven. Here, we inquire about their similarities, differences, and possible trajectories. Their often unintended ripple effects have varied considerably, depending on time, polity, and policy arena; their social, cultural, political, and economic impacts range from concrete legislation, demographic, and economic trends to more diffuse outcomes, such as changing attitudes regarding gender, support for new energy policies, or pressures to recalibrate educational institutions. They also fuse gradually with unexpected and rapid change. After the nuclear accident in Fukushima, Japan, for example, energy policy catapulted to the top of the political agenda, and the government decided to immediately shut down older nuclear plants and set up a plan to phase out this energy source in Germany.

Unification, Europeanization, and globalization share at least four characteristics:

- they have deepened and accelerated since the 1990s,
- they expose an open-ended dynamic of integration and interdependence with uncertain endpoints,
- they rely on political decisions and diffusion, and
- they often evoke strong feelings and opposing views.

Their synchrony is illustrated by the impact of unification on Germany's institutions, policies, and role in the world. It brought major change to eastern citizens; their state, familiar surroundings, and important identity markers disappeared. They had to get used to new political institutions and a new currency twice (first the DM, then the euro), and, for most, new jobs or early retirement changed their life trajectory and recast their biographies. For western Germans, the impact was more indirect.

However, unification did not occur in a vacuum. It was part of the breakdown of the post–World War II world order that divided much of the globe into two ideologically opposed blocs. Europe's desire to integrate deepened, and Germany's international role increased as a result. Germany overall became the most populous country in Europe except for Russia. Once it was no longer on the front line of the potential east-west confrontation, it could act as a bridge builder. Unification pressured Germany to augment its role on the international stage but also, along with demographic trends and international competition, heightened internal pressures for labor market and pension reform. In strictly institutional terms, unification had the greatest impact on the party system and voting behavior, but even here, the effects were often more diffuse than direct. After all, CDU/CSU and SPD are still the major parties, and loss of votes to smaller parties characterizes all Western democracies. The merger of the two states also tested the federal structure through functional modifications that are still unfolding.

Europeanization and Unification

Faster and Deeper

Europeanization and unification are distinct yet overlapping categories that both accelerated and deepened in the 1990s. Most of the decade was absorbed in merging the two formerly divided countries. Following jubilation, reality soon set in. Western Germans could no longer enjoy politics as usual, and new opportunities for many eastern Germans would be paired with difficult adjustments. Deindustrialization in the east, financial cost, and attitudinal barriers—Germans were said to have trouble breaking down "the wall in the head"—were some problems maintaining division.

These processes coincided with a new phase of European integration. Its rejuvenation started in the mid-1980s, and implementation of the Maastricht Treaty in 1993 established border-free trade, travel, and transnational policies among members. The treaty merged EC organizations with the EU, laid out a framework for introducing the euro currency, and expanded cooperation in many areas, including foreign and security policy, justice, and home affairs. In the next years, the EU expanded; membership rose from twelve to fifteen states, and negotiations began with many others, ultimately allowing thirteen more to join in 2004, 2007, and 2013. The Maastricht Treaty was amended several times, but the Lisbon Treaty (2009) marked the end of efforts to adjust institutionally to the widening EU; it became the first pillar supporting the European canopy and increasing its legitimacy and efficiency.

Europeanization is not completed. Rather, new and at times difficult processes of institutional adjustment are in the offing. The consequences of Britain's decision to leave the EU reach beyond economics into the realm of politics; institutions and policies must adjust to this unprecedented change. Germany will be crucial in shaping the future of European integration.

Interdependence

Many narratives portray German unification and European integration as interdependent; Germany's integration into the EU and NATO were crucial prerequisites to unification. Had Germany not been "contained" by the evolving multinational structures in Europe, the considerable reluctance of many European leaders to accede to the merger of the two Germanies would have been more difficult to overcome. International reservations about unification were assuaged only by Germany's firm commitment to European integration. German Chancellor Helmut Kohl famously reassured his counterparts in other capitals that unification and Europeanization are two sides of the same coin. Václav Havel, famous playwright and dissident turned first Czechoslovak and later Czech president, echoed these words and carried them a step further to promote the inclusion of Central and Eastern European countries into the EU: "It is difficult to imagine a united Germany in a divided Europe" (Zantovský 2014, 372).

Germany's firm mooring in the European project facilitated international acceptance of unification and accelerated overall European integration, often with unintended consequences. For example, deeper integration of monetary policy aimed to secure a united Germany within the EU but paradoxically also elevated its power and influence. The relationship is not one-sided: as Europe's economic powerhouse, Germany elevates the EU's standing in the world; it also acts as a crucial intermediary between Western and Eastern Europe. In other words, European integration both restrains and frees German influence in Europe and the world.

As a result, Germany has taken on a greater leadership role. In the Ukrainian crisis, for example, the German chancellor forged unity among EU countries to support sanctions against Russia, despite some domestic opposition from businesses and parts of the political left. Relations with the United States, whose government favored sanctioning Russia, were particularly close at that time, but the common stance against Russia also signaled a more coherent European foreign and security policy. Here again, Germany's and Europe's actions were interdependent; sanctions depended upon Germany's consent and represented both German and European interests.

Open-Ended Processes

Unification and Europeanization expose an open-ended dynamic of integration and interdependence with uncertain endpoints. Is German unity achieved when political, social, and economic similarities outweigh differences? The application of this standard is beset with difficulties since regional diversity is common in all countries, and in Germany, east-west differences coincide with pronounced north-south differences. The reference point also matters (Welsh 2013). Depending on policy area, the former East Germany can be viewed and analyzed as an economic trouble spot, a laboratory for new forms of labor relations, the vanguard in childcare coverage, or a vestige of distinct differences in religious affiliation and voting behavior. Younger generations may feel that any distinction between east and west is of purely historical value, but for others, it is still lived reality. For some, the division may end when the east no longer depends on transfer payments, but reducing German unification to economics short-changes the complexity of the process.

The future of European integration is even more open to interpretation. The last decade has given new significance to the crisis narrative that has accompanied it from the outset. In the past, national and EU elites managed most crises, with the public as bystander, but in recent years, European integration has polarized the broader public. Not surprisingly, voices critical of the loss of sovereignty in policy areas—in particular, monetary policy—have intensified; European integration is under fire from both right and left, and even pro-European parties call for reform. On the flip side, the Brexit galvanized support for integration. "Pulse of Europe," a citizen's initiative, regularly calls for public demonstrations championing the economic and political integration of Europe. The election of the pro-integrationist French president Emmanuel Macron was a vote for Europe.

While the need for change is widely conceded, how best to integrate or disintegrate Europe remains contested. The consensus holds that the EU will not become a United States of Europe, but just how much integration, the form it takes, and the territory it covers are matters of debate and disagreement (Schimmelfennig 2015, 28–29). Which areas require more integration, and where should the EU retreat to leave room for more sovereignty? Alternatively, is renationalization on the agenda, and will the EU lose stature? Did integration proceed too quickly?

These questions are not new; for example, politicians and scholars have long wondered whether membership preferences will produce disparate levels of integration (Pfetsch 2007). Core countries, among them Germany and France, pursue deeper integration with others that follow EU rules and regulations in selected policy areas. Indeed, the links between the EU and Norway, Switzerland, and Turkey are modifications of one model of tiered integration, and the distinction between EU members and the eurozone is another. In the area of security policy, EU member states rely on NATO since most belong to it, but some, such as Austria, Ireland, and Sweden, do not even though they still participate in the EU's Common Foreign and Security Policy. The EU has also established the European Neighborhood Policy (ENP) to facilitate cooperation and closer trade and political relations with states to the east and south, like Ukraine, whose full membership is not desirable or not yet on the agenda. The EU has signed similar agreements with several North African countries, yet relations remain tense. The openness of the European integration process presents both internal and external challenges.

Europeanization and Globalization

Europeanization is ultimately linked with globalization; both evolved over centuries and focus on economic integration, formal networks and institutions, and the flow of goods, people, finances, and ideas. Interdependence works both ways: Does the growth of EU competencies represent an embrace of globalization or a way to counter its effects? In the first interpretation, a strong, united Europe enhances the competitiveness of its member states. EU policies and institutions mediate the impact of global forces, which, some argue, may require its transformation into a new "republic" (Guérot 2016) or open space for renewed political discourse on the perils and problems of globalization. In the second interpretation, the Maastricht Treaty was designed in the late 1980s and early 1990s to respond to a progressively more globalized market and new economic players, such as Japan and, later, China. Most European countries preferred participating in the regional integration of an "ever closer" union to navigating the global market on their own, and their arguments were not limited to the economic realm. Support for a more integrated CFSP, for example, is high in most member states. Evidence suggests that an integrated Europe can withstand global challenges better (Jacoby and Meunier 2010).

Both Europeanization and globalization complicate governing and test traditional notions of sovereignty. Separating the national from the supranational has become increasingly difficult in many areas of policy making. The EU's reach into the lives of citizens has become more direct and critical voices more prominent. In the past decade, all European countries have witnessed a rise of Euroskeptic parties and movements, representing a new cleavage in European party systems. Antiglobalization protests, increasingly directed against the expansion of free trade agreements, have also been on the rise. In trade negotiations with Canada (CETA) and the United States (TTIP), EU critics and globalization critics joined forces. While the CETA agreement was finally signed in 2016 after several years of negotiation, opposition against TTIP continues and negotiations are on hold.

The backlash against Europeanization as a process of transferring sovereignty to the European level includes the rise of nationalist sentiments in many European countries. The "old specter of nationalism is back again and for many has greater popular appeal than the EU, which has been made the scapegoat for all sorts of social and economic problems" (Ther 2016, vii) even when problems are rooted elsewhere. Nationalism feeds on Euroskepticism; it is a reaction against, and, for some, an alternative to, the processes of globalization and Europeanization.

Globalization and Europeanization have made borders in Europe more porous; the new political map of Europe is not etched in stone. Although doomsday scenarios about European integration are not new and may again prove wrong, new problems are arising from within and outside the EU. Within the EU, the alleged legitimacy crisis is perceived differently in different countries, creating friction and deepening fractures; outside challenges are even harder to control as European economies are intertwined with global developments.

Globalization and Europeanization are also intimately linked to Europe's ties with the United States. The rise of a stable, democratic Western Europe after World War II has greatly benefited both sides. Today, the EU and the United States are each other's leading trade partners by volume (imports plus exports), and their cooperation has secured peaceful interaction rather than competition and war. Will these ties remain strong, given the resurgence of nationalism and populism in many European countries and the United States? Or will the two continents drift apart? How important are common transatlantic values and trajectories? Will the Western-oriented, liberal international order survive new strains within the Western alliance, some prompted by its former anchor, the United States? How will its opponents, particularly in Russia, affect the alliance or benefit from its strains? These questions will engage politicians and political observers in the years to come.

A WORLD IN MOTION

At times, writing about contemporary politics seems a Sisyphean task, in particular when developments and events shake up established assumptions. In the United States, a new administration lays out different goals and strategies in global politics. In Europe, Brexit negotiations have resumed, but far from calming domestic politics, they have opened new divisions. The outcome of the Dutch and French elections in spring 2017 reduced anxieties about a right-wing shift in major European capitals, yet our understanding of European affairs and the future trajectories of global politics remains troubled. Germany is often seen as a steady beacon above the changing sea. The outcome of the 2017 national election qualified, but did not negate, this characterization. In tandem with France, it is still called upon to reform the EU and shape the future of Europe.

Leaving aside electoral outcomes and a potential nationalist resurgence, the enduring threat of terrorism; the rise of Russia and China on the international stage; civil wars, conflicts, poverty, and environmental changes that feed the flow of refugees; worries about the stability of international financial markets and free trade; and uncertainty about the path that the United States will take under President Donald Trump are among the many factors that governments in Germany and all Western democracies must consider. Developments in the EU add to the challenges. The euro crisis is contained but not solved; solidarity among member states has also been tested by questions about immigration; antiestablishment parties and growing societal inequalities complicate national politics.

Germany sits at the center of European and global developments. As the largest, economically strongest, and politically most influential country in the EU, it must take on greater responsibility for the future of the European continent.

References

Acemoglu, Daron, and James A. Robinson. 2012. *Why Nations Fail: The Origins of Power, Prosperity and Poverty*. New York: Crown.

Alba, Richard, and Nancy Foner. 2015. *Strangers No More: Immigration and the Challenges of Integration in North America and Western Europe*. Princeton, NJ: Princeton University Press.

Albrecht, Ulrich. 1992. *Die Abwicklung der DDR: Die "2+4-Verhandlungen." Ein Insider Bericht*. Wiesbaden: Westdeutscher Verlag.

Allen, Christopher S. 2010. "Ideas, Institutions and Organized Capitalism: The German Model of Political Economy Twenty Years after Unification." *German Politics & Society* 28 (2): 130–50.

Alscher, Mareike, and Eckhard Priller. 2016. "Zivilgesellschaftliches Engagement." In *Datenreport 2016: Ein Sozialbericht für die Bundesrepublik Deutschland*, 383–89. Bonn: Bundeszentrale für politische Bildung.

Anders, Carsten, Hendrik Biebeler, and Hagen Lesch. 2015. "Gewerkschaftsmitglieder. Mitgliederentwicklung und politische Einflussnahme: Die deutschen Gewerkschaften im Aufbruch?" *IW-Trends: Vierteljahresschrift zur empirischen Wirtschaftsforschung* 42 (1): 21–36.

Arendt, Hannah. 1958. *The Origins of Totalitarianism*. 2nd enlarged edition. New York: Meridian.

Armingeon, Klaus, and Besir Ceka. 2014. "The Loss of Trust in the European Union during the Great Recession since 2007: The Role of Heuristics from the National Political System." *European Union Politics* 15 (1): 82–107.

Arnold, Felix, Ronny Freier, and Martin Kroh. 2015. "Geteilte politische Kultur auch 25 Jahre nach der Wiedervereinigung?" *DIW Wochenbericht*, no. 37: 803–14.

Ash, Timothy Garton. 1990. "The Revolution of the Magic Lantern." *New York Review of Books*, January 18. http://www.nybooks.com/articles/1990/01/18/the-revolution-of-the-magic-lantern.

———. 2013. "The New German Question." *New York Review of Books*, August 15. http://www.nybooks.com/articles/2013/08/15/new-german-question.

Ayoub, Phillip M. 2016. *When States Come Out: Europe's Sexual Minorities and the Politics of Visibility.* Cambridge, UK: Cambridge University Press.

Bach, Jonathan P. G. 1999. *Between Sovereignty and Integration: German Foreign Policy and National Identity after 1989.* Münster, Germany: LIT Verlag.

Bäck, Hanna, Patrick Dumont, Henk Erik Meier, Thomas Persson, and Kåre Vernby. 2009. "Does Europeanization Lead to a 'Presidentialization' of Executive Politics?" *European Union Politics* 10 (2): 226–52.

Baldwin, Peter. 2009. *The Narcissism of Minor Differences: How America and Europe Are Alike—An Essay in Numbers.* Oxford, UK: Oxford University Press.

Bannas, Günter. 2006. "Sie inszeniert sich nicht. Angela Merkel's Stil." *Frankfurter Allgemeine Zeitung*, November 22, 3. http://germanhistorydocs.ghi-dc.org/sub _document.cfm?document_id=3802.

Bartlett, Robert. 1993. *The Making of Europe: Conquest, Colonization, and Cultural Change, 950–1350.* Princeton, NJ: Princeton University Press.

Beck, Ulrich. 2013. *German Europe.* Cambridge, UK: Polity.

Behrens, Martin. 2015. "Weakening Structures, Strong Commitment: The Future of German Employment Relations." In *The German Model—Seen by Its Neighbors*, edited by Brigitte Unger, 135–45. Lexington, KY: SE Publishing.

Behrens, Martin, and Andreas H. Pekarek. 2016. "Umkämpfte Einheit: Neue und alte Muster der Lagerbildung in der deutschen Gewerkschaftsbewegung." *Zeitschrift für Politikwissenschaft* (Supp 2) 26: 117–34.

Bertelsmann Foundation, ed. 2015. "Religion Monitor. Understanding Common Ground. Special Study of Islam, 2015. An Overview of the Most Important Findings." https://www.bertelsmann-stiftung.de/en/our-projects/religion-monitor.

Betts, Paul. 2005. "Germany, International Justice and the Twentieth Century." *History and Memory* 17 (1–2): 45–86.

Bittner, Jochen. 2014. "What Germany Can Teach Japan." *New York Times*, April 16. http://www.nytimes.com/2014/04/17/opinion/what-germany-can-teach-japan.html.

Blackbourn, David, and Geoff Eley. 1984. *The Peculiarities of German History: Bourgeois Society and Politics in Nineteenth-Century Germany.* Oxford, UK: Oxford University Press.

Blohm, Michael, and Jessica Walter. 2016. "Einstellungen zur Rolle der Frau und des Mannes." In *Datenreport 2016: Ein Sozialbericht für die Bundesrepublik Deutschland*, 426–31. Bonn: Bundeszentrale für Politische Bildung.

Blyth, Mark. 2013. *Austerity: The History of a Dangerous Idea.* Oxford, UK: Oxford University Press.

Bönke, Timm, Matthias Giesecke, and Holger Lüthen. 2015. "The Dynamics of Earnings in Germany: Evidence from Social Security Records." *DIW Discussion Paper* no. 1514. Berlin: German Institute for Economic Research.

Borchert, Jens, and Klaus Stolz. 2011. "German Political Careers: The State Level as an Arena in Its Own Right?" *Regional & Federal Studies* 21 (2): 205–22.

Börzel, Tanja, and Thomas Risse. 2009. "Venus Approaching Mars? The EU as an Emerging Civilian World Power." *Berliner Arbeitspapiere zur EU*, no. 11.

Bozo, Frédéric. 2005. *Mitterrand, the End of the Cold War, and German Unification.* New York: Berghahn.

Brubaker, Rogers. 1992. *Citizenship and Nationhood in France and Germany*. Cambridge, MA: Harvard University Press.

Bujard, Martin. 2015. "Consequences of Enduring Low Fertility—A German Case Study. Demographic Projections and Implications for Different Policy Fields." *Comparative Population Studies* 40 (2): 131–64.

Bulmer, Simon, and William E. Paterson. 2013. "Germany as the EU's Reluctant Hegemon? Of Economic Strength and Political Constraints." *Journal of European Public Policy* 20 (10): 1387–1405.

Bundesgesetzblatt, ed. 2016. "Integrationsgesetz vom 31. Juli 2016." Bundesanzeiger Verlag.

Bundeskriminalamt. 2017. "Kriminalität im Kontext von Zuwanderung. Kernaussagen. Betrachtungszeitraum: 1.01.–30.09.2016," March 31. Wiesbaden.

Bundesministerium für Wirtschaft und Energie, ed. 2016. "Erneuerbare Energien auf einen Blick." Accessed November 27. https://www.bmwi.de/DE/Themen/Energie/Erneuerbare-Energien/erneuerbare-energien-auf-einen-blick.html.

Busch, Andreas. 2005. "Shock-Absorbers under Stress: Parapublic Institutions and the Double Challenges of German Unification and European Integration." In *Governance in Contemporary Germany: The Semisovereign State Revisited*, edited by Simon Green and William E. Paterson, 94–114. Cambridge, UK: Cambridge University Press.

Chambers, Simone, and Jeffrey Kopstein. 2001. "Bad Civil Society." *Political Theory* 29 (6): 837–65.

Cohen, Roger. 2015. "The German Question Redux." *New York Times*, July 13. http://nyti.ms/1Hplxq1.

Colino, César. 2013. "Varieties of Federalism and Propensities for Change." In *Federal Dynamics: Continuity, Change, and the Varieties of Federalism*, edited by Arthur Benz and Jörg Broschek, 48–69. Oxford, UK: Oxford University Press.

Conradt, David P. 2015. "The Civic Culture and Unified Germany: An Overview." *German Politics* 24 (3): 249–70.

Cooke, Lynn Prince. 2011. *Gender-Class Equality in Political Economies*. New York: Routledge.

Crawford, Beverly. 2007. *Power and German Foreign Policy: Embedded Hegemony in Europe*. Basingstoke and New York: Palgrave Macmillan.

Dalton, Russell J., Susan E. Scarrow, and Bruce E. Cain. 2004. "Advanced Democracies and the New Politics." *Journal of Democracy* 15 (1): 124–38.

Dalton, Russell J., and Steven Weldon. 2010. "Germans Divided? Political Culture in United Germany." *German Politics* 19 (1): 9–23.

Daniel, William T. 2015. *Career Behaviour and the European Parliament: All Roads Lead through Brussels?* Oxford, UK: Oxford University Press.

Datenhandbuch zur Geschichte des Bundestages seit 1990. Edited by Deutscher Bundestag. https://www.bundestag.de/datenhandbuch

Datenreport 2016. Ein Sozialbericht für die Bundesrepublik Deutschland. Edited by Statistisches Bundesamt (Destatis) and Wissenschaftszentrum für Sozialforschung (WZB) in cooperation with Das Sozio-oekonomische Panel (SEOP) am

Deutschen Institut für Wirtschaftsforschung (DIW Berlin). Bonn: Bundeszentrale für Politische Bildung.

Davidson-Schmich, Louise. 2015. "LGBT Politics in Germany: Unification as a Catalyst for Change." Paper presented at the Annual Meeting of the German Studies Association, Washington, DC.

———. 2016. *Gender Quotas and Democratic Participation.* Ann Arbor: University of Michigan Press.

Decker, Frank. 2016. "The 'Alternative for Germany': Factors behind Its Emergence and Profile of a New Right-Wing Populist Party." *German Politics & Society* 34 (119): 1–16.

Della Porta, Donatella, Hanspeter Kriesi, and Dieter Rucht, eds. 1999. *Social Movements in a Globalising World.* London: Palgrave Macmillan.

Dette-Koch, Elisabeth. 2003. "German Länder Participation in European Policy through the Bundesrat." In *German Public Policy and Federalism: Current Debates on Political, Legal and Social Issues,* edited by Arthur B. Gunlicks, 182–96. New York: Berghahn.

Deutscher Paritätischer Wohlfahrtsverband, ed. 2016. Zeit zu handeln. Bericht zur Armutsentwicklung in Deutschland 2016. https:/www.de-paritaetische.de/armuts-bericht

Deutschland Magazine. 2007. Special Issue on Berlin 6 (4).

Die Beauftragte für die neuen Bundesländer. 2016. *Jahresbericht der Bundesregierung zum Stand der Deutschen Einheit. 2016.* Edited by Bundesministerium für Wirtschaft und Energie. Berlin: Bundesministerium für Wirtschaft und Energie.

Doerschler, Peter. 2015. "Die Linke: Still an Eastern Cultural Icon?" *German Politics* 24 (3): 377–401.

Downs, William M. 2012. *Political Extremism in Democracies: Combating Intolerance.* New York: Palgrave Macmillan.

Drakulic, Slavenka. 2016. "Competing for Victimhood: Why Eastern Europe Says No to Refugees." *Eurozine.* http://www.eurozine.com/articles/2015-11-04-drakulic-en .html.

Dustmann, Christian, Bernd Fitzenberger, Uta Schönberg, and Alexandra Spitz-Oener. 2014. "From Sick Man of Europe to Economic Superstar: Germany's Resurgent Economy." *Journal of Economic Perspectives* 28 (1): 167–88.

Dyevre, Arthur. 2011. "The German Federal Constitutional Court and European Judicial Politics." *West European Politics* 34 (2): 346–61.

Economist. 2013. "The Reluctant Hegemon." June 15. http://www.economist.com/ news/leaders/21579456-if-europes-economies-are-recover-germany-must-start -lead-reluctant-hegemon.

———. 2015a. "The Silent Minority." February 7. http://www.economist.com/news/ united-states/21642222-americas-largest-ethnic-group-has-assimilated-so-well -people-barely-notice-it.

———. 2015b. "The Indispensable European." November 7. http://www.economist .com/node/21677643/pring.

———. 2017. "How to Understand Angela Merkel's Comments about America and Britain." May 28. http://www.economist.com/blogs/kaffeeklatsch/2017/05/what-s -brewing-germany.

Edinger, Michael. 2009. "Profil eines Berufsstands: Professionalisierung und Kar- rierelogiken von Abgeordneten im vereinten Deutschland." In *Parlamentarismus- forschung in Deutschland: Ergebnisse und Perspektiven 40 Jahre nach Erscheinen von Gerhard Loewenbergs Standardwerk zum Deutschen Bundestag*, edited by Helmar Schöne and Julia von Blumenthal, 177–205. Baden-Baden: Nomos.

Ekiert, Grzegorz, and Jan Kubik. 1999. *Rebellious Civil Society: Popular Protest and Democratic Consolidation in Poland, 1989-1993*. Ann Arbor: University of Michigan Press.

Elazar, Daniel Judah. 1987. *Exploring Federalism*. Tuscaloosa: University of Ala- bama Press.

Esping-Andersen, Gøsta. 1990. *The Three Worlds of Welfare Capitalism*. Princeton, NJ: Princeton University Press.

Eurobarometer. 2013. "Public Opinion in the European Union," *Standard Euroba- rometer* 80 (Spring 2013). Accessed August 11, 2015. http://ec.europa.eu/public _opinion/archives/eb/eb80/eb80_first_en.pdf.

European Commission. 2014. "European Citizenship. Standard Eurobarometer 81." http://ec.europa.eu/public_opinion/archives/eb/eb81/eb81_citizen_en.pdf.

———. 2016. "Gender Pay Gap." http://ec.europa.eu/justice/gender-equality/gender -pay-gap/situation-europe/index_en.htm.

European Council. 1993. "Official Positions of the Other Institutions and Organs— European Council, Presidency Conclusions." Art. 7, A, iii. http://www.europarl .europa.eu/enlargement/ec/cop_en.htm.

Eurostat. 2016a. "Shedding Light on Energy in the EU: A Guided Tour of Energy Statistics." http://ec.europa.eu/eurostat/cache/infographs/energy/.

———. 2016b. "Energy Production and Imports." http://ec.europa.eu/eurostat/statis tics-explained/index.php/Energy_production_and_imports#Imports.

"Facts: The Bundestag at a Glance." 2016. German Bundestag, Public Relations Division.

Federal Ministry of Economics and Technology. 2015. "Energy Concept for an En- vironmentally Sound, Reliable and Affordable Energy Supply: Complete Source." http://www.bmwi.de/English/Redaktion/Pdf/energy-concept,property=pdf,bereich =bmwi,sprache=en,rwb=true.pdf.

Federal Ministry of the Interior, ed. 2014. *Migration and Integration: Residence Law and Policy on Migration and Integration in Germany*. http://www.bmi.bund.de.

Feldman, Gardner Lily. 2012. *Germany's Foreign Policy of Reconciliation: From Enmity to Amity*. Lanham, MD: Rowman & Littlefield.

Ferree, Marx Myra. 2012. *Varieties of Feminism: German Gender Politics in Global Perspective*. Stanford, CA: Stanford University Press.

Fichter, Michael. 1997. "Trade Union Members: A Vanishing Species in Post-Unifi- cation Germany." *German Studies Review* 20 (1): 83–104.

Fish, M. Steven, and Matthew Kroenig. 2009. *The Handbook of National Legisla- tures: A Global Survey*. New York: Cambridge University Press.

Fix, Liana. 2015. "The Different Shades of German Power: A 'Germanification' of EU Foreign Policy during the Ukraine Crisis?" Bilbao: UACES.

Fleckenstein, Timo, Adam M. Saunders, and Martin Seeleib-Kaiser. 2011. "The Dual Transformation of Social Protection and Human Capital: Comparing Britain and Germany." *Comparative Political Studies* 44 (12): 1622–50.

Forschungsgruppe Wahlen. 2016. "Gewünschte Koalition seit 1997." http://www .forschungsgruppe.de/Umfragen/Politbarometer/Langzeitentwicklung_-_Themen _im_Ueberblick/Politik_I/#KoalWunsch.

Frankfurter Allgemeine Zeitung. 2016. "Große Mehrheit der Deutschen steht zur EU." June 22. http://www.faz.net/aktuell/politik/brexit/deutsche-waeren-fuer-die -eu-zeigt-sih-vor-brexit-abstimmung-14301521.html.

Geißler, Rainer. 2011. "Migranten und Kriminalität: Wissenschaftliche Erkenntnisse zur Darstellung in den Medien." In *Nationale Identität und Integration: Herausforderungen an Politik und Medien in Frankreich und Deutschland*, edited by Roland Löffler, 142–57. Freiburg: Herder.

German Marshall Fund of the United States. 2014. "Transatlantic Trends 2014." http://www.gmfus.org/publications/transatlantic-trends-2014.

Göktürk, Deniz, David Gramling, Anton Kaes, and Andreas Langenohl, eds. 2011. *Transit Deutschland: Debatten zu Nation und Migration*. Paderborn: Konstanz University Press.

Goodwin, Matthew, and Caitlin Milazzo. 2015. *UKIP: Inside the Campaign to Redraw the Map of British Politics*. Oxford, UK: Oxford University Press.

Gress, Franz. 2010. "Federalism and Democracy in the Federal Republic of Germany." In *Federal Democracies*, edited by Michael Burgess and Alain-G. Gagnon, 178–201. Abingdon: Routledge.

Gross, Stephen. 2013. "The German Economy and East-Central Europe: The Development of Intra-Industry Trade from Ostpolitik to the Present." *German Politics & Society* 31 (3): 83–105.

Guérot, Ulrike. 2016. *Warum Europa eine Republik werden muss: Eine politische Utopie*. Bonn: Dietz Verlag.

Haas, Ernst B. 1958. *The Uniting of Europe: Political, Social, and Economic Forces, 1950–1957*. Stanford, CA: Stanford University Press.

Habermas, Jürgen. 1994. "Citizenship and National Identity." In *The Condition of Citizenship*, edited by Bart van Steenbergen, 20–35. London: Sage.

———. 2010. "Leadership and Leitkultur." *New York Times*, October 28. http://www .nytimes.com/2010/10/29/opinion/29Habermas.html.

———. 2012. *The Crisis of the European Union: A Response*. Cambridge, UK: Polity.

Haftendorn, Helga. 1983. *Sicherheit und Entspannung: Zur Außenpolitik der Bundesrepublik Deutschland 1955–1982*. Baden-Baden: Nomos.

———. 1996. "Gulliver in the Center of Europe: International Involvement and National Capabilities for Action." In *Germany and Europe in the Nineties*, edited by Bertel Heurlin. London: Macmillan.

———. 2006. *Coming of Age: German Foreign Policy since 1945*. Lanham, MD: Rowman & Littlefield.

Hall, Peter A. 2012. "The Economics and Politics of the Euro Crisis." *German Politics* 21 (4): 355–71.

Hall, Peter A., and David Soskice. 2001. *Varieties of Capitalism: The Institutional Foundations of Comparative Advantage*. Oxford, UK: Oxford University Press.

Hamilton, Daniel S. 2015. "TTIP's Geostrategic Implications." Testimony at the Hearing on National Security Benefits of Trade Agreements with Asia and Europe, Committee on Foreign Affairs, U.S. House of Representatives, May 17, 2015. http://docs.house.gov/meetings/FA/FA18/20150317/103161/HHRG-114-FA18 -Wstate-HamiltonD-20150317.pdf.

Harnisch, Sebastian. 2014. "Deutsche Führung in der internationalen Gesellschaft: ein rollentheoretischer Ansatz." In *Deutsche Außenpolitik und internationale Führung: Ressourcen und Praktiken und Politiken in einer veränderten Europäischen Union*, edited by Sebastian Harnisch and Joachim Schild, 17–55. Baden-Baden: Nomos.

Harnisch, Sebastian, and Hanns W. Maull, eds. 2001. *Germany as a Civilian Power? The Foreign Policy of the Berlin Republic*. Manchester: Manchester University Press.

Hassel, Anke. 2014. "The Paradox of Liberalization—Understanding Dualism and the Recovery of the German Political Economy." *British Journal of Industrial Relations* 52 (1): 57–81.

Hellmann, Gunther. 2016. "Zwischen Gestaltungsmacht und Hegemoniefalle: Zur neuesten Debatte über eine 'neue deutsche Außenpolitik.'" *Aus Politik und Zeitgeschichte* 66 (28–29): 4–12.

Hepburn, Eve. 2008. "The Neglected Nation: The CSU and the Territorial Cleavage in Bavarian Party Politics." *German Politics* 17 (2): 184–202.

Heun, Werner. 2011. *The Constitution of Germany*. Oxford, UK: Hart.

Hillebrand, Rainer. 2015. "Germany and Its Eurozone Crisis Policy: The Impact of the Country's Ordoliberal Heritage." *German Politics & Society* 33 (1/2): 6–24.

Hobolt, Sara B. 2016. "The Brexit Vote: A Divided Nation, a Divided Continent." *Journal of European Public Policy* 23 (9): 1259–77.

Hobsbawm, Eric J. 1994. *The Age of Extremes: The Short Twentieth Century, 1914–1991*. New York: Pantheon Books.

Hofmann, Gunter. 2013. "Nazis rein, Linke raus." *Die Zeit*, July 11. http://www.zeit .de/2013/29/berufsverbote-radikalenerlass-1972.

Hooghe, Liesbet, and Gary Marks. 2001. *Multilevel Governance and European Integration*. Lanham, MD: Rowman & Littlefield.

———. 2009. "A Post-Functionalist Theory of Integration: From Permissive Consensus to Constraining Dissensus." *British Journal of Political Science* 39 (1): 1–23.

Hooghe, Liesbet, Gary Marks, and Arjan H. Schakel. 2008. "Operationalizing Regional Authority: A Coding Scheme for 42 Countries, 1950–2006." *Regional & Federal Studies* 18 (2–3): 123–42.

Howard, Marc Morjé. 2012. "Germany's Citizenship Policy in Comparative Perspective." *German Politics & Society* 30 (1): 39–51.

Inglehart, Ronald. 1977. *The Silent Revolution: Changing Values and Political Styles Among Western Publics*. Princeton, NJ: Princeton University Press.

"Interview with Joachim Gauck." 1995. *Deutschland Archiv* 28 (11): 1228–32.

Irwin-Zarecka, Iwona. 1993. "In Search of Usable Pasts." *Society* 30 (2): 32–36.

Jacobsen, Lenz, and Veronika Völlinger. 2016. "Zuwanderung und Kriminalität: Wenn man es nur genauer wüßte." *Zeit Online*, December 29. http://www.zeit.de/gesell schaft/zeitgeschehen/2016-12/zuwanderung-kriminalitaet-statistik-polizei-migration.

Jacoby, Wade. 2001. *Imitation and Politics: Redesigning Modern Germany*. Ithaca, NY: Cornell University Press.

———. 2015. "Europe's New German Problem: The Timing of Politics and the Politics of Timing." In *The Future of the Euro*, edited by Matthias Matthijs and Mark Blyth, 187–209. Oxford, UK: Oxford University Press.

———. 2017. *Surplus Germany*. Paper Series No. 8. Washington, DC: Transatlantic Academy.

Jacoby, Wade, and Sophie Meunier. 2010. "Europe and the Management of Globalization." *Journal of European Public Policy* 17 (3): 299–317.

James, Paul, and Manfred B. Steger. 2014. "A Genealogy of 'Globalization': The Career of a Concept." *Globalizations* 11 (4): 417–34.

Jarausch, Konrad H. 2006a. *After Hitler: Recivilizing Germans, 1945–1995*. Oxford, UK: Oxford University Press.

———. 2006b. "Drifting Apart: Cultural Dimensions of the Transatlantic Estrangement." In *Safeguarding German-American Relations in the New Century*, edited by Hermann Kurthen, Antonio V. Menéndez-Alcarcón, and Stefan Immerfall, 17–31. Lanham, MD: Lexington.

Jeffery, Charlie, and Nicole M. Pamphilis. 2016. "The Myth and the Paradox of 'Uniform Living Conditions' in the German Federal System." *German Politics* 25 (2): 176–92.

Jeřábek, Martin. 2011. *Deutschland und die Osterweiterung der Europäischen Union*. Wiesbaden: VS Verlag für Sozialwissenschaften.

Joppke, Christian. 2010. *Citizenship and Immigration*. Cambridge, UK: Polity.

Kagan, Robert. 2003. *Of Paradise and Power: America and Europe in the New World Order*. New York: Random House.

Kahlert, Heike. 2015. "Nicht als 'Gleiche' vorgesehen. Über das 'akademische Frauensterben' auf dem Weg an die Spitze der Wissenschaft." *Beiträge zur Hochschulforschung*, no. 3: 60–78.

Karapin, Roger. 2007. *Protest Politics in Germany: Movements on the Left and Right since the 1960s*. University Park: Pennsylvania State University Press.

Katzenstein, Peter J. 1987. *Policy and Politics in West Germany: The Growth of the Semisovereign State*. Philadelphia: Temple University Press.

———, ed. 1997. *Tamed Power: Germany in Europe*. Ithaca, NY: Cornell University Press.

Keane, John. 2003. *Global Civil Society?* Cambridge, UK: Cambridge University Press.

Kielmannsegg, Peter Graf. 2000. *Nach der Katastrophe: Eine Geschichte des geteilten Deutschland*. Berlin: Siedler.

Kintz, Melanie. 2014. "Many New Faces, But Nothing New? The Sociodemographic and Career Profiles of German Bundestag Members in the Eighteenth Legislative Period." *German Politics & Society* 32 (2): 16–25.

Kirchheimer, Otto. 1966. "The Transformations of Western European Party Systems." In *Political Parties and Political Development*, edited by Joseph La Palombara and Myron Weiner, 237–59. Princeton, NJ: Princeton University Press.

Kitschelt, Herbert. 1989. *The Logics of Party Formation: Ecological Politics in Belgium and West Germany*. Ithaca, NY: Cornell University Press.

———. 2000. "The German Political Economy and the 1998 Election." In *Power Shift in Germany: The 1998 Election and the End of the Kohl Era*, edited by

David P. Conradt, Gerald R. Kleinfeld, and Christian Soe, 200–220. New York: Berghahn Books.

Kitschelt, Herbert, and Wolfgang Streeck. 2004. "From Stability to Stagnation: Germany at the Beginning of the Twenty-First Century." In *Germany: Beyond the Stable State*, edited by Herbert Kitschelt and Wolfgang Streeck, 2–32. London: Frank Cass.

Kleine-Brockhoff, Thomas, and Hanns W. Maull. 2011. "The Limits of German Power: Berlin Has Much Potential for Global Influence, and Just as Many Shortcomings." *IP-Journal, Deutsche Gesellschaft für Auswärtige Politik.* https://ip-journal.dgap.org/en/ip-journal/regions/limits-german-power.

Klusmeyer, Douglas B., and Demetrios G. Papademetriou. 2009. *Immigration Policy in the Federal Republic of Germany*. New York: Berghahn Books.

Kneip, Sascha. 2011. "Gegenspieler, Vetospieler oder was? Demokratiefunktionales Agieren des Bundesverfassungsgerichts 1951–2005." *Politische Vierteljahresschrift* 52 (2): 220–47.

———. 2015. "Von rügenden Richtern und richtenden Rügen. Das Bundesverfassungsgericht und die Regierung Merkel II." In *Politik im Schatten der Krise. Eine Bilanz der Regierung Merkel 2009–2013*, edited by Reimut Zohlnhöfer and Thomas Saalfeld, 273–301. Wiesbaden: Springer VS.

Kocka, Jürgen. 1988. "German History before Hitler: The Debate about the German Sonderweg." *Journal of Contemporary History* 23 (1): 3–16.

———. 2016. "A New Special Path for Germany." *Telos* 176 (Fall): 209–12.

Kommers, Donald P., and Russell A. Miller. 2012. *The Constitutional Jurisprudence of the Federal Republic of Germany: With a New Foreword by Justice Ruth Bader Ginsberg*. 3rd and exp. ed. Durham, NC: Duke University Press.

König, Thomas, and Lars Mäder. 2008. "Das Regieren jenseits des Nationalstaates und der Mythos einer 80-Prozent-Europäisierung in Deutschland." *Politische Vierteljahresschrift* 49 (3): 438–63.

Kopstein, Jeffrey. 1997. *The Politics of Economic Decline in East Germany, 1945–1989*. Chapel Hill: University of North Carolina Press.

Korteweg, Anna C., and Gökce Yurdakul. 2014. *The Headscarf Debates: Conflicts of National Belonging*. Stanford, CA: Stanford University Press.

Kundnani, Hans. 2015. *The Paradox of German Power*. Oxford, UK: Oxford University Press.

Ladrech, Robert. 2009. "Europeanization and Political Parties." *Living Review in European Governance* 4 (1): 4–21.

Lang, Sabine. 2013. *NGOs, Civil Society, and the Public Sphere*. Cambridge, UK: Cambridge University Press.

Leggewie, Claus. 2004. "Renaissance des Antiamerikanismus? Zur Unterscheidung von Amerikakritik und Antiamerikanismus am Beginn des 21. Jahrhunderts." In *Amerika und Europa—Mars und Venus? Das Bild Amerikas in Europa*, edited by Rudolf Thadden and Alexandre Escudier, 105–15. Göttingen: Wallstein Verlag.

Lehmbruch, Gerhard. 1976. *Parteienwettbewerb im Bundesstaat: Regelsysteme und Spannungslagen im Institutionengefüge der Bundesrepublik Deutschland*. Stuttgart: Kohlhammer.

Leibfried, Stephan, Evelyn Huber, Matthew Lange, Jonah D. Levy, Frank Nullmeier, and John D. Stephens, eds. 2015. *The Oxford Handbook of Transformations of the State*. Oxford, UK: Oxford University Press.

Lemke, Christiane. 1991. *Die Ursachen des Umbruchs: Politische Sozialisation in der ehemaligen DDR*. Opladen: Westdeutscher Verlag.

———. 1997. "Nachholende Mobilisierung: Demokratisierung und politischer Protest in post-kommunistischen Gesellschaften." *Aus Politik und Zeitgeschichte* 47 (5): 29–37.

Lenard, Patti Tamara. 2010. "What Can Multicultural Theory Tell Us about Integrating Muslims in Europe?" *Political Studies Review* 8 (3): 308–21.

Le Pen, Marine. 2016. "After Brexit, the People's Spring Is Inevitable." *New York Times*, June 28. http://www.nytimes.com/2016/06/28/opinion/marine-le-pen-after -brexit-the-peoples-spring-is-inevitable.html.

Linn, Susanne, and Frank Sobolewski. 2015. *The German Bundestag: Functions and Procedures: 18th Electoral Term*. Rheinbreitbach: NDV GbmH & Co.

Lijphart, Arend. 2012. *Patterns of Democracy: Government Forms and Performances in Thirty-Six Countries*. 2nd ed. New Haven, CT: Yale University Press.

Lukas, Julius, and Doreen Reinhard. 2016. "Wer beherrscht den Osten?" *Zeit Online*, May 24. http://www.zeit.de/2016/22/ostdeutschland-2016-macht-einfluss-mdr -doku/komplettansicht.

Mabbatt, Deborah. 2016. "What Brought the State In: Minimum Wage in Germany." *Journal of European Public Policy* 23 (8): 1240–58.

Maier, Charles S. 1997. *Dissolution: The Crisis of Communism and the End of East Germany*. Princeton, NJ: Princeton University Press.

Mair, Peter, and Cas Mudde. 1998. "The Party Family and Its Study." *Annual Review of Political Science* 1 (1): 211–29.

Markovits, Andrei S. 2007. *Uncouth Nation: Why Europe Dislikes America*. Princeton, NJ: Princeton University Press.

Marshall, T. H. 1964. *Class, Citizenship, and Social Development: Essays*. 1st US ed. Garden City, NY: Doubleday.

Maull, Hanns W. 2011. "Deutsche Außenpolitik: Orientierungslos." *Zeitschrift für Politikwissenschaft* 21 (1): 95–119.

———. 2015. "Von den Schwierigkeiten des Regierens in Zeiten der Globalisierung." *Aus Politik und Zeitgeschichte* 65 (31–32): 34–39.

Mearsheimer, John J. 1990. "Back to the Future: Instability in Europe after the Cold War." *International Security* 15 (4): 5–56.

Menz, Georg. 2009. *The Political Economy of Managed Migration: Nonstate Actors, Europeanization, and the Politics of Designing Migration Policies*. Oxford, UK: Oxford University Press.

Messina, Anthony M. 2009. "The Politics of Migration to Western Europe: Ireland in Comparative Perspective." *West European Politics* 32 (1): 1–25.

Meulemann, Heiner. 2016. "Religiösität und Säkularisierung." In *Datenreport 2016: Ein Sozialbericht für die Bundesrepublik Deutschland*, 378–82. Bonn: Bundeszentrale für politische Bildung.

Moravscik, Andrew. 1998. *The Choice for Europe: Social Purpose and State Power from Messina to Maastricht*. Ithaca, NY: Cornell University Press.

Mouritsen, Per. 2013. "The Resilience of Citizenship Traditions: Civic Integration in Germany, Great Britain and Denmark." *Ethnicities* 13 (1): 86–109.

Mudde, Cas. 2016. "Europe's Populist Surge: A Long Time in the Making." *Foreign Affairs* 95 (6): 25–30.

Mushaben, Joyce Marie. 2008. *The Changing Faces of Citizenship: Integration and Mobilization among Ethnic Minorities in Germany*. New York: Berghahn Books.

———. 2017. *Becoming Madam Chancellor: Angela Merkel and the Berlin Republic*. Cambridge, UK: Cambridge University Press.

Müller, Jan-Werner. 2006. "On the Origins of Constitutional Patriotism." *Contemporary Political Theory* 5 (3): 278–96.

———. 2016a. "Populismus: Symptom einer Krise der politischen Repräsentation." *Aus Politik und Zeitgeschichte* 66 (40–42): 24–29.

———. 2016b. "The EU's Democratic Deficit and the Public Sphere." *Current History*, no. 779 (March): 83–88.

Münkler, Herfried. 2009. *Die Deutschen und ihre Mythen*. Berlin: Rowohlt.

———. 2015. *Macht in der Mitte: Die neuen Aufgaben Deutschlands in Europa*. Hamburg: Edition Körber Stiftung.

Newman, Abraham. 2015. "The Reluctant Leader: Germany's Euro Experience and the Long Shadow of Reunification." In *The Future of the Euro*, edited by Matthias Matthijs and Mark Blyth, 117–35. Oxford, UK: Oxford University Press.

Newport, Frank. 2013. "Most in U.S. Still Proud to Be American." http://www.gallup.com/poll/163361/proud-american.aspx.

Niclauß, Karlheinz. 2004. *Kanzlerdemokratie: Regierungsführung von Konrad Adenauer bis Gerhard Schröder*. Paderborn et al.: Ferdinand Schoeningh.

Niedermayer, Oskar. 2015a. "Staatliche Parteienfinanzierung I." Bonn: Bundeszentrale für politische Bildung. http://www.bpb.de/politik/grundfragen/parteien-in-deutschland/42240/staatliche-parteienfinanzierung-bundestagsparteien.

———. 2015b. "Wahlkampfausgaben der Parteien." Bonn: Bundeszentrale für politische Bildung. http://www.bpb.de/politik/grundfragen/parteien-in-deutschland/140330/wahlkampfausgaben.

———. 2016. "Deutsche Parteien und Europa." In *Handbuch zur deutschen Europapolitik*, edited by Katrin Böttger and Mathias Jopp, 171–86. Baden-Baden: Nomos.

Nolan, Mary. 2012. *The Transatlantic Century: Europe and America, 1890–2010*. Cambridge, UK: Cambridge University Press.

———. 2014. "Americanization? Europeanization? Globalization? The German Economy since 1945." *Bulletin of the German Historical Institute* 54 (Spring): 49–63.

Norris, Pippa, and Ronald Inglehart. 2001. "Cultural Obstacles to Equal Representation." *Journal of Democracy* 12 (3): 126–40.

Nye, Joseph S. 1991. *Bound to Lead: The Changing Nature of American Power*. New York: Basic.

Offe, Claus. 2015. *Europe Entrapped*. Cambridge, UK: Polity.

O'Malley, Eoin. 2007. "The Power of Prime Ministers: Results of an Expert Survey." *International Political Science Review* 28 (1): 7–27.

Packer, George. 2014. "The Quiet German: The Astonishing Rise of Angela Merkel, the Most Powerful Woman in the World." *New Yorker*, December 1. http://www.newyorker.com/magazine/2014/12/01/quiet-german.

Pappas, Takis S. 2016. "The Specter Haunting Europe: Distinguishing Liberal Democracy's Challengers." *Journal of Democracy* 27 (4): 22–36.

Patton, David F. 2011. *Out of the East: From PDS to Left Party in Unified Germany*. Albany: State University of New York Press.

Peck, Jeffrey M. 2006. *Being Jewish in the New Germany*. New Brunswick, NJ: Rutgers University Press.

Pew Research Center. 2015. "Germany and the United States: Reliable Allies. But Disagreement on Russia, Global Leadership and Trade." May 7. http://www.pewglobal.org/2015/05/07/germany-and-the-united-states-reliable-allies.

Pfaff, Steven, and Hyojoung Kim. 2003. "Exit-Voice Dynamics in Collective Action: An Analysis of Emigration and Protest in the East German Revolution." *American Journal of Sociology* 109 (2): 401–44.

Pfetsch, Frank. 2007. *Das neue Europa*. Wiesbaden: VS Verlag für Sozialwissenschaften.

Pickel, Gert. 2009. "Secularization as a European Fate? Results from the Church and Religion in an Enlarged Europe Project 2006." In *Church and Religion in Contemporary Europe: Results from Empirical and Comparative Research*, edited by Gert Pickel and Olaf Müller, 89–122. Wiesbaden: VS Verlag für Sozialwissenschaften.

Poguntke, Thomas, and Paul Webb, eds. 2005. *The Presidentialization of Politics: A Comparative Study of Modern Democracies*. Oxford, UK: Oxford University Press.

Pond, Elizabeth. 2015. "Germany's Real Role in the Ukraine Crisis: Caught Between East and West." *Foreign Affairs* 94 (2): 173–76.

Port, Andrew. 2013. "The Banalities of East German Historiography." In *Becoming East German: Socialist Structures and Sensibilities after Hitler*, edited by Mary Fulbrook and Andrew Port, 1–30. New York: Berghahn.

"Press Release no. 345." 2016, September 28. https://www.destatis.de/DE/PresseService/Presse/Pressemitteilungen/2016/09/PD16_345_225.html.

Puetter, Uwe. 2014. *The European Council and the Council: New Intergovernmentalism and Institutional Change*. Oxford, UK: Oxford University Press.

Quint, Peter E. 1997. *The Imperfect Union: Constitutional Structures of German Unification*. Princeton, NJ: Princeton University Press.

Reuband, Karl-Heinz. 2015. "Wer demonstriert in Dresden für Pegida? Ergebnisse empirischer Studien, methodische Grundlagen und offene Fragen." *Mitteilungen des Instituts für Parteienrecht und Parteienforschung* 21: 133–44.

Risse, Thomas. 2010. *A Community of Europeans? Transnational Identities and Public Spheres*. Ithaca, NY: Cornell University Press.

Ritter, Gerhard Albert. 2011. *The Price of German Unity: Reunification and the Crisis of the Welfare State*. Oxford, UK: Oxford University Press.

Roberts, Geoffrey K. 2002. "Political Education in Germany." *Parliamentary Affairs* 55 (3): 556–68.

Rome Declaration. 2017. March 25. http://www.consilium.europa.eu/en/press/press-releases/2017/03/25-rome-declaration.

Roth, Roland, and Dieter Rucht, eds. 2008. *Die sozialen Bewegungen in Deutschland seit 1945: Ein Handbuch*. Frankfurt a.M. and New York: Campus.

Rucht, Dieter, Britta Baumgarten, and Simon Teune. 2010. "Befragung von Demonstranten gegen Stuttgart 21 am 18.10.2010" Press Conference. Berlin: Science Center Berlin.

Rudolf, Peter. 2010. *Das "neue" Amerika: Außenpolitik unter Barack Obama*. Frankfurt a.M.: Suhrkamp Verlag.

Sarotte, Mary Elise. 2009. *1989: The Struggle to Create Post-Cold War Europe*. Princeton, NJ: Princeton University Press.

———. 2014. *The Collapse: The Accidental Opening of the Berlin Wall*. New York: Basic.

Sarrazin, Thilo. 2010. *Deutschland schafft sich ab: Wie wir unser Land aufs Spiel setzen*. Munich: Deutsche Verlags-Anstalt.

Scheller, Henrik. 2015. "Der erschöpfte Föderalstaat." *Aus Politik und Zeitgeschichte* 65 (28–30): 17–23.

Schieder, Friedrich. 2014. "Führung und Solidarität in der deutschen Europapolitik." In *Deutsche Außenpolitik und internationale Führung: Ressources, Praktiken und Politiken in einer veränderten Europäischen Union*, edited by Sebastian Harnisch and Joachim Schild, 56–91. Baden-Baden: Nomos.

Schimmelfennig, Frank. 2001. "The Community Trap: Liberal Norms, Rhetorical Action, and the Eastern Enlargement of the European Union." *International Organization* 55 (1): 47–80.

———. 2015. "Mehr Europa—oder weniger? Die Eurokrise und die europäische Integration." *Aus Politik und Zeitgeschichte* 65 (52): 28–34.

Schmidt, Manfred G. 2001. "Still on the Middle Way? Germany's Political Economy at the Beginning of the Twenty-First Century." *German Politics* 10 (3): 1–12.

———. 2011. *Das politische System Deutschlands: Institutionen, Willensbildung und Politikfelder*. 2nd rev. and exp. ed. Munich: C. H. Beck.

———. 2015. "The Four Worlds of Democracy: Commentary on Arend Lijphart's Revised Edition of Patterns of Democracy (2012)." In *Complex Democracy: Varieties, Crises, and Transformations*, edited by Volker Schneider and Burkard Eberlein, 29–50. Heidelberg: Springer.

Schneider, Volker, and Burkard Eberlein, eds. 2015. *Complex Democracy: Varieties, Crises, and Transformations*. Heidelberg: Springer.

Schwartz, Herman. 1999. "A Brief History of Judicial Review." In *The Self-Restraining State: Power and Accountability in New Democracies*, edited by Andreas Schedler, Larry Diamond, and Marc F. Plattner, 145–50. Boulder, CO: Lynne Rienner.

Shafer, Byron E. 1999. "American Exceptionalism." *Annual Review of Political Science* 2 (1): 445–63.

Shell. 2015. *Jugend 2015.17. Shell Jugendstudie*. http://www.shell.de/ueber-uns/die-shell-jugendstudie/new-world-agenda.html.

Siddi, Marco. 2016. "German Foreign Policy towards Russia in the Aftermath of the Ukraine Crisis." *Europe-Asia Studies* 68 (4): 665–77.

Silvia, Stephen J. 2013. *Holding the Shop Together: German Industrial Relations in the Postwar Era*. Ithaca, NY: Cornell University Press.

Smith, Helmut Walser. 2008. "When the Sonderweg Debate Left Us," *German Studies Review* 31 (2): 225–40.

Sperling, Stefan. 2013. *Reasons of Conscience: The Bioethics Debate in Germany*. Chicago: University of Chicago Press.

Statista. 2014. "Juden in Deutschland." http://de.statista.com/statistik/daten/studie/1232/umfrage/anzahl-der-juden-in-deutschland-seit-dem-jahr-2003.

Stefes, Christoph H. 2010. "Bypassing Germany's *Reformstau*: The Remarkable Rise of Renewable Energy." *German Politics* 19 (2): 148–63.

Steinmo, Sven. 2008. "Historical Institutionalism." In *Approaches and Methodologies in the Social Sciences: A Pluralistic Perspective*, edited by Donatella Della Porta and Michael Keating, 118–36. Cambridge, UK: Cambridge University Press.

Stent, Angela E. 1999. *Russia and Germany Reborn: Unification, the Soviet Collapse and the New Europe*. Princeton, NJ: Princeton University Press.

Stern, Fritz. 1993. "Freedom and Its Discontents." *Foreign Affairs* 72 (4): 108–25.

———. 2005. "Lessons from German History." *Foreign Affairs* 84 (3): 14–18.

Streeck, Wolfgang. 2009. *Re-Forming Capitalism: Institutional Change in the German Political Economy*. Oxford: Oxford University Press.

———. 2011. "The Crisis of Democratic Capitalism." *New Left Review*, no. 71. http://newleftreview.org/II/71/wolfgang-streeck-the-crises-of-democratic-capitalism.

Strunz, Sebastian, Erik Gawel, and Paul Lehmann. 2014. "On the Alleged Need to Strictly Europeanise the German Energiewende." *Intereconomics* 49 (5): 244–67.

Sweet, Alex Stone. 2012. "Constitutional Courts." In *The Oxford Handbook of Comparative Constitutional Law*, edited by Michel Rosenfeld and András Sajó, 816–30. Oxford, UK: Oxford University Press.

Szabo, Stephen F. 2015. *Germany, Russia, and the Rise of Geo-Economics*. London and New York: Bloomsbury.

Thelen, Kathleen. 1999. "Historical Institutionalism in Comparative Politics." *Annual Review of Political Science* 2 (1): 369–404.

———. 2004. *How Institutions Evolve: The Political Economy of Skills in Germany, Britain, the United States and Japan*. Cambridge, UK: Cambridge University Press.

———. 2014. *Varieties of Liberalization and the New Politics of Social Solidarity*. New York: Cambridge University Press.

Ther, Philipp. 2016. *Europe since 1989: A History*. Princeton, NJ: Princeton University Press.

Tolley, Michael C. 2012. "Judicialization of Politics in Europe: Keeping Pace with Strasbourg." *Journal of Human Rights* 11 (1): 66–84.

Tsebelis, George. 2002. *Veto Players: How Political Institutions Work*. Princeton, NJ: Princeton University Press.

Ullrich, Sebastian. 2009. *Der Weimar Komplex: Das Scheitern der ersten deutschen Demokratie und die politische Kultur der frühen Bundesrepublik 1945–1949*. Göttingen: Wallstein.

von Wahl, Angelika. 2011. "A 'Women's Revolution from Above'? Female Leadership, Intersectionality, and Public Policy under the Merkel Government." *German Politics* 20 (3): 392–409.

von Winter, Thomas. 2016. "Die Europapolitik der deutschen Interessenverbände." In *Handbuch zur deutschen Europapolitik*, edited by Katrin Böttger and Mathias Jopp, 187–200. Baden-Baden: Nomos.

Vorländer, Hans, Naik Herold, and Steven Schäller. 2016. *Pegida: Entwicklung, Zusammensetzung und Deutung einer Empörungsbewegung.* Wiesbaden: Springer.

Welsh, Helga A. 2010. "Policy Transfer in the Unified Germany: From Imitation to Feedback Loops." *German Studies Review* 33 (3): 531–38.

———. 2013. "Debates and Perceptions about Unification: The Centrality of Discourse." In *United Germany: Debating Processes and Prospects*, edited by Konrad H. Jarausch, 64–80. New York: Berghahn Books.

Wendel, Mattias. 2016. "The Refugee Crisis and the Executive: On the Limits of Administrative Discretion in the Common European Asylum System." *German Law Journal* 17 (6): 1005–32.

Weßels, Bernhard. 2016. "Politische Integration und politisches Engagement." In *Datenreport 2016: Ein Sozialbericht für die Bundesrepublik Deutschland*, 400–415. Bonn: Bundeszentrale für politische Bildung.

Wicke, Christian. 2015. *Helmut Kohl's Quest for Normality: His Representation of the German Nation and Himself.* New York: Berghahn Books.

Wike, Richard. 2016. "Where Americans and Germans Agree, Disagree on Foreign Policy," *Pew Research Center.* June 14. http://www.pewresearch.org/fact-tank/2016/06/14/where-americans-and-europeans-agree-disagree-on-foreign-policy.

Winkler, Heinrich August. 2007. *Germany: The Long Road West.* Vol. 2: 1933–1960. Oxford, UK: Oxford University Press.

Wolfram, Edgar. 2006. *Die geglückte Demokratie: Geschichte der Bundesrepublik Deutschland von ihren Anfängen bis zur Gegenwart.* Stuttgart: Klett-Cotta.

Yoder, Jennifer. 2010. "The Integration of Eastern German Political Elites since 1989." *German Studies Review* 33 (3): 549–64.

Zantovský, Michael. 2014. *Havel: A Life.* New York: Grove Press.

Zelikow, Philip, and Condoleezza Rice. 1995. *Germany Unified and Europe Transformed: A Study in Statecraft.* Cambridge, MA: Harvard University Press.

Zimmer, Annette, and Rudolf Speth. 2015. "Von der Hierarchie zum Markt. Zur Koordination von Interessenvertretung heute." In *Lobby Work: Interessenvertretung als Politikgestaltung*, edited by Rudolf Speth and Annette Zimmer, 31–52. Wiesbaden: Springer VS.

Zimmermann, Hubert. 2014. "A Grand Coalition for the Euro: The Second Merkel Cabinet, the Euro Crisis and the Elections of 2013." *German Politics* 23 (4): 322–36.

Zolleis, Udo, and Carina Wertheimer. 2013. "Is the CSU Still a Volkspartei?" *German Politics* 22 (1–2): 97–113.

Index

About the Authors

Christiane Lemke is professor of political science and director of international relations and European studies at Leibniz University, Hannover, Germany. She received her PhD from the Free University Berlin, where she also earned her Habilitation *venia legendi* in political science. She has served as Visiting Professor at Harvard University, DAAD Visiting Professor at the University of North Carolina at Chapel Hill, and was the Max Weber Chair in German and European Studies at New York University. She has published widely on European affairs and the politics of the European Union, including studies of democratic transitions in east central Europe, citizenship, human rights, the eurozone crisis, and Germany's role in Europe.

Helga A. Welsh is professor of politics and international affairs at Wake Forest University in Winston-Salem, North Carolina. She received her PhD in political science from Ludwig Maximilians University in Munich and began her academic career at the Institute for Contemporary History in Munich before moving to the United States. Her publications have focused on the history and politics of the former East Germany, German unification, democratic transitions in Central and Eastern Europe, transitional justice, and German education policy. She is one of the editors of "German History in Documents and Images," a project administered by the German Historical Institute in Washington, DC, and coeditor of the journal *German Politics*.

EUROPE TODAY
Series Editor: Erik Jones
Founding Editor: Ronald Tiersky